ECONOMICS AND ECONOMIC POLICY IN BRITAIN,
1946 – 1966

MODERN REVIVALS IN ECONOMICS

Series Editor: Professor Mark Blaug

Mark Blaug
An Introduction to the Economics of Education
(0 7512 0022 0)

Mark Casson
The Entrepreneur: An Economic Theory
(0 7512 0023 9)

Mark Casson
Multinationals and World Trade: Vertical Integration and the Division of Labour in World Industries
(0 7512 0024 7)

A J Culyer
The Political Economy of Social Policy
(0 7512 0025 5)

John Cullis and Peter West
The Economics of Health: An Introduction
(0 7512 0026 3)

G C Harcourt
Some Cambridge controversies in the theory of capital
(0 7512 0027 1)

Ian Steedman
Fundamental Issues in Trade Theory
(0 7512 0028 X)

Melvin L Greenhut
A Theory of the Firm in Economic Space
(0 7512 0074 3)

Carl S Shoup
Ricardo on Taxation
(0 7512 0060 3)

T W Hutchison
The Politics and Philosophy of Economics: Marxians, Keynesians and Austrians
(0 7512 0089 1)

T W Hutchison
'Positive' Economics and Policy Objectives
(0 7512 0090 5)

T W Hutchison
Economics and Economic Policy in Britain 1946 – 1966: some aspects of their inter-relations
(0 7512 0091 3)

T W Hutchison
On revolutions and progress in economic knowledge
(0 7512 0093 X)

J Creedy and D P O'Brien (eds)
Economic Analysis in Historical Perspective
(0 7512 0088 3)

D P O'Brien
J R McCulloch: A Study in Classical Economics
(0 7512 0096 4)

D M Nuti (ed)
V K Dmitriev: Economic Essays on Value, Competition and Utility
(0 7512 0095 6)

J C Dodds and J L Ford
Expectations, Uncertainty and the Term Structure of Interest Rates
(0 7512 0097 2)

J L Ford and S Sen
Protectionism, Exchange Rates and the Macroeconomy
(0 7512 0098 0)

Mark Blaug (ed)
The Economics of the Arts
(0 7512 0099 9)

ECONOMICS AND ECONOMIC POLICY IN BRITAIN, 1946 – 1966

Some Aspects of Their Interrelations

T W Hutchison

Emeritus Professor of Economics
University of Birmingham

Gregg Revivals

First published in Great Britain in 1968 by
George Allen & Unwin Ltd

Reprinted in 1992 by
Gregg Revivals
Gower House
Croft Road
Aldershot
Hampshire GU11 3HR
England

Gregg Revivals
Distributed in the United States by
Ashgate Publishing Company
Old Post Road
Brookfield
Vermont 05036
USA

A CIP catalogue record for this book is available
from the British Library

A CIP catalogue record for this book is available
from the US Library of Congress

ISBN 0 7512 0091 3

Printed in Great Britain by
Ipswich Book Co. Ltd., Ipswich, Suffolk

TO E. B. & R.

Je ne suis pour rien. Je suis pour qu'on ne déraisonne pas. L'exportation du sens commun est la seule qui me fâche. . . .

Cette science d'administration, cette science qu'on appelle économie politique . . . est bien plus compliquée et bien plus difficile qu'on ne pense. . . .

Tous les problèmes d'économie politique se réduisent à faire du bien aux hommes; mais il n'y a aucun bien qui ne soit allié à quelque mal qui souvent l'affaiblit, quelquefois le balance.

Ferdinando Galiani, *Dialogues sur le Commerce des Blés* (1770).

ACKNOWLEDGMENTS

I was extremely fortunate while writing much of this book to be the holder of a Visiting Fellowship of the Institute of Advanced Studies in the Australian National University. No place, as far as I am aware, so happily combines a delightful atmosphere and surroundings with conduciveness to research and writing, and I am deeply indebted for friendly and stimulating hospitality to more Canberrans than I can list here. I am specially grateful to Mr David Bensusan-Butt for reading my typescript and for making many valuable comments. Of course the entire responsibility for all the statements and opinions, historical and critical, in this volume is mine. For their skilful assistance in preparing the typescript I am grateful to Miss Jean Taylor, of Birmingham, and Mrs G. McIntyre, of Canberra, and for help with the index to Mr D. G. Mussenden.

T.W.H., November 1967

CONTENTS

Preface to the *Gregg Revivals* Edition

At certain periods the then dominant economic theories and ideas have been regarded as having helped to bring about highly successful phases in economic history and policy; and have, for a decade or two, actually coincided with such phases of success, before institutional changes, in due course, rendered obsolete, or inadequate, the policy prescriptions which had till then appeared so successful. One such period occurred in this country in the middle decades of the nineteenth century, when the theories of the English Classical economists regarding free markets and free trade seemed to bring about, and then coincide with, the increasing economic success of the fifties and sixties, when Britain became the leading economic and industrial power, and 'workshop of the world', until, in the late sixties and seventies problems and changes occurred, not envisaged in the then dominant policy prescriptions.

A somewhat similar coincidence occurred approximately a hundred years later, after the end of World War II, when those in Britain who had grown up, or lived through, the decade of the thirties, dreaded the recurrence of depression and large-scale unemployment. This fear or foreboding was, however, never realized after the war. The great post-war depression never came about, and very high and stable levels of employment lasted for two decades or longer. Again economists, and the prevailing economic doctrines, like the English classicals a century earlier – perhaps not without justification – gained immensely in prestige and confidence – (or over-confidence). In particular, some rather crude versions of Keynesianism became highly influential – (though Keynes himself would almost certanly have rejected these versions, as, in a famous phrase of his, 'modernist stuff, gone wrong and turned sour and silly'). With considerable over-confidence it was influentially held that not only could, and should, the level of unemployment be held down to around 2%, but that, at the same time, the lagging British growth rate could, and should, be raised considerably by government measures. For example, Lord Kaldor (as he was shortly to become) proclaimed (1963) that 'we could raise our economic strength considerably by a vigorous policy of comprehensive planning', while Lord Balogh maintained that centralized investment controls were an essential measure for raising the British rate of growth to 5–6%, because: 'This was the way the Soviet obtained its results, and I doubt whether we can do better' (1963; v. below, p. 217).

II

This book was written in the mid-sixties at what must have been somewhere near a peak of confidence, on the part of economists, in the power of their subject. By August 1968, when the book was published, the crest of this wave had probably broken, or was just about to break, with institutional changes having produced new problems which the previously prevailing ideas and theories did not cope with adequately.

It would not be at all easy to find a book on economics which has met with more extremely contrasting and conflicting reviews. In *The New Statesman* (I. XI. 1968) an Oxford expert described it as 'the publishing outrage of the year'. According to *The Economist*, however, this was 'the most entertaining – though not the most informative – economics book to appear for many years' (28. IX. 1968). In *The Times*, the Economics Editor complained of its 'unscholarly (dare I say journalistic?) method', claiming that it 'would have thrilled Senator Joe McCarthy' (15. VII. 1968).

On the other hand, in the other '*Times*' organ, the '*Literary Supplement*', the anonymous reviewer described the book as 'courageous and careful' . . . 'a flabbergasting confrontation of our academic economic counsellors with their own words' . . . 'which deserves wider approbation than naturally it is likely to get from most economist critics in this country' (26. IX. 1968). Finally, Harold Wincott, in *The Financial Times*, commented that the book 'must have involved him – [the author] – in a fantastic amount of research, for much of it is based on a meticulous study of the writings and speeches of our leading economists'. Wincott noted that the concluding critical-methodological section was 'not wholly pessimistic', and, after quoting from my methodological suggestions (pp. 271–6) remarked: 'Fairer than that, no man could say'.

III

At the time these various reviews were appearing my morale was much fortified by a meeting, and some correspondence with, Sir Robert Hall (as he then was) who, for fourteen of the twenty years covered by this book had been the senior economic adviser to H.M. Government. I had ventured to send him a copy and remain deeply grateful for his response. Sir Robert wrote to me regarding my book (25. VII. 1968): 'I have read it with almost feverish interest . . . I thought a book like this was badly needed . . . and congratulate you on doing it'. As to academic economists at that time, citing some well-known names Sir Robert continued: 'They also developed extraordinary powers of forgetting what they had said before and glossing over very lightly their past errors. It is not at all surprising that people should behave in this way, but it is a great reproach to economics that they can get away with it with no damage to their careers and reputations . . . I think the profession shows up very badly in the ease with which anyone can get away with almost anything'. (In other words, the effective methodological prescription of the time, with regard to the contributions of academic economists to the discussion of economic policy, was 'anything goes' – or 'went').

IV

To me, it is of great interest that, in his Presidential address to the Royal Economic Society (1959), on 'the Practical Application of Economics', Sir Robert displayed a great concern with, and grasp of, basic methodological principles and distinctions. This interest and grasp is surely all the more important and noteworthy coming from someone concerned, for so long and so intensively, at the highest level, with the enlightenment and guidance of policy and policy decisions. For such enlightenment and guidance had, of course, been, for the most part, the prime aim of economists and economics since Sir William Petty, nearly three hundred years ago; – (though by the 1960s this aim was beginning to be obscured, fudged, and replaced, by an increasing number of economists, especially mathematical economists).

In his address, however, Sir Robert remarked that it was 'an illusion to suppose that the dispassionate economist beloved of those who labour the distinction between ends and means, between normative and positive economics, can live in the practical world' (*Economic Journal*, 69, 276, p. 640). However this may be with regard to 'the practical world' of government and business, this remark about the normative-positive distinction does not imply that the distinction should not, in the prime interest of clarity, be pursued, as far as possible – (which is surely pretty far, given an academic commitment to clarity) – in the academic, as contrasted with the 'practical' world. Indeed, to pursue such distinctions, as far as they will go, might be regarded as just what the *academic* world is for; (although, actually, the first man to introduce the normative-positive distinction into economics was that eminently 'practical' self-made millionaire Richard Cantillon). Moreover, Sir Robert himself seemed ready to criticise academic economists for their failure to observe this elementary distinction, and for not keeping separate their normative inclinations from their positive theorizing and analysis, when he observed that 'most economists started with emotional views either because they were temperamentally inclined to favour planning like . . . , or felt that the market mechanism was a work of providence . . . ' (Letter to this writer, 25. VII. 1968). Indeed it seems reasonable to suggest that Sir Robert's own great and lengthy success in being 'admired and trusted by Labour and Conservative Chancellors – by men with as differing views as Cripps and Thorneycroft', must have been due, in significant measure, to the extent and clarity with which he was able effectively to distinguish, in his advice and guidance, between his own positive economics and his ethical and political principles; (see Lord Plowden on 'Robert Hall remembered', in *The Robert Hall Diaries 1954 – 1961*, ed. Alec Cairncross, 1991, p. XIV).

Sir Robert also laid the greatest emphasis on another vital and fundamental logical or methodological distinction. Calling for 'the explicit formulation of hypotheses . . . in ways which would have a precise meaning to economic statisticians' – so that these hypotheses could be tested – Sir Robert pointed out that formulating hypotheses in a testable form 'would help to guard against what I regard as a besetting sin of economists; that of enunciating purely definitional relationships when they purport to be making statements about reality. . . . This sin is so pervasive that I almost wish that it were within our power to mark out in some way any economist who failed to use consistently the identity symbol when writing a definitional equation and to confine the use of the equals symbol to empirical relationships or hypotheses' (*Economic Journal*, 69, 276, pp. 650 – 1).

Thirty years later this still 'besetting sin' is even more confusingly obscured by the highly and purely mathematical form in which it is now more often perpetrated, in pursuit of purely mathematical criteria and aims, which have increasingly supplanted the criteria and aims of economics as an empirical and historical subject, directed, primarily at elucidating and guiding policy decisions.

V

I am very glad that this book is being reprinted. I hope first that it may be of interest to students of the economic thought and policies of the period. But – (believe it or not) – the book had a possibly even more serious purpose, that of indicating briefly that certain elementary logical and methodological principles were of importance in the practical application of economic theory, analysis and knowledge to the elucidation and guidance of policy decisions. So I hope, secondly, that the elementary methodological principles suggested in the concluding pages may, – as they seem perennially to be – worthy of repetition.

Terence Hutchison
August 1992

FOREWORD

The application of economics or economic 'theories' to policies, which this book is about, may be due for some reconsideration, since its problems have been considerably transformed, in two respects, in the decades following the Second World War. First, the range of economic policies has become much more extensive, and their objectives much more ambitious and complex. Secondly, and more recently, economists have aimed at formulating their theories, and the predictions they provide as bases for policies, in much more precise quantitative terms than previously (though how far this aim has been successfully achieved obviously varies from case to case, and might be a matter of controversy).

Of course *any* deliberate or 'rational' proposals for, or criticisms of policies can be said to be based more or less formally or informally on some kind of 'theory'. Cabinet ministers, politicians, civil servants and journalists all employ 'theories', formulated more or less precisely and explicitly, or imprecisely and inexplicitly. Here however, we are particularly concerned to discover how far the economic theories set out in textbooks of economics and in specialist treatises, now mainly the work of university economists, have been contributing to the elucidation of recent policy problems. Insofar as these more formal economic theories can influence or enlighten policy proposals or criticisms, or the diagnoses and prognoses involved, one might expect to find such enlightenment most thoroughly and accurately demonstrated and exploited in the actual contributions to policy discussions volunteered by university economists, of which there have been many in Britain in the last two decades. For university economists have not confined themselves to the forging of 'tools' or instruments to be wielded by others, civil servants or politicians. They have not merely devoted themselves to the craft of making golf-clubs, or even simply to composing textbooks on the general principles of golf, or to the coaching of beginners, but have ventured out on to the course in the middle of the open championships. We shall be surveying their play at some of the longer and more problematic holes.

Much methodological theorizing and criticism, normative and positive, in austere essays, inaugural proclamations and lectures, or in the exhortatory introductions to conventional textbooks, seems to be concerned with rather pure, ideal, rarified and abstract intellectual processes, or with severely 'rigorous' models, of mathematical precision, yielding, so the student is advised, 'scientific' predictions, tested 'against the evidence of what actually happens in the economy', as a basis for policy.[1] But it sometimes appears that the processes thus described bear about as close a relation to the 'impure' processes and manoeuvres of actual policy discussions, whether of economists or non-economists, as the pure models of competitive equilibrium, or steady growth and the like, bear to actual economic behaviour and processes. Moreover these methodological disquisitions are usually illustrated by much simpler applications of elementary price theory and Keynesian theory than are involved in the central policy issues of the last twenty years with which we are concerned here.

We are, therefore, exploring the actual inter-relations of economic theorizing and policy discussion by trying, first, to set out a positive record of the recent pronouncements of university economists on current policy issues (though we have occasionally veered outside the strictly 'university' field for significant examples). This essay attempts to set out such a record of the contributions of university economists regarding the central problems of British economic policy after 1945: regarding the familiar complex of the domestic problems of full employment, inflation and the rate of growth, and of prices, productivity and incomes: and, abroad, of the balance of payments, trade policies and our economic relations with the Commonwealth, the United States and Europe. If some authors are quoted much more than others it is because they have written much more on these policy problems. While aiming at a fairly comprehensive outline regarding this central group of issues, we are not attempting anything like a complete coverage of the application of economics to policies from 1946 to 1966, and we pass over almost entirely such more technical fields as banking, monopoly and restrictive practices, taxation policies, the details of convertibility, as well as many others. Having set out our historical outline, we shall then attempt to draw some brief conclusions, positive and normative, regarding the processes, the methods and the criteria actually and observably employed by economists in formulating their pro-

[1] R. G. Lipsey, *An Introduction to Positive Economics*, 2nd ed., 1966, p. 43.

nouncements on policies and the necessary underlying predictions. We shall try to perceive to what extent and in what form the economic theories of the textbooks, the treatises and the lecture room actually underly or come through into current policy proposals and criticism or establish the diagnoses and predictions on which these are based; or how far, on the contrary, the actual policy proposals and criticisms are being based—inevitably or otherwise—on sheer guesswork, 'hunch' and speculation, which are liable to be, and often actually are, swayed and coloured by ideological prejudices or the swings of fashion.

We shall be quoting below from works of very different sorts and sizes, from letters to *The Times*, articles in *The New Statesman* and in the bank reviews, and from topical pamphlets, as well as from contributions to learned journals and from weighty volumes, the fruit of profound research. The assumption, however, is made here that whatever the setting in which it may be published, any significant public pronouncement by a university economist on a major issue of economic policy should be taken and judged seriously, as an important, duly weighed statement and not dismissed, or excused, as ephemeral or trivial. When addressing specialist colleagues in a book or article, remote from policy applications, economists expect to be judged by high standards in respect of logical or mathematical precision, the avoidance of bias and the reliability of the empirical evidence. We assume here that we may expect correspondingly high standards, for instance in respect of avoiding unjustifiable dogmatism, deliberate distortion and bias, in pronouncements on economic policy wherever they may be published. When contributing to or influencing public opinion the economist is operating, however marginally or ineffectively, on the living body politico-economic. Surely at least as strict standards are relevant in these operations as are requisite for the abstract manipulation of plastic models in a learned journal, or in academic dissections or *post mortems* on theoretical corpses remote from policy applications.

In attempting to present a record of economists' policy proposals, criticisms, predictions and diagnoses, it has been necessary to sketch, at least in bare outline, the parallel record of events and policies to which economists were responding: the different phases of the struggle with inflation and incomes, the succession of 'stops' and 'goes', and, abroad, the story, sometimes slightly depressing but always deeply interesting, of Britain's attempts and failures at readjustment to her rapidly changing economic and political position in the world. In composing this background of events and policies I have, as will be obvious, relied for most of the period heavily and confidently on the great work of Mr J. C. R. Dow, *The Management of the British Economy 1945-60*. I have also been much helped by the topical commentaries of *The London and Cambridge Economic Bulletin* and *The National Institute Economic Review*, as well as by the valuable books of Mr Andrew Shonfield and Mr Samuel Brittan. As regards the Diaries of Events for the four main periods into which the story divides I am also much indebted to these sources.

Inevitably it has been rather difficult to avoid the air of trying to appear wise after the event (especially regarding the years after 1960). But, of course, what I am appearing or trying to appear, if anything, is of no relevance. The problems of economic policy are such that every crumb of wisdom must be sought in whatever direction one may be found, and even such crumbs as can be derived in the *ex post* form are not to be despised. Though it may be much easier to come by, even wisdom *after* the event does not always seem to be attained, and at least its quest may help towards the acquisition of that fundamental basis of all wisdom—not conspicuous by its presence in our period—which derives from a clear, firm grasp of the extent of one's ignorance. Moreover, wisdom *after* the last 'event' is one of the less unreliable, if pedestrian, directions in which to seek such wisdom as is achievable *before* the next 'event'. It is not too early to attempt such a process, impossible though it is, as yet, to write a definitive history of the economic ideas and policies of the period.

1. 1946-1951

DIARY OF EVENTS

(1) Full Employment in Britain

(2) Britain in the World Economy

(3) Planning and the Price Mechanism

(4) From Devaluation to Korea

(5) The Labour Record

DIARY OF EVENTS
(Dates in some cases approximate)

1945	May 8	VE Day
	July 5	General Election: Lab. 393; Cons. 203
	July 27	New Government: Dr Dalton Chancellor
	August 14	VJ Day
	August 24	End of Lend-Lease announced
	December 6	US Loan Agreement signed: £1,000m. loan
1946	March 1	Bank of England nationalized
	April 21	Death of Lord Keynes
	July 13	US Loan Agreement ratified by Congress
	July 21	Bread rationing
	September 19	Winston Churchill, at Zurich, calls for 'United States of Europe'
1947	January 1	Coal industry nationalized
	June 5	General Marshall's proposals for European Recovery Programme
	July 15	Sterling made convertible
	August 15	Independence of India
	August 20	Convertibility of sterling ended
	November 13	Autumn Budget
		Dr Dalton resigns. Sir Stafford Cripps Chancellor
1948	January 1	Railways nationalized
	February 4	Statement on Personal Incomes, Costs and Prices: Wage Pause
	March 13	American loan exhausted
	April 16	OEEC established
	July 5	National Health Service started
	November 4	Mr Harold Wilson's 'bonfire of controls'
1949	March 13	'Benelux' agreement
	March 26	Franco-Italian customs agreement
	May 5	Council of Europe established
	September 18	Devaluation of £ from \$4·03 to \$2·80
	October 24	Economy measures

1950	February 23	General Election: Lab. 315; Cons. 298
	May 9	France and German Federal Republic invite other European democracies to join in Coal and Steel Community. Britain declines
	June 25	South Korea invaded from North Korea
	September 19	EPU established
	October 19	Sir Stafford Cripps resigns; Mr Gaitskell Chancellor
	December 13	Marshall aid to Britain ceases
1951	April 10	Budget: tax increases and Health Service charges
	April 18	Agreement signed on European Iron and Steel Community
	April 22	Mr Bevan and Mr Wilson resign
	July 26	Bank credit restrictions: price controls: dollar imports cut
	October 25	General Election: Cons. 321; Lab. 295
	October 27	Mr Butler becomes Chancellor
	November 7	Economy measures: Bank Rate raised from 2 to 2½ per cent — (first post-war increase)

1. 1946-1951

(1) THE DOMESTIC PROBLEM: 'FULL EMPLOYMENT'

In the inter-war years there had been less disagreement among university economists regarding policies against unemployment than some subsequent myths have suggested.[1] The extent of agreement, which was reasonably far-reaching, had been considerably obscured by the ferocious theoretical and terminological disputes stirred up in the later thirties by Keynes's *General Theory*, regarding such questions as the definitions of 'savings' and 'investment', the 'essential' determinants of the rate of interest and the logic and history of the 'classical', self-adjusting employment model. It is at least possible that these strenuous analytical disputes during the rest of the thirties may have hindered the development of a confident agreement on measures against unemployment, which had previously existed at least to the extent of denying the main classical policy maxims.

One of the main classical *policy* dogmas, of obvious Smithian and Ricardian lineage, was what had come to be known as 'The Treasury View', that is, in the words of Churchill's budget speech of 1929,

'the orthodox Treasury doctrine which has steadfastly held that . . . very little additional employment can in fact and as a general rule be created by State borrowing and expenditure'.[2]

For as the White Paper of May 1929 argued (with unemployment at 10 per cent or more):

'The large loans involved, if they are not to involve inflation, must draw on existing capital resources. These resources are on the whole utilized at present in varying degrees of active employment; and the great bulk is utilized for home industrial and

[1] A fuller account of economists' views on employment policies in the thirties is given in the Appendix at the end of the book.

[2] *Parliamentary Debates*, Vol. 227, April 15, 1929, col. 54.

commercial purposes. The extent to which any additional employment could be given by altering the direction of investment is therefore at the best strictly limited.'[1]

This dogma had been attacked by Pigou twenty-one years earlier in his 1908 inaugural lecture on succeeding Marshall, and by D. H. Robertson in 1915 in a criticism of R. G. Hawtrey.[2] Indeed, Keynes himself, on the appearance of the White Paper in May 1929, at once criticized the Treasury experts as completely mistaken in believing in their own orthodoxy and (seven deeply depressed years before the appearance of *The General Theory*) as 'not familiar with modern economic thought':

'Not one of the leading economists of the country who has published his views, or with those opinion I am otherwise familiar, would endorse the general character of their argument.'[3]

A *second* main classical policy doctrine, of pure Smithian descent, much proclaimed by establishment experts in the great 'Economy' campaign of 1931, was that of the general beneficence of saving or frugality and especially of keeping down government expenditure. Together with the balanced budget doctrine, this implied rigid 'economy' and cuts in expenditure by governments during depressions. This might be called the classical built-in de-stabilizer. On the other hand, as an example of advanced opinion at the bottom of the slump (October 1932), with unemployment over 20 per cent, we may cite a letter which appeared in *The Times* attacking the orthodox classical maxims of saving and economy in the following terms:

'One thing is, in our opinion, clear. The public interest in present conditions does not point towards private economy; to spend less money than we should like to do is not patriotic.

Moreover, what is true of individuals acting singly is equally true of groups of individuals acting through local authorities. If the citizens of a town wish to build a swimming bath, or a library,

[1] Cmd. 3331, 1929, p. 53.
[2] A. C. Pigou, *Economic Science in Relation to Practice*, 1908, pp. 27-8; and D. H. Robertson, *A Study in Industrial Fluctuations*, 1915, p. 253.
[3] *Nation and Athenaeum*, May 18, 1929.

or a museum, they will not, by refraining from doing this promote a wider national interest . . . . Through their misdirected goodwill the mounting wave of unemployment will be lifted still higher.'[1]

This letter was signed by Keynes, but alongside his signature were five others, those of Professors Pigou and Macgregor, Sir Walter Layton, Sir Arthur Salter and Sir Josiah Stamp. But the Smithian doctrine on saving was still upheld not only by establishment figures in the City, Whitehall and the Conservative Party. The above letter was answered, two days later, by four London University economists (Professors Gregory, von Hayek, Plant and Robbins). They argued in a letter to which James Mill and Ricardo—and presumably Adam Smith—would enthusiastically have added their signatures:

'We are of the opinion that many of the troubles of the world at the present time are due to improvident borrowing and spending on the part of public authorities . . . . The depression has abundantly shown that the existence of public debt on a large scale imposes frictions and obstacles to readjustment very much greater than the frictions and obstacles imposed by the existence of private debt. Hence we cannot agree with the signatories of the letter that this is a time for new municipal swimming baths, etc., merely because people "feel they want" such amenities.

If the Government wish to help revival, the right way for them to proceed is, not to revert to their old habits of lavish expenditure, but to abolish those restrictions on trade and the movement of capital (including restrictions on new issues) which are at present impeding even the beginning of recovery.'[2]

'The Treasury View', and the doctrine of the beneficence of saving and 'economy', especially by governments and in depressions, both stemmed from the classical, Smithian doctrine of

[1] *The Times*, October 17, 1932. See also Pigou's letter to *The Times* of June 7, 1932, and his lecture on 'Economy and Waste', in *Economics in Practice*, 1935, pp. 26 ff. For the considerable measure of agreement between Pigou and Keynes (and other leading economists) on policies against unemployment in 1930, see R. Skidelsky's very interesting account in *Politicians and Unemployment*, 1967, which appeared after this chapter was written.

[2] *The Times*, October 19, 1932.

saving and investment. It might be suggested that, in addition to these two, there was a *third* classical policy doctrine, that of seeking to reduce employment by wage cuts. In this case, however, a very clear distinction would have to be made between (1) those who at the time actually recommended wage cuts as a cure for unemployment; and (2) those who were prepared to argue that in a system, or 'model', with perfectly flexible wages, unemployment would disappear, but who did not propose to attack unemployment, under the actual conditions of the time, by wage cuts but by acting on demand. It was this *second* view which was held by Pigou. Earlier Keynes himself had argued that

'a drastic reduction of wages in certain industries and a successful stand-up fight with the more powerful Trade Unions might reduce unemployment in the long run'.[1]

But he dismissed such a policy as quite impracticable. Pigou and Robertson also were certainly not in favour of attacking unemployment by wage reductions in the thirties, though some recent writings have suggested this. Mr Lekachman, quoting passages from Pigou's and Robertson's evidence to the Macmillan Committee (which do not imply anything more than the *second* view distinguished above), claims:

'Once more a leader of his profession committed himself to the conclusion that the route to full employment in 1939 [sic, 1930?] ran through a series of wage reductions terminating in a lower average level of wages.'[2]

[1] *The Nation and Athenaeum*, June 7, 1924.

[2] *The Age of Keynes*, 1967, p. 51. Mr Michael Stewart has also recently maintained that Professors Pigou and Robbins held the view that 'until wages were reduced, unemployment would persist', or that 'if employment was to be increased, the unions must agree to wage reductions' (*Keynes and After*, 1967, pp. 68 and 115). Mr Stewart seems to imply that Pigou in 1933 advocated direct reductions in money wages, in contrast with Keynes. Mr Stewart supports this charge by stating that Pigou 'concluded that provided there are no obstacles to the free working of the market, "There will always be at work a strong tendency for wage rates to be so related to demand that everybody is employed. Hence, in stable conditions, everyone will actually be employed".' Mr Stewart does not observe that Pigou was here concerned with an abstract, simplified case or model, as the whole passage (to which Mr Stewart gives no page reference) makes perfectly clear. Pigou wrote: 'With perfectly free competition among workpeople and labour perfectly mobile, the nature of the

As regards *actual policy* during the depression, Pigou (1933) in fact maintained:

'For prosperity to be restored either money costs must fall or money prices must rise. The practical difficulties in the way of the former solution have proved so serious and the friction to be overcome so great that *the main body of instructed opinion has turned towards the latter.*'[1]

Pigou further committed himself to the maxim 'when in doubt, expand'.[2] In fact his view in the early thirties was broadly the same as the one he expressed later when he explicitly denied that he was

'in favour of attacking the problem of unemployment by manipulating wages rather than by manipulating demand'.[3]

As regards Robertson, in his evidence to the Macmillan Committee (1930) one of his main arguments was for public investment and 'a conscious direction of capital investment', to counter 'the gluttability of wants'. He was less ready even than Keynes, at that time, to rely on lower interest rates and credit expansion at the bottom of the slump:

'The doctrine of temporary gluttability which I have tried to outline above is in direct conflict not only with the so-called "Treasury View" that such a policy of promoting public works

relation will be very simple. There will always etc., etc. . . .' In his policy recommendations at this time, Pigou did not assume that these perfectly simplified conditions existed, or advocate a direct attack on money wages. Only two pages earlier Pigou made it clear that his arguments were not opposed to 'large-scale public works', or 'bounties, guarantees of interest and, if successful in their purpose, protective duties' (*Theory of Unemployment*, 1933, pp. 250-2). Mr Stewart's claims seem to be supported by less irrelevant and misleading quotations in the case of Professor Robbins (v. *The Great Depression*, 1934, p. 186). Incidentally Mr. Stewart, though referring to 'the sheer indency of calling for wage cuts' (p. 68) at this time, agrees that Keynes also held that if employment was to be increased 'there must be a fall in average wages' in real terms (p. 116). See Appendix.

[1] *The Times*, January 6, 1933 (italics added).
[2] *The Times*, February 21, 1933.
[3] *Lapses from Full Employment*, 1945, p. v.

absorbs resources which would otherwise anyhow be employed by private enterprise, but also with the doctrine which has been maintained, for instance, by Mr Hawtrey, that the public works are a "mere piece of ritual", achieving nothing which could not equally well be achieved by the banking system acting alone, through a sufficiently great alteration in its terms of lending. When the spirit of investment is really costive unto death, I do not feel confident that the most enlightened group of bankers have it in their power to administer a sufficient purge, unless they are backed and utilized by authorities even higher than they.'[1]

As regards wage reductions, Mr Robertson was hesitant:

'I find it very difficult to express an opinion as to how far the maintenance of an uneconomically high real wage-level is a *practically* important cause of unemployment in this country today.'

He asserted that:

'the demand for labour in many directions today is pretty inelastic, in the sense that considerable wage concessions would not be likely to lead to a great increase in the numbers employed'.

Mr Robertson concluded:

'I should, I think, expect smaller results on employment from a successful drive against wages, unaccompanied by any other change, than some people would. I should not, however, if I were Minister for Employment, feel justified in refusing an offer by the Trade Union Congress to bring all wages down by 10 per cent; and if it were accompanied by a vigorous effort to revive the demand for labour by other means, I should hope for appreciable results on the volume of employment.'[2]

Until the outbreak of war there seems to have been little or no prospect in Britain of significant measures against unemployment

[1] See his memorandum to the Macmillan Committee, 1930, reprinted in *Economic Essays and Addresses*, by A. C. Pigou and D. H. Robertson, 1931, p. 124; also A. J. Youngson, *The British Economy*, 1920-57, 1960, p. 248.
[2] A. C. Pigou and D. H. Robertson, *Economic Essays and Addresses*, 1931, pp. 128-9.

on the lines Keynes and others advocated. In 1940 Keynes himself complained:

'It is, it seems, politically impossible for a capitalistic democracy to organize expenditure on the scale necessary to prove my case—except under war conditions.'[1]

In fact it was war conditions that broke up any significant remaining adherence to classical policy doctrines and soon enabled Keynes to develop the essential *means for* employment policies, in peace as well as war, in his *How to Pay for the War* and in the National Income White Papers dating from 1941. The abstract disputes stirred up by *The General Theory* proved of little relevance when it came to policy formation, though they continued to smoulder on after the war in some quarters.

Wide agreement emerged during the war that a high level of employment was a practicable objective of the highest priority. But in 1946 public opinion was still, and was to remain, profoundly affected by the experience of the inter-war years. Sir Oliver Franks (as he then was) described (1947) the forebodings of that time:

'The citizens and governments of most nation states fear the occurrence of large-scale unemployment more than any other disaster that can happen in peace. No government of the future can hope to stay for long in power if it lets large-scale unemployment destroy the physical and spiritual conditions of life among the people. The great depression of 1929-35 made in many ways a deeper and more permanent mark on this country than the war of 1939-45. It is noticeable in the present generation of undergraduates at my university . . . almost all of them are deeply worried about securing employment. . . . The world to which they look forward seems insecure, impoverished and uncertain. Their frame of mind looks back beyond the forties to the thirties. What they fear is large-scale unemployment.'[2]

However, economics and economists had come out of the war

[1] *New Republic*, July 20, 1940, quoted by A. E. Holmans, *United States Fiscal Policy, 1945-1959*, 1961, p. 318.
[2] *Central Planning and Control in War and Peace*, 1947, p. 21.

with enhanced prestige. Economically the war had been organized with much efficiency; and considerable official planning and unofficial thought had been given to the post-war employment problem. In spite of the fears of Oxford undergraduates, there seems to have been wide and justified confidence among economists that the appalling economic sickness of the inter-war years could be largely warded off or at least kept in check. But there were wide differences as to what was a feasible target. In the Government White Paper of 1944 all parties accepted 'as one of their primary aims and responsibilities the maintenance of a high and stable level of employment after the war'. But in explaining the proposal for variations in social insurance contributions to help stabilize aggregate demand, the assumption was made at least by way of an example, in the White Paper, of 'an average level of 8 per cent unemployment' or about 1½ million.[1]

Sir William Beveridge, on the other hand, called for a policy which ensured 'always having more vacant jobs than unemployed men' and put forward a figure of 3 per cent 'as a conservative, rather than an unduly hopeful, aim to set for the average unemployment rate of the future under conditions of full employment'.[2] But this was considered optimistic, even rather wild, in some quarters (as well as terminologically contradictory).[3] Even Keynes himself commented in a letter to Beveridge: 'No harm in aiming at 3 per cent unemployment, but I shall be surprised if we succeed.'[4] An Oxford symposium, *The Economics of Full Employment* (1944), assumed a minimum of frictional or seasonal un-

[1] Cmd. 6527, May 1944, p. 3 and p. 30. See G. D. N. Worswick and P. Ady, *The British Economy 1945-1950*, 1952, p. 16.

[2] *Full Employment in a Free Society*, 1944, p. 128.

[3] v. *Lapses from Full Employment*, by A. C. Pigou, 1944, p. 2.

[4] Quoted by Professor R. F. Kahn, *The Listener*, May 3, 1956, p. 543. Regarding Keynes's idea of full employment, Lord Robbins has called attention to a very interesting article in *The Times* of April 17 and 18, 1939, in which Keynes predicted that processes then in train would reduce unemployment by at least 750,000 (that is from 1,300,000 to about 550,000 which still represented about 5-6 per cent unemployment). Keynes wrote: 'The problem of abnormal unemployment will cease to exist during the financial year 1939-40. . . . It is full time for a complete readjustment of our mental outlook.' But this was in what Keynes himself called a 'twilight' period between peace and war, and it is difficult to conclude what his conception of 'normal' peacetime employment or unemployment was, or what his percentage target would have been. (See L. C. Robbins, *The Economist in the Twentieth Century*, 1954, p. 32.) See Appendix.

unemployment between 'say 5 per cent or 2 per cent'.[1]

It must be remembered that in 1945-6 the bogy of stagnation, so vividly conjured up by Keynes before the war, was still very much alive in some minds. For one thing, incidentally, the prospects for population seemed to point to a marked, even alarming, decline. Two quotations from the number of the *Economic Journal* (June 1946) in which Keynes's last article appeared, may be taken as illustrative. A review of a book, *Britain and her Birthrate,* after noting with approval that the authors have 'lined up with those who do not want the English people to disappear', concluded: 'Pride in large families must somehow be restored.' Secondly, a few pages later, Mr R. F. Harrod (who had also claimed three years earlier that as regards population, 'we are in the midst of a major crisis'), urged the stagnationist thesis as follows:

'It may be that waiting will soon no longer be a scarce factor, in the sense that enough waiting will be forthcoming at zero interest to satisfy all demands arising at zero interest. . . . It may be that we have so far been held back from Bliss not by an insufficient propensity to save, but by the forces described by Lord Keynes, and that some interference by a central authority will be necessary to overcome these forces.'[2]

That is, supply and demand for loan capital might '*soon*' be such that the Government should take steps to bring down rates of interest, perhaps to zero, if they did not reach that level of their own accord.

However, if there was considerable range of disagreement as to what level of employment it would prove practicable to maintain, there was an unusually wide measure of agreement as to the dangers and problems of 'too high' or 'over-full' or even simply of 'full' employment. There was certainly a remarkable consensus regarding the problems that would arise, though not, of course, as to how they could or should be treated or what was the 'right' target level of unemployment.

For example, Pigou (1944), though holding that 'a moderate

[1] *The Economics of Full Employment*, ed. F. Burchardt, 1944, p. iii.

[2] *Economic Journal*, June 1946, p. 286, p. 288 and p. 313. See also R. F. Harrod, *Britain's Future Population*, 1943, p. 25, and the Report and Papers of the Royal Commission on Population, 1949.

inflationary tendency, if it enables unemployment to be kept at a low level would be well forth enduring', argued that maintaining a very high level of employment might well require that

'a spiralling movement of inflation is allowed to develop, so that the money demand for labour is not merely stabilized upwards, but perpetually moves higher and higher ahead of the pursuing wage rate'.[1]

In fact, the concept of a full employment 'equilibrium' might prove an illusion.

Even Beveridge himself warned that:

'There is a real danger that sectional wage bargaining, pursued without regard to its effect on prices, may lead to a vicious spiral of inflation, with money wages chasing prices and without any gain in real wages for the working class as a whole. . . . The fact remains that there is no inherent mechanism in our present system, which can with certainty prevent competitive sectional bargaining for wages from setting up a vicious spiral of rising prices under full employment.'[2]

Beveridge suggested that compulsory arbitration would be necessary, and that,

'in peace in a free society, men should not be imprisoned for striking, though they may rightly be deprived of all support if the strike is contrary to a collective bargain or an agreed arbitration'.[3]

However, in Mr Kaldor's quantitative appendix to Beveridge's book, it seems to have been rather optimistically assumed that (without any further controls being explicitly mentioned) the full employment or 3 per cent unemployment target, could and would be combined with price stability:

'It will be assumed that post-war governments will pursue a monetary and wage policy which maintains the prices of final

[1] *Lapses from Full Employment*, 1944, p. 72.
[2] *Full Employment in a Free Society*, 1944, p. 199.
[3] *Op. cit.*, p. 200.

commodities constant. This implies that given the share of wages in the total value of output (which in the past showed remarkably little change over long periods), the average rate of money wages will rise in the same proportion as productivity per man hour. A policy of a falling price level, implying constant money wages, quite apart from its other disadvantage of enhancing rentier incomes, would make the task of monetary stabilization under full employment needlessly difficult; while a policy of a rising price level might be incompatible with the maintenance of stability in the long run."[1]

In the years immediately after the war a number of economists repeated these warnings more strongly than Beveridge. Mrs Robinson argued (1946):

'Nor is completely full employment desirable. The attainment of full employment, in this absolute sense, would require strict controls, including direction of labour. To raise the average of employment from 86 per cent (the average for Great Britain, 1921-38) to say, 95 per cent, would be compatible with a much greater amount of individual liberty than to raise it from 95 per cent to 98 per cent. To raise it from 95 per cent to 98 per cent (not momentarily—but on the average) would involve great sacrifices of liberty, and to raise it from 98 per cent to 100 per cent would involve complete conscription of labour. No one regards 100 per cent employment as a desirable objective.'[2]

Professor Meade (1948) held that the then existing level of unemployment of about 1½ per cent was 'an altogether abnormally low figure which is a result of the present excess inflationary pressure of demand for goods and services'. He went on:

'The real danger, however, is that the unemployment percentage

[1] Mr Kaldor added that there was 'one particular case in which a policy of rising prices would be preferable to that of constant prices', that is if the supply of goods and services freely provided by the State were to form an increasing proportion of the national real income', Beveridge, *op. cit.*, p. 398.
[2] Joan Robinson, *Collected Economic Papers*, 1951, p. 106 (from a paper dated 1946). See also *Essays in the Theory of Employment*, 1937 and 1947, p. 26: 'In general it may be said that something appreciably short of full employment must be regarded as the optimum.'

will have to be much higher than the technical minimum for a progressive society of, say, 4 per cent. It is possible that at this level of unemployment the trade unions, in exercising to the full their monopolistic bargaining power in the labour market, would push wage-rates up at so high a rate as to cause an intolerable rate of rise in money costs and so in prices. . . . Suppose that at 4 per cent unemployment the bargaining power of the trade unions were so great that the general level of money wage-rates rose by 5 per cent per annum, and that it required an unemployment percentage of 10 per cent so to reduce the bargaining position of the trade unions that the general level of money wage-rates was not pushed up by more than the tolerable 2 per cent per annum. Society would be faced with a most bitter dilemma.'[1]

Professor Meade pointed out that 'we have, in fact, a choice between four ways of dealing with this problem: the methods of Stagnation, Starvation, Slavery or Seduction'. He favoured 'Seduction', that is the use of the price mechanism to get labour to move 'where society most needs its effort'.[2]

Professor Kahn (as he then was), in reviewing Professor Meade's work, did not criticize his general conception of the dilemma. But he held that 'Seduction' was 'a poor method of securing a movement of labour', and favoured some control of engagements:

'I should contend that the motive of security is the dominant one in the minds of workers; and the combination of unemployment in one industry with scarcity of labour in another would, I should have thought, be far more effective in driving labour from one to the other than any conceivable wage differential. . . . Professor Meade believes that this alternative method, which he attempts to decry by describing as the method of *Starvation*, as compared with his method of *Seduction*, would necessitate withholding unemployment benefit from those whom it was desired to transfer. I do not think that this would be necessary at all.

[1] J. E. Meade, *Planning and the Price Mechanism*, 1948, pp. 70-1.

[2] *Op. cit.*, pp. 72-3. Later Professor Meade observed (*The Times*, August 2, 1949): 'At the moment we have only 1½ per cent unemployment as compared with the pre-war minimum of practically 10 per cent. There is still much inflation to be taken out of the system.'

What would be necessary is that the redundant workers should become *permanently* unemployed in their previous occupation and that we should not be influenced outside the proper context by Professor Meade's advocacy, designed to render more palatable the technical minimum of unemployment which he feels it is necessary to establish, of "adequate measures to ensure that this unemployment takes the form of short bouts of unemployment for many persons rather than long-period unemployment for a few unfortunate individuals".'[1]

Dr Thomas Balogh, holding that more extensive controls than Mr Kahn's were inevitable, maintained:

'All historical and theoretical evidence points to the conclusion that a "free" system in modern conditions needs at least 10 per cent, but more probably 15 to 20 per cent unemployment for stability, that is to say an industrial reserve army of between 1½ and 2½ million.'[2]

Professor Arthur Lewis, on the other hand, took a less severe view. Assuming 3 per cent unemployment as the technical or 'frictional' minimum, he argued:

'Unemployment is such an evil that it is hard to reject any means that would abolish it completely. But some ways of achieving an end are better than others. The way to abolish the 3 per cent of frictional unemployment is to improve the organization of the labour market. To abolish it by bringing down the evils of inflation and direction of labour is like cutting off an arm to save a finger. The level of unemployment can therefore be used as a gauge for monetary policy. In the present state of the British labour market if unemployment is less than 2 per cent of the gainfully occupied population there is inflationary pressure, and if it is more than 3 per cent the monetary tap should be turned on.'[3]

[1] *Economic Journal*, March 1949, p. 9.
[2] *New Statesman and Nation*, January 24, 1948. On the other hand, Mr F. W. Paish held: 'If we are to stabilize wages and so to stabilize prices we must be prepared to contemplate an unemployment level of not less than four per cent.' (*The Listener*, March 4, 1948.) This was more pessimistic than his later estimates.
[3] *Principles of Economic Planning*, 1949, p. 47.

On the other side of the political spectrum, Professor Jewkes (1948), highly critical of Beveridge's proposals, took a decidedly tougher line:

'The target of employment set should not be too high. . . . It would be unwise to try to exceed, *by the use of this method of increasing national expenditure,* a level of about 94 or 95 per cent of employment, i.e. 5 or 6 per cent of unemployment. We cannot work to finer limits than that. Used beyond that point increasing national expenditure is also certain to slip over the edge into inflation and everything it involves. Unemployment of 5 or 6 per cent should not be a matter for concern.'[1]

Like Mrs Robinson, Professor Jewkes pointed out that 'the more controls we are prepared to put up with, the lower would be the average level of unemployment'. He seems to have been over-optimistic, however, in supposing that ' a decade of full employment would completely obliterate the bogy of labour immobility'.[2]

Professor Robbins (1949), also highly critical of Beveridge's proposals, emphasized that 'a world of difference separated the conceptions of the White Paper from the conceptions of *Full Employment in a Free Society*'. He argued that:

'The objective of equality between the demand for and supply of labour, implies essentially, if it is to be acceptable, *that the average level of wages is not rising faster than the average increase in productivity.*

The conception of a certain kind of balance between vacancies and applications . . . if adopted without reserve, was open to objection, first because it might appear to guarantee jobs regardless of the wage level and secondly because it appeared to ignore the possible requirements of international equilibrium.'

Professor Robbins concluded:

'To frame policy with an eye *inter alia* to the maintenance of high levels of employment is wisdom. To frame it with regard to full employment *only* is likely to lead to disappointment and

[1] *Ordeal by Planning*, 1948, p. 79.
[2] *Op cit.*, pp. 82-3.

even, perhaps, to something worse than disappointment.'[1]

Professor Robbins did not then offer any quantitive estimate of the percentage of unemployment that might, on his criteria, prove necessary or desirable. Elsewhere, however, he maintained:

'We get the contemporary picture quite out of perspective if we suppose that an unemployment percentage below two represents a normal state of "full employment". On the contrary, it is one of the surest signs of a state of inflationary pressure. Few things can be more certain than that such a state of affairs cannot persist for ever. But, while it lasts, the same force which imposes a direct drag on the increase of exports at the same time damages the situation still further by undermining industrial discipline.'[2]

Sir Hubert Henderson, in one of his last papers (1950), was even more trenchant:

'It seems to me inevitable, that wage-rates and labour-costs will rise steadily and indefinitely, so long as that sellers' labour market is maintained. Nothing is more chimerical than to suppose that this could be avoided by making an amicable agreement with trade unions about wages policy. . . . Official appeals for a wage standstill can do a good deal to slow down the pace of a wage inflation; but they can no more arrest it in what I have called a sellers' labour market, than King Canute could stop the waves from wetting his feet when the tide was flowing in. It is equally chimerical to suppose that a wage inflation can continue in Great Britain, after inflation has been arrested in other countries, without tending to a progressive loss of British export trade. The idea that it can be avoided by clever devices, or what I should call silly clever devices, designed to keep down the price of our exports will not bear examination. If we were to begin subsidizing exports, we should have to subsidize them increasingly.'[3]

[1] 'Full Employment as an Objective', in *The Economist in the Twentieth Century*, 1954, pp. 33, 34, 38, and 40. Professor D. H. Robertson, in a subsequent review, warmly supported Professor Robbins's arguments on 'full employment'. (*Economic Journal*, March 19, 1955, p. 107).
[2] *Lloyds Bank Review*, October 1949, p. 15.
[3] *Economia Internazionale*, November 1950, p. 960.

We would add to these views of university economists two indications that Labour Chancellors, in the years after the war, were prepared, on occasions at any rate, to be markedly more severe than Chancellors of either party in later years. As regards Sir Stafford Cripps, Mr Shonfield has pointed out:

'There is the extraordinary statement in the Economic Survey of 1948 of his objective to increase the number of unemployed by 50 per cent in the course of the year, and to do so by deliberately putting a damper on the building industry. Unemployment was 300,000 at the end of 1947, and Cripps said that in order to achieve more mobility of labour it would have to go up to 450,000 by the end of 1948. No Cabinet Minister, Labour or Conservative, since that time has been prepared to take his courage in both hands in any comparable way.'[1]

Later, Mr Gaitskell, also, was prepared to try to get back at least to Beveridge's standard, then far exceeded for several years, in March 1951, when he stated that 'the Government has therefore decided . . . to express the full employment standard of the United Kingdom as a level of unemployment of 3 per cent at the seasonal peak'.[2]

We have pointed out that there was very wide agreement that 'full' or a very high level of employment would pose serious problems with regard to wages, inflation and 'freedom', but that there was little agreement as to how these problems could or should be treated. It was not simply that there were, of course, normative differences about the desirable or tolerable level of unemployment. There were, mixed in with, and not sufficiently clearly distinguished from the normative disagreements, also positive disagreements about the effects of different policies or about what combinations of competing objectives were possible or feasible. As Mr Worswick wrote (1952), surveying the post-war years:

'Quite a number of theories about the *optimum* level of employment appeared in the years 1946 to 1950, which purported to

[1] *British Economic Policy since the War*, 1958, p. 166. See also Economic Survey for 1948, Cmd. 7344, pp. 43-4.
[2] Written Parliamentary answer, March 22, 1951.

demonstrate that productivity (and even, in some theories, total production) would rise if the level of employment was less full than was in fact the case. There is far too little evidence about the many conflicting influences mentioned above to put any such theory to a satisfactory test.'

However, despite the paucity of evidence, Mr Worswick was prepared to conclude that:

'In fact, the view that the very high level of employment, which reigned after the war, contributed to the rapid increase in industrial productivity, has more to be said for it than the opposite.'[1]

Fifteen years later (1967), disagreement and ignorance still persisted on much the same scale:

'The trouble is that no accepted body of knowledge exists which would enable one to compare the probable effects of alternative long-term strategies towards demand (not even of that half-knowledge which exists in other fields of economics). The research that has been done on demand management could give a Chancellor some useful information on *how* to reduce the pressure of demand over the next twelve months by a given amount, and even on the delayed repercussions that such measures might have in a further twelve months. But there is very little generally-agreed doctrine which would help him to decide whether this would be a sensible thing to do or not. The real intellectual uncertainty concerns the difference—if any—that alternative policies towards demand would make to the growth of productive capacity in the long run.'[2]

Over fifteen or twenty years, the climate of opinion about the criteria or objectives of employment policy underwent a considerable change. For example, we noticed Mrs Robinson in 1946 arguing that completely full employment was not desirable, and that to raise the level of employment

'from 95 per cent to 98 per cent (not momentarily—but on the

[1] *The British Economy 1945-1950*, edited by G. D. N. Worswick and P. H. Ady, 1952, p. 9.
[2] Samuel Brittan, *Inquest on Planning in Britain*, P.E.P., 1967, p. 38

average) would involve great sacrifice of liberty, and to raise it from 98 per cent to 100 per cent would involve complete conscription of labour'.[1]

But twenty years later Professor Robinson denounced acceptance of as low a level as 2 per cent unemployment as 'cold-blooded' and 'out of the question':

'There is one school of thought which contends that, since the trouble arises from near-full employment, let us give it up. Supporters of this view maintain that a "moderate" amount of unemployment, say between 2 and 3 per cent over all, would be sufficient to keep wages in check and secure stable prices. The evidence for this view is very sketchy. It might need much more. But, in any case, deliberately to adopt such a cold-blooded policy is out of the question.'[2]

Something, or probably several things, have changed and the changes are obviously pretty crucial for policy. But it is not easy to say precisely *what* has changed, that is, how far it has been positive estimates of what is possible, normative views of what is right, or simply blood temperatures; or some combination of all three. Economists, for their part, have not been very lucid or explicit about it. It has certainly turned out to be 'easier', or more practicable, to maintain a 98 per cent level of employment, or more, than was expected twenty years ago. Nevertheless, the view can hardly have changed that levels of employment over about 98 per cent bring serious costs and problems. Professor Robinson herself remarked (1966) that 'pursuing full employment as an end in itself is precisely what has landed the British economy in its present difficulties'.[3]

Of course, a major force at work has been party political competition. No other single index has been more closely, though not invariably, correlated with the ups and downs of the Government's standing in the opinion polls, than the unemployment percentage. But economists' preferences have also changed, along with the national taste for 98½-99 per cent employment levels.

[1] *Collected Economic Papers*, 1951, p. 106 (from a paper dated 1946).
[2] *Economics: An Awkward Corner*, 1966, p. 20.
[3] *Op. cit.*, p. 46.

Certainly no economists twenty years ago would have uttered as a kind of moral proclamation:

'With benefits at their present level the deliberate creation of unemployment much above 1½ per cent for any significant period of time is quite intolerable.'[1]

In fact, as we shall discuss later, the position seems to have been reached, after twenty years of full employment, that economists in Britain, while not boldly proceeding to the New Zealand objective of total employment, according to which 0·5 per cent unemployment is regarded as intolerable[2] and a matter for public demonstrations against the Government, nevertheless argue heatedly as to whether 1½ or 2 per cent of unemployment is 'tolerable' or 'intolerable', with little attempt to analyse the issue further in terms of opportunity costs.

(2) BRITAIN IN THE WORLD ECONOMY

It was, of course, international questions which took up most of Keynes's attention in the last years of his life, questions regarding the nature of the post-war world economic order and of the economic aspects and basis of Britain's rôle in the world (the subject of so many delusions in the decades ahead). In international economic policy-making and discussion, the political assumptions are usually more controversial, weigh more heavily and need more explicit formulation and analysis even than in domestic

[1] See *New Society*, March 2, 1967, p. 327, in a review by Professor M. H. Peston of Mr R. Pryke's book, *Though Cowards Flinch* (1967). Mr Pryke writes (p. 40): 'For a Labour Government deliberately to throw men out of work must rank as one of the great betrayals of principle by a political party.' Perhaps: but, as we have seen, at least there are precedents. One need not go back to Snowden, simply to Sir Stafford Cripps.

[2] However, Sir Roy Harrod has expressed the view that 'any measures deliberately designed to increase the level of unemployment are morally wrong', and that he prefers 'the Swedish target . . . of having the unemployment at 0 per cent'. (*Towards a New Economic Policy*, 1967, pp. 16-7). But as Sir Roy also holds (*op. cit.*, p. 70) that 'growth, always subject to any desirable increase in leisure, has priority over all other objectives', it is difficult to derive from his statements any clear order of priorities, if, as it sometimes will, 'full employment' clashes with the pursuit of 'growth' (e.g. with regard to the choice between pit closures, and continuing subsidies or dearer fuel).

issues. As Mr Harrod put it regarding the much debated question of the sterling balances:

'Of this issue I would say that it is not one that can be settled by economic theorizing, that it is not even one of economic policy in the ordinary sense, but that it is one in which economic policy is raised to the plane of the highest statesmanship.'[1]

Similar in kind was the general issue crudely summarized, or oversimplified, as 'multilateralism' *versus* 'bilateralism', along with the question as to how far Britain should have co-operated with America in the post-war international economic settlement, or should have tried to organize a separate bloc. (Similarly complex, of course, was the Common Market issue of later years.)

We shall present economists' views on Britain's international or external problems (1945-51) under three headings:

(1) the United States Loan Agreement;
(2) the issue of 'multilateralism' and 'bilateralism' and the problem of dollar shortage; and
(3) the problem of the sterling balances.

(i) *The Loan Agreement*

The main international policy issues really began to come under political and public focus towards the end of 1945 with the sudden and unexpectedly early ending of the war and Lend-Lease, and with the negotiation of the Loan Agreement. Those interested in 'shock' effects or 'cold shower' stimuli may study the sudden ending of Lend-Lease and the terms of the US loan of December 1945.

As Mr Dow says:

'It was expected that the war against Japan would continue for some years longer than the war in Europe, during which the economy could be partially demobilized and exports expanded. Beyond this, continued American financial assistance was counted on. Both expectations were to be falsified almost immediately after the end of the war. . . . That there was to be a problem had long been foreseen. But the unexpectedly quick end of the war with Japan removed the year or two's breathing space which it

[1] *Policy Against Inflation*, 1958, p. 111.

had been hoped would allow some rebuilding of our export trade. The abrupt ending of Lend-Lease, that equally unexpectedly followed, removed the assistance which we had come to count on almost as a moral right.'[1]

Some, apparently including Keynes, had hoped for a free gift or at least an interest-free loan, perhaps considerably greater than that eventually made. Thanks largely to the sudden ending of the war by the atomic bomb, the terms of the Loan Agreement certainly emerged with something of the sudden shock of a cold shower, the first dose of post-war reality. But in December 1945, to Chancellor Dalton's blunt question, in the debate on the Agreement, 'What is your alternative?', the only, not very convincing, lines of argument were either: (i) that somehow or other better terms could have been obtained from the Americans; or (ii) that, if better terms were not obtainable, Britain should not have signed the Agreement, and should have tried to have organized a closed 'bloc' of Commonwealth and other countries. However, Dr Balogh, in a letter to *The Times* (December 12, 1945), put it like this:

'In the absence of alternatives or transitional arrangements a substantial immediate loan from the United States was forced on us, at whatever long run cost.'[2]

Later (1952) Dr Balogh maintained:

'A small loan enabling Britain to mobilize her economic power after the abrupt discontinuation of Lend-Lease was probably necessary. It might have been obtained without any strings attached.'[3]

However, still later (1963) Dr Balogh retrospectively took the view:

'The criticism against British policy was not, ultimately, that it

[1] *The Management of the British Economy*, 1945-60, 1964, pp. 9 and 17.
[2] *The Times*, December 2, 1945. See *Unequal Partners*, Vol. II, 1963, p. 148.
[3] *The British Economy 1945-1950*, ed. by G. D. N. Worswick and P. Ady, 1952, p. 480.

accepted American dictation. Britain was in practice (though perhaps not in principle) in no position to resist. It would have entailed too much sacrifice on the part of an exhausted people.'[1]

On the other hand, Professor Robbins argued at the time (January 1947):

'Much as has been said against the agreements . . . no other practical plan for bridging the gap has been brought to the notice of the public. The critics who urged that we could meet the situation by assistance from elsewhere have failed to reveal the sources they had in mind; and the gradual realization of the magnitude of our external disequilibrium has done much to discredit their point of view. Meanwhile, debates in Congress have perhaps gone some way to dispose of the view that the bargaining was all on one side, always a somewhat comic version of the proceedings to those who ever knew Lord Keynes in argument.'[2]

Professor Robbins warned against using the loan to finance 'unrequited exports':

'There is, however, another danger which perhaps is less apparent. We make no contribution to the solution of this problem if we sell our exports on credit or if they are paid for by drafts of existing sterling balances. When the balance of payments is adverse, only sales against hard cash bring advantages. . . . We are, in effect, handing over to others the benefits of the loan which we ourselves need so desperately. How far this is happening today it is not possible to say precisely.'

Professor Robbins concluded:

'There is no way out by attempting to create a closed bloc against the United States. We have neither the means to make it acceptable nor the resources to carry on while it is in the process of formation. Moreover, if it were a question of creating closed blocs, it is not to be believed that the United States, with her almost limitless capacity to lend and to subsidize, would remain quies-

[1] *Unequal Partners*, Vol. II, 1963, p. 12.
[2] *Lloyd's Bank Review*, January 1947, p. 22.

cent; and it is not pleasant to think of the damage to the political equilibrium of the world which might follow from such economic warfare. The men who have urged this course have given bad advice, discreditable to their understanding and dangerous to our future well-being."[1]

Though there was much rather vague grumbling, very few economists were prepared to say bluntly that the Loan Agreement should not have been signed by Britain. One who did oppose Britain's signature was Professor G. D. H. Cole, who argued for the stimulating effects of a still colder shower of post-war reality, in that, by foregoing the loan, Britain would have been forced, and enabled, to go all out for some form of comprehensive 'planning':

'In effect, the taking of the American loan made it possible for Great Britain not to plan the reorganization of British industry, and impossible for her to plan her overseas trade. . . . We should have had to plan, and plan thoroughly not merely in patches but over the entire economic field' [sc. if the loan had been rejected].[2]

The particular clause in the Loan Agreement with immediately dangerous implications was the provision that Britain was to make sterling convertible within one year of the agreement coming into operation. As was pointed out by Sir Hubert Henderson immediately after the conclusion of the agreement:

'Any country can call upon us, within little more than a year from now, to supply it with dollars to an amount represented by its favourable balance of payments with us . . . together with that part of the accumulated balances that we agree to release. Since the world is hungry for goods, most of which can be obtained most easily from the United States, we must expect to be called on to supply dollars to virtually the full extent of this twofold liability.'[3]

[1] *Op. cit.*, pp. 23 and 24.
[2] *New Statesman and Nation*, April 5, 1947, p. 230. See also *New Statesman and Nation*, May 4, 1946, p. 322.
[3] *Bulletin of the Oxford University Institute of Statistics*, January 1946, p. 7; quoted by J. C. R. Dow, *The Management of the British Economy 1945-1960*, 1964, p. 25n.

Again, eighteen months later, just as the convertibility crisis was descending, Sir Hubert emphasized:

'It may prove, I greatly fear, that by agreeing to resume convertibility, years before the Bretton Woods obligation to do so becomes generally operative (if it ever does), we have in effect set up a large notice-board reading "To Countries Short of Dollars: To obtain these, cut down your imports from Britain." If so, we shall not be able to maintain convertibility for very long.'[1]

But unless Sir Hubert was implying that the removal of the convertibility condition could have been obtained from the Americans, or the agreement should not have been signed, these comments were relevant rather as warnings about future difficulties, which certainly arrived rapidly and massively in August 1947.

As Mr Dow points out:

'The Government had fought hard about a rigid commitment to the early resumption of convertibility. Even after the negotiations, Dr Dalton noted in his diary the "secret reflection" that "even in the next year or two, circumstances may require a large revision" of the conditions.'[2]

However, Mr Dow continues:

'What is surprising is that, despite forebodings in 1945 the Government did not suspect that convertibility would lead to trouble; and was slow to believe the mistake would have to be undone.'[3]

(ii) *'Multilateralism', 'Bilateralism' and the Dollar Shortage*

The debate regarding Britain's post-war trade policy was sometimes summarized (and over-simplified) as an issue of 'multilateralism' *versus* 'bilateralism'. But as Mr MacDougall argued, the issue was one of degree rather than of 'key principle'. No one

[1] *Bulletin of the Oxford University Institute of Statistics*, August 1947, p. 279.
[2] *The Management of the British Economy 1945-1960*, 1964, p. 25n.
[3] *Op. cit.*, p. 25.

was maintaining that in no circumstances whatsoever was discrimination to be permitted. Nor was any serious authority arguing for complete freedom for *any* country to discriminate at *any* time or place. Mr MacDougall held:

'Many—perhaps most—of those who think seriously about this subject hold views that would fall into the half-and-half category.'[1]

Mr MacDougall concluded:

'Freedom to discriminate will lead to discrimination not only where this is right and proper, but also for purposes that are destructive of trade. . . . It is particularly important at present that, in applying discriminatory principles for good reason, the world should not allow discrimination to get out of hand.'[2]

The international monetary and trade plans evolved by British and American experts in the later years of the war were on a 'multilateralist' pattern. A most keen supporter of 'multilateralism' was Mr R. F. Harrod who complained of

'lack of enthusiasm in many quarters for international co-operation. This is a deplorable state of affairs. . . . It is the greatest possible folly since there is no alternative method by which we can secure our own prosperity.'

He held that when the scarce currency clause was passed by both Houses of Congress in Washington in July 1945,

'then was the time for national thanksgiving: was a single voice raised?'[3]

Keynes, in his speeches in the House of Lords and his last article (June 1946), inclined towards an optimistic but not un-

[1] *Bulletin of the Oxford University Institute of Statistics*, November 1947, p. 375.
[2] *Op. cit.*, pp. 386 and 389.
[3] *A Page of British Folly*, 1946, pp. 15 and 26. See also *The Life of John Maynard Keynes*, 1951, pp. 544-5, for Mr Harrod's enthusiastic reactions on first reading the Scarce Currency clause in war-time.

qualified 'multilateralism'. Regarding the American proposals on trade and employment which of course followed the 'multilateral' pattern, Keynes argued:

'We have here sincere and thoroughgoing proposals, advanced on behalf of the United States, expressly directed towards creating a system which allows the classical medicine to do its work. It shows how much modernist stuff, gone wrong and turned sour and silly, is circulating in our system, also incongruously mixed, it seems, with age-old poisons, that we should have given so doubtful a welcome to this magnificent, objective approach which a few years ago we should have regarded as offering incredible promise of a better scheme of things. I must not be misunderstood. I do not suppose that the classical medicine will work by itself or that we can depend on it. We need quicker and less painful aids of which exchange variation and overall import control are the most important. But in the long run these expedients will work better and we shall need them less, if the classical medicine is also at work. And if we reject the medicine from our systems altogether, we may just drift on from expedient to expedient and never get really fit again. The great virtue of the Bretton Woods and Washington proposals, taken in conjunction, is that they marry the use of the necessary expedients to the wholesome long-run doctrine.'[1]

Thus Keynes was insisting, repeatedly, on 'necessary expedients'. But his rhetorical question as to whether one was not justified in concluding

'that the chances of the dollar becoming dangerously scarce in the course of the next five to ten years are not very high?'[2]

seems to have amounted to a serious underestimate of the length of the recovery period. Productive capacity was wiped out, or production and trade disrupted, over most of Europe and Asia. Naturally the United States, where production and capacity were completely undamaged and had soared during the war to unparalleled heights not only of war supplies but for civilian con-

[1] *Economic Journal*, June 1946, p. 186.
[2] *Op. cit.*, p. 185.

sumption as well, found her goods desperately sought after all round the world.

As Sir Hubert Henderson, an early critic of enthusiastic 'multilateralism' put it:

'The question is whether plans based on non-discrimination as the key principle are likely, in the conditions left behind by a second major war, to secure a large volume of international trade.'[1]

But the counter-question to Sir Hubert's question was whether these conditions should be assumed by decision-makers to be permanent or long-run, or whether, rather, they should be regarded as transitional, pending reconstruction in Europe, and how long recovery would eventually take? Anyhow, the question of multilateralism and non-discrimination *versus* bilateralism and discrimination, turned largely on attitudes to the phenomenon of 'dollar shortage', and whether this was conceived as requiring the sufferers from this ailment—Britain, Western Europe and much of the world—to undertake the organization, in self-defence, of 'a full-employment bloc', to withstand the predicted disastrous consequences of the economic power of the United States.

The predictions of 'dollar shortage' were not, of course, simply based on the difficulties of some ultimately limited reconstruction period, however prolonged this was regarded as likely to be. Much of the opposition to the 'multilateralist' international settlement was based on fears of American instability and another great American depression, then being widely and expertly predicted. As so often, Keynes himself had provided the main arguments of his opponents twenty years previously (1925), when he was criticizing the objectives or effects of the old gold standard as being 'to link rigidly the City and Wall Street':

'The United States lives in a vast and unceasing crescendo. Wide fluctuations, which spell unemployment and misery for us, are swamped for them in the general upward movement. A country, the whole of whose economic activities are expanding, year in, year out, by several per cent per annum, cannot avoid, and at the

[1] *Bulletin of the Oxford University Institute of Statistics*, August 1947, p. 281.

same time can afford, temporary maladjustments. This was our own state during a considerable part of the nineteenth century. Our rate of progress was so great that stability in detail was neither possible nor essential. This is not our state now. Our rate of progress is slow at the best, and faults in our economic structure which we could afford to overlook whilst we were racing forward and which the United States can still afford to overlook, are now fatal. . . . The United States may suffer industrial and financial tempests in the years to come, and they will scarcely matter to her; but we, if we share them, may almost drown.'[1]

Though Keynes would, presumably, not have wished to deny that the Great Depression of 1929 and the thirties 'scarcely mattered' to the United States, his insight had much validity when it was written (1925). But the question in 1945 was whether things were not going to turn out differently after the war. Dr Thomas Balogh thought that they would not. He saw (November 1945)

'no reason why such a change in the American economic and social structure and political organization is to be expected which would render a full employment of that country and the balancing of its foreign payments in any way likely'.[2]

He alleged:

'The US may at last have found the elixir of a "stable and high" level of employment. But Lord Keynes has on at least two previous occasions—1929 and 1936—congratulated them on their success. On those occasions he was, unfortunately, somewhat premature.'[3]

Dr Balogh maintained:

'The difficulties of maintaining stability in the United States

[1] *Essays in Persuasion*, 1931, p. 233. See E. F. Schumacher, *Export Policy and Full Employment*, 1944, p. 29.
[2] *Unequal Partners*, Vol. II, 1963, p. 146.
[3] *The Economist*, January 5, 1946. (References were not provided regarding Keynes's predictions in 1929 and 1936).

have increased as a result of the war and are, at the moment, different in order of magnitude from those experienced by other countries.'[1]

But, of course, it was not simply instability and depression in the United States economy which it was predicted would provoke dollar shortage for Europe and the rest of the world: alternatively its 'dynamism', or more rapidly increasing technological and competitive power, would do the same. As Professor Kindleberger put it, it was a case of 'heads-I-win, tails-you-lose'.[2] The position attained by the United States economy was of unique epoch-making significance, according to Dr Balogh (1948):

'The rise of the United States to a position unparalleled since the Roman Empire has placed the world in a dilemma unless indeed, as we shall argue below, conscious measures are taken to restore equilibrium. We either have to envisage prodigious investment activity in the United States which increases the competitive power of that country faster than productivity rises elsewhere and thereby *leads to periodic pressure abroad and probable break-downs*, or continued depression which makes nonsense of the classical mechanism of adjustment towards a "creditor position".'[3]

The problem was held to be of very long-run dimensions: it had, as well, something to do with sheer size:

'Even after the fundamental disequilibrium in the world's balance of payments arising from the war and the slow recovery of the old world has been overcome the disequilibrium between the United States and the rest of the world is likely to persist. This disequilibrium is due to the discrepancy in order of magnitude of the economic power of the United States and any other single country, except perhaps the USSR in the long run. . . .'

'Western Europe's crisis is not a temporary or short-lived

[1] *Bulletin of the Oxford University Institute of Statistics*, October 1946, p. 320; see *Unequal Partners*, Vol. II, 1963, p. 157.
[2] *The Dollar Shortage*, 1950, p. 78
[3] 'The United States and International Economic Equilibrium', in *Foreign Economic Policy for the United States*, edited by Seymour Harris, 1948, p. 467. Dr Balogh held (1954) that this argument 'does not seem to need amendment'. (*Oxford Economic Papers*, September 1954, p. 283).

departure from an "equilibrium position" to which it is easy to return. It is a historically unique, harsh break with all that has gone before, a fundamental structural crisis which, if it can be cured at all, can be cured only by a set of carefully planned and discriminating policies."[1]

Dr Balogh was able to imagine very alarming possibilities for Europe: (though important, long-run policies, of course, should be based on reasonable estimates of what is probable, not simply on what 'it is possible to imagine'):

'Even in the more distant future it is possible to imagine so large a superiority in US technical progress over Europe, as to turn the terms of trade sufficiently against the latter to cause an actual fall in the standard of life. In any case, most of Europe's efforts to raise herself might be perpetually stultified by this pressure on the terms of trade even if her standard of life did not actually fall. . . .'

'The discrepancy between American productivity and that of the rest of the non-Communist world is so great that a relatively small decline in the US might strike like a tornado elsewhere.'[2]

However, it surely did not require very profound economic *expertise* to discern that if and when European and Asian recovery advanced, an important element in the 'dollar problem' would be removed. In 1951 Dr Balogh observed:

'It is also obvious that with the recovery of Europe the external dependence of Europe on American crude food exports has dwindled. In the same way the American exports of machinery will not be quite as needed as they were just immediately after the war. The advantages of America in third markets will not any longer derive from the physical impossibility of obtaining machines elsewhere. . . . In the long run, however, there seems no reason to change the sceptical view put forward on earlier occasions. . . . In the long run the "propensity" to import of

[1] *Op. cit.*, p. 476 and p. 478.
[2] *The Dollar Crisis, Causes and Cure*, 1949, p. 138 and p. 140.

America so far as primary goods are concerned is likely to decrease rather than increase.'[1]

It must be emphasized that the long-run dollar shortage was predicted not simply as a British, but as a European or world problem. Anyhow, by the early fifties, American vices in the form of instability and depression having failed to strike quite like 'a tornado', the emphasis shifted in Oxford to American virtues, that is, to the other horn of the dilemma, in the form of 'dynamism' and rapidly rising productivity, which then came to be emphasized as a cause of chronic dollar shortage. This argument had a brief if intellectually high-powered run for its money, but was, of course, nicely timed to coincide with the onset of nearly a decade of some sluggishness in the American economy under Eisenhower, though not with anything reasonably to be described as a 'depression' occurring. The course actually taken lay fairly precisely between instability, on the one hand, and 'dynamism' on the other, that is, as we shall discuss below, rather neatly between the two horns of the predicted dilemma.

(iii) *Sterling Balances: the Level of Investment*

In the autumn of 1947 the Government was a sitting target for criticism. The American loan had been spent in a fraction of the period for which it had been intended to last. Of course it had gone either on consumption, investment or the repayment of debt. In the most extreme of the attacks on the Government, Mr Harrod concentrated on the two latter categories. His first line of criticism was against the freeing of the sterling balances, accumulated largely by poorer countries in the Commonwealth (later to be called 'underdeveloped' or 'developing') in return for supplying war resources and facilities. He regarded the use of the loan to repay the balances not simply as incompetent, but as dishonourable, 'a veritable economic Munich':

'It is clearly wrong for us to begin paying out these sums now, while we are still dependent on foreign assistance and while the rations of our own people remain insecure.'[2]

[1] *Bulletin of the Oxford University Institute of Statistics*, May 1951, p. 160.
[2] *Are These Hardships Necessary?* ('Mr Harrod says No!'), 1947, pp. 53 and 178.

Mr Harrod specified the case of India, to whom balances had been released, and who was then (August 1947) achieving her independence. He went on:

'Primitive peoples who have struggled in hard conditions through centuries, which we cannot count, must be educated and raised to a higher degree of civilization. But there is no categorical imperative to take action on a large scale for another two, three or five years.'[1]

Later Mr Harrod concluded (1952):

'In my judgment this was the most momentous policy issue which has confronted Britain in the present century. . . . Each balance should have been replaced by a non-negotiable acknowledgment of indebtedness of like amount by the British Government.'[2]

Professor Robbins, in more moderate terms, took a rather similar line (1949):

'So long as there are outstanding the abnormally large balances accumulated during the war by governments and persons abroad, whose withdrawal is limited only by special arrangements made *ad hoc* at frequent special negotiations, so long will the situation have an incurable instability and uncertainty, utterly inimical to the restoration of more normal conditions. It is not only that with the type of temporary settlement which at present prevails in this field, our negotiators (i.e. the Chancellor and other Ministers concerned) seem chronically unable to refrain from making concessions which are obviously out of all relation to what is prudent—witness the amazing terms recently accorded to India—it is also that while there is this abnormally large volume of "old" sterling about in the world, it is almost impossible to make any real progress to the re-establishment of convertibility. Until this problem is settled on a more permanent footing, it is safe to say that we shall have to continue to endure exchange control of the most ferocious nature

[1] *Op. cit.*, p. 56.
[2] *The Pound Sterling*, 1952, p. 11.

and that nevertheless our balance of payments will continue to be in jeopardy.'[1]

Professor Robbins went on:

'Although there should be no question of repudiation, there can be no obligation to repay at a rate which endangers our general stability.'

However, he admitted:

'Despite the fact that more rapid release creates intolerable embarrassments here at home, it cannot be denied that there are political considerations which make it difficult to discontinue the process.'[2]

Dr Balogh (1949) also complained of 'unrequited exports' and of the flow of capital to 'the Empire', and called for 'the judicious use of controls':

'The damning of the flood of British funds to the sterling area which might be used to finance unrequited exports, together with energetic measures to push exports, should once more restore the sterling area dollar balance. There has been no indication, however, that the present policy of the Bank of England, which fails in preventing the flow of capital into the Empire and thus permits the finance of unrequited exports, will be reversed.'[3]

The issue was certainly one of painful difficulty, one, as we have noticed Mr Harrod saying, of 'economic statesmanship', not to be settled by economic theorizing. It might have been *just* possible that some agreement could have been entered into which would not have caused undue 'hardships' to poor creditors but which would have significantly eased the British position. But it seems difficult to assert dogmatically that any such arrangement could obviously have been arrived at. Indeed, as Professor Robertson subsequently put it:

[1] *Lloyds Bank Review*, October 1949, p. 25.
[2] *Op. cit.*, pp. 26 and 27.
[3] *The Dollar Crisis, Causes and Cure*, 1949, p. XXXI.

'Repaying debt is seldom such an agreeable process as incurring it; and there was a good deal of rather intemperate talk in England, by politicians of both the leading parties and economists of diverse schools, about the flood of "unrequited exports" which was supposed to be pouring into Asia in repayment of war debt incurred in her defence, and to be causing an unwarranted strain on Britain's productive capacity.' . . .

'India can argue that only by means of her lavish dollar expenditure and of those "unrequited exports" from Britain which Mr Churchill and Mr Dalton vied with one another in grudging in 1947 was she able to avert famine and chaos and turn herself into the main bulwark against Communist engulfment of the East.'[1]

Mr Harrod's second main line of attack was on the level of capital investment undertaken, or allowed, by the Labour Government, which we discuss here since he linked it so closely with the balance of payments difficulties as its immediate cause. He held:

'What we did, and had no right to do, was to make plans for capital outlay greatly in excess of the easement that was being provided for us.'[2]

He expressed some nostalgia for the austerities of the old classical political economy:

'Indeed it might well be argued that we should be better off with the old Political Economy which, with all its shortcomings, succeeded for a long time in retaining its hold upon the mind of the average well-informed citizen. . . . The old school would have said, quite rightly in existing circumstances, that if foreign

[1] *Britain in the World Economy*, 1954, p. 41 and p. 46. India could also have argued that under British rule during the war, in addition to her military casualties, she had in fact suffered a famine in Bengal in 1943 in which 'three million people died of hunger' (T. Zinkin, *India*, 1965, p. 73)—'hardships', or 'insecure rations', of rather a different order of magnitude as compared with Britain's.

[2] *Are These Hardships Necessary?*, 1947, p. 37.

trade was out of balance it was because we were living beyond our means.'[1]

Mr Harrod deplored that the Government was still giving first priority to the 'reconstruction of our basic industries and services'. He went on:

'We must abandon the foolish idea that it helps our balance of trade to cut imports as such. Only a cut in the capital programme can make a substantial improvement in the balance of trade. Import cuts are particularly undesirable, because on the whole imports are especially important, whether materials for industry or food. When people are left free to economize in their consumption in their own way, it is unlikely that those economies will be mainly directed against imported goods. There is no harm in that.'[2]

Looking ahead Mr Harrod inquired:

'Supposing that the international plans were in full working order, would this country have the right, having embarked upon capital programmes far beyond its means and far beyond what is needed to maintain full employment, and having thereby created a large adverse balance of trade, to claim that some international adjustment must be made to allow this adverse balance of trade to continue?'[3]

Mr Harrod later (December 1947) elaborated his point of view further:

'According to free trade doctrine, if foreign trade is not in balance, that must be because the individuals in the nation are trying to live beyond their means. The cure would be retrenchment, not specifically in the purchase of foreign goods, but in the purchase of goods generally. In the particular case of Britain today, of course, it is in the great capital instal-

[1] *Op. cit.*, pp. 58 and 62.
[2] *Op. cit.*, p. 151.
[3] *Op. cit.*, p. 136.

lation programmes that retrenchment should be made.'[1]

Mr Harrod was far from alone in his criticism of the Government's investment plans. But from across the Atlantic Professor Schumpeter, in a review of English writings on policy (1949), expressed his great surprise at finding English economists disapproving of the Government's attitude towards investment. He suggested that 'England's economy suffers from excess consumption and under-saving.' He concluded:

'A Labour Government that is still more than are any other governments under the temptation to neglect its nation's future deserves credit and not blame for its efforts to foster industrial investment.'[2]

Professor Schumpeter probably never actually tasted the watery post-war beer or snoek or whale-meat steak. All the same, his surprise at finding a majority of English economists so vigorously condemning the Government's investment plans does not itself seem very surprising. Schumpeter also found surprising the thorough-going defence of 'multilateralism' indulged in by some English economists during this arduous period:

'In England's present situation I, for one, find it difficult to accept, e.g. Harrod's brief argument for all but unrestricted multilateralism, non-discrimination, and freely interchangeable currencies. . . . As we have seen, England, her economic and social structure being what they are, cannot take the course that would have appealed to Ricardo. Instead she has to manoeuvre

[1] *And So It Goes On, further thoughts on present mismanagement*, 1951, p. 117. On this and other matters Mr Harrod stated 'I have much confidence in the general drift of my pleading' (p. viii).

[2] *Journal of Political Economy*, October 1949, p. 379. Another critic of over-ambitious investment plans was Dr J. R. Hicks (*Lloyds Bank Review*, July, 1947, p. 9): 'One of our difficulties is that we have got into a state of mind which looks upon a major reconstruction of British industry as one of our most urgent obligations. But, as things are, major reconstruction is not a thing which we can possibly afford. If we try to undertake it, we shall merely experience recurrent breakdowns of the kind we experienced in the coal crisis of this spring.' On the other hand, Mr R. F. Kahn strongly favoured more investment and cuts in consumption at this time. See *The Listener*, May 6, 1948, and February 3, 1949. The two leading and closest disciples of Keynes, Mr Kahn and Mr Harrod, diverged sharply both on points of policy, and later on theory, when in their evidence to the Radcliff Committee they took diametrically opposite views on the distinction between cost-push and demand-pull inflation. See below p. 154n 2.

back to a normal position by *all* the means at her command—credit policy, taxation, rationing, exchange and trade controls of all kinds, with devaluation, perhaps as a final measure to help over the last few steps towards abandoning the discrimination against the dollar: her case is not one for specious simple measures à la Keynes."[1]

(3) PLANNING AND THE PRICE MECHANISM

Three main factors in the years just after the war combined to pose for debate the general issues of planning and the price mechanism: (i) the problems of reconversion from the war economy, and the question of the peace-time rôle of government both in the transition and in the longer run, in view, particularly, of Britain's difficult foreign trade position; (ii) the question as to how far the new, agreed governmental task of maintaining a high level of employment would affect the balance between central regulation and the price mechanism; (iii) the rather nebulous and variegated notions of the Labour Government (and Party) regarding 'planning'.

In this chapter then, we are standing back somewhat from specific issues of contemporary policy and considering views on general principles. But although subsequently the debate was not pursued much in terms of general principle, in fact, throughout our whole period, regarding almost all the main questions of policy (except devaluation), economists tended to group themselves, on both positive and normative issues, into those favouring more planning as against those favouring freer use of the price mechanism. The former were usually in favour of a rather higher level of aggregate demand, in positive terms preferred 'cost-push' to 'demand-pull' explanations of inflation, supported more 'purposive' growth policies, with an often hostile attitude to Britain's joining the European Common Market. The latter, the price-mechanists, tended to favour slightly lower levels of aggregate demand, explanations of inflation in terms of 'demand-pull', showed more preference for price stability, were more prepared to subordinate the pursuit of growth to this and other objectives, and were rather more likely to favour Britain's entry into the European Common Market.

[1] *Op. cit.*, p. 382.

Anyhow most of the leading economists took the opportunity of pronouncing on the issues in general terms (1946-1949). Some of these contributions have lasting value as statements of the general principles of economic policy in a mixed economy. Others were more concerned with detailed topical proposals and comment, and others with ideological self-expression. One general feature of these writings is their little attempt to distinguish and make explicit the different objectives of policy, and to set out the assumptions being made about them. There was a tendency to imply that these were obvious, compatible and agreed.

A provocative prelude had been provided in 1944 by Professor Hayek's *The Road to Serfdom*, with its clarion call to Britain to go back to the nineteenth century, with regard, at least, to 'ideals', adding dire warnings of woe if she did not.[1] Professor Hayek's line of thought was followed up by Professor Jewkes, who in his *Ordeal by Planning* (1948) offered a wholesale tirade against 'planning' and 'planners'. We have already cited his views regarding 5 or 6 per cent as a suitable target for the level of unemployment. Perhaps more significant today than his general denunciations, is his catalogue of well-documented examples of planning in Britain at the time:

'A market gardener requires a new shaft for a wheel-barrow, a piece of wood costing perhaps ninepence. A licence must be applied for from the surveyor of the district council on the appropriate form. The licence has to be registered and filed by the district surveyor and then presented to, registered and filed by the timber merchant. A local authority for roads wishes to improve visibility at a dangerous junction by substituting some twenty yards of iron fence for the existing hedge. To obtain permission to do this five enormous forms and nine maps, some of them coloured, have to be prepared and submitted. The despatch of a small shipment of six drums of lubricating oil involves the filling in of forty-six forms, requiring forty-two signatures, not including the customer's invoice or delivery notes. A local authority cannot increase the pocket-money of a child under its care without first obtaining sanction from the Home

[1] 'Though we can neither wish nor possess the power to go back to the reality of the nineteenth century, we have the opportunity to realize its ideals.' Phoenix Books edition, p. 240.

Office. Newspapers are fined for exceeding more than 55 per cent of advertising matter. A firm is fined for making 60,000 frying-pans for the home market, although it is established by evidence that the firm had done this only because of long delays by the Board of Trade in providing an export licence, a licence which in fact had been received after the fine had been imposed. A provincial corn merchant operates under fourteen licences and 160 fixed prices. His books have been minutely investigated five times since control began; inspectors drop in at least four times a year to see if they can catch him; the Costings Department of his Ministry require his trading accounts and balance sheets; he is expected to remember the salient points of hundreds of Orders and Regulations. Orders are couched in language open to all sorts of meanings so that the public could not know whether they were acting legally or not unless they took counsel's opinion or a solicitor's advice. Four Lincolnshire farmers are fined £1,200 for growing canary seed. Mrs Shenton, aged 79, is fined £10 for growing too few potatoes; she said she had responded to a Ministry broadcast appeal to grow more wheat. . . .

The detail of the control is incredible. The *Board of Trade Journal* warns retailers that it is illegal to embellish utility furniture. The women of Pangbourne wanted to run a bazaar to raise funds for a village hall; they were informed by the Board of Trade that a pair of boy's trousers made out of an adult's skirt or trousers are regarded as new and, therefore, coupons must be charged. The Board of Trade finds time to fix maximum prices for haircuts. Churchers College, Petersfield, receives a form from the Ministry of Fuel and Power informing them that their previous allocation of coke had been cancelled and that their basic allocation for the twelve months to April 30, 1948, was nil tons, that it was possible only to allocate nil tons, divided as to nil tons a month in the summer and nil tons a month in the winter, and that the name of the supplier was also indicated. Boxes containing fragments of wedding-cake sent to friends abroad are emptied and sent on empty because the export of confectionery is prohibited. The Government seeks to impose an Order preventing a householder from decorating his own house, without getting a licence, if the cost of the raw materials plus the estimated cost of his own labour comes to more than £10. Strong protests forced the Government to exclude the cost of labour but not to drop the control. The owners of private gardens are prohibited, except under licence, to bottle fruit and sell it to the public. A householder cannot obtain a replacement for a cracked wash-bowl without getting a licence from the local authority and having the bowl examined to prove it is unusable.'[1]

For all that, and much more, the question remained as to what to do next, in a very difficult situation of massive inflationary potential, with the extensive apparatus of controls left over from the war.

On the other wing, Sir Oliver Franks was one of the most vigorous champions of central planning (1947). To some extent he seemed to be wanting to carry over into peace the methods and motives of war. As regards foreign trade he maintained

'that no government in the foreseeable future, say, the next dozen years is likely to dare to do without export programmes and import programmes centrally planned and controlled. The fear of scarcity and the threat of crisis will never be sufficiently far away. The struggle for the standards of life will be too grim and the issue too precarious.'[2]

As regards the rôle of government in economic planning:

'It is engaged on a far greater adventure than an experiment with certain measures and methods in novel circumstances. It is engaged on a radical redefinition of the function of government in the economic field and is asserting its job to be the shaping of situations before they arise. In short, it has gone into business management and become general manager of the national economy.'[3]

Sir Oliver (invoking both Churchill and Stalin), called for a 'miracle of statesmanship', anticipating many subsequent appeals to the spirit of 1940:

'How the quantitative, abstract and generalized expressions

[1] *Ordeal by Planning*, 1948, pp. 217 and 220. References for each case are, of course, cited by Professor Jewkes.
[2] *Central Planning and Control in War and Peace*, 1947, p. 24.
[3] *Op. cit.*, p. 35.

which represent the goal to which the economy is directed are to be given flesh and blood so that they live as the hope and desire of the people I do not know. It is at once the task and the miracle of statesmanship to translate them into terms which have meaning and inspiration to ordinary men in ordinary circumstances. I am aware that such leadership has to effect a revolution in men's minds: that it has to change their conception of the rôle of the State in industry and commerce and therefore alter their idea of their own parts. That is the measure of its necessity in a democracy. It is comparable to what was done by Winston Churchill amid the events of 1940. It may be compared, too, to a very different task, undertaken in a different context with very different methods by Stalin in the Five Years' Plan.'[1]

Sir Oliver noted the kind of *expertise* required:

'Since central planning concerns the future and what can be done in it, it is necessarily occupied with extrapolation from the present. Trends and tendencies must be isolated and analysed so that forecasts can be built up and estimates made. This cannot be done by purely intellectual processes: or if it is, the results are certain to be unreal and bad guides for practice. An awareness of how things happen is required, of the interrelations of commercial and industrial processes, of the factors which enter into the business decisions of business men. That is why good forecasting and estimating is an art though using all the scientific techniques that the study of statistics has made available. It is not the art of what war-time nomenclature called the back-room boy. It requires knowledge of the world as well as highly specialized training. It is no criticism of the Civil Service to say that it has not enough experts of this kind. There are not enough in existence.'[2]

More towards the middle of the road, between Sir Oliver and Professor Jewkes, though with varying shades of emphasis, were the contributions from Professors Robbins and Robertson, Meade and Lewis (as they then were). The first pair might perhaps be described as rather to the right of centre, and the second perhaps rather to the left.

[1] *Op cit.*, p. 37.
[2] *Op. cit.*, p 52.

Professor Robbins in *The Economic Problem in Peace and War* (1947) discussed lucidly and judiciously the continuing rôles of government in peace, and the desirability of a wider scope for market mechanisms, as contrasted with war-time. Rejecting, in peace, 'a system of economic totalitarianism', Professor Robbins saw the first requirement of policy as being to remove 'the disintegrating effects of suppressed inflation'. He did not favour 'here and now' a rise in interest rates, nor a drastic surgical deflationary operation on the monetary system as had been carried out in Belgium. But he wanted to 'begin to make more use of the price system', though certainly not 'an immediate abandonment of all controls':

'My conception rather is to ease the strain by letting prices rise by stages.'[1]

But though he saw 'no reason against proceeding internally at a fairly smart pace in the direction I have indicated',

'I see much greater difficulty in moving towards a rapid approach to decontrol in the external sector. . . . The degree of our external disequilibrium is so great and the uncertainty and disorganization of the world is so extensive that I see no immediate prospect of the abandonment of control of imports.'[2]

Acknowledging an earlier 'tendency to ignore certain deep-seated possibilities of disharmony', Professor Robbins concluded:

'For the avoidance of both inflation and deflation, I favour something which, if you like, you can call overall financial planning.'[3]

But he warned very cogently that:

'The promise of planning for full employment tends to elide rather too slickly the very real problem of wages policy. The theory of wages is not in a very satisfactory condition at the present day.'[4]

[1] *The Economic Problem in Peace and War*, 1947, pp. 61-3.
[2] *Op. cit.*, pp. 64-5.
[3] *Op cit.*, p. 68.
[4] *Op. cit.*, p. 70.

Professor Robertson, reviewing current controversies (1947), was on major points often in close agreement with Professor Robbins. He gently criticized 'the amiable woolliness' of the Government's conception of 'planning' in its Economic Survey for 1947, and also Sir Oliver Franks's ideas about planning and control, not feeling

'disposed to admit that the seamless robe of Frankish corporativism is the only, or indeed likely to be the most efficient, wear in which to face whatever permanent readjustment of the national life is forced upon us by the ending, if it *has* ended, of that chapter which began when we set out with such splendid improvidence to become the workshop of the world'.[1]

Professor Meade in his *Planning and the Price Mechanism* (1948) argued in favour of what he called 'the Liberal-Socialist Solution'. The four immediate steps he recommended were:

(i) 'Effective but equitable measures must be taken to reduce the present inflationary pressure of excessive monetary demand.' . . .

(ii) 'The working of the price mechanism should be restored piecemeal in particular markets.' . . .

(iii) 'Steps must be taken to control the export of capital.' . . .

(iv) 'We should do everything we can to restore the international working of the price mechanism."[2]

Professor Meade opposed 'planning without prices', and criticized the inefficiency and waste of controls, holding that

'there can be no doubt that money and the pricing system are among the greatest social inventions of mankind'.[3]

Professor Meade proclaimed a middle way:

'This middle way, which . . . I have called the Liberal-Socialist Solution, must proceed by making full use of the money and pricing systems, but so controlling those systems that three fundamental conditions are fulfilled: first, that the total monetary

[1] 'The Economic Outlook', *Economic Journal*, December 1947, p. 436.
[2] *Planning and the Price Mechanism*, 1948, pp. vi-x.
[3] *Op. cit.*, p. 9.

demand for goods and services is neither too great nor too small in relation to the total supply of goods and services that can be made available for purchase; secondly, that there is a tolerably equitable distribution of money income and property so that no individual can command more than his fair share of the community's resources; and thirdly, that no private person or body of persons should be allowed to remain uncontrolled in a sufficiently powerful position to rig the market for his own selfish ends."[1]

Professor Meade went on to a more detailed examination of these three headings, including under monopoly the wage-fixing functions of the trade unions. (We have already cited Professor Meade's views on 4 per cent unemployment as a technical minimum in a dynamic society and Professor Kahn's comments thereon.)[2]

Professor Arthur Lewis's study, *The Principles of Economic Planning*, prepared for the Fabian Society, came fairly close to Professor Meade's 'Liberal-Socialist' ideas. Professor Lewis warned the Fabians of the dangers of hampering enterprise:

'The stifling effect of direction on enterprise, . . . is a consideration of the utmost importance in a country like the United Kingdom. This is a country which lives by foreign trade. We built up this trade by being first in the field of mass production of standard commodities. But today other nations are as good as we are at this game, if not better, and we can hold our own only if we are constantly in the vanguard pioneering new ideas; inventing new goods and processes, trying them out on the market, adjusting rapidly in accordance with consumer reaction, and so on. None of this can be foreseen, and so none of this can be planned from the centre. The future of the country depends on bold and free entrepreneurship; on people with new ideas being free to back them against all opposition, to get what resources of capital, labour and raw materials they need without bureaucratic hindrance and to test out the market for themselves. Any form of planning which prevents this permanently, or for long periods, will be the ruin of Great Britain. . . .

[1] *Op. cit.*, p. 11.
[2] See above, I(i) p. 30.

The obvious moral of all this is that our aim should be to preserve free markets wherever possible. The manager of an industrial establishment, whether private or public, should be left free to adjust his concern to market condition; to make what he can sell, and to make it with whatever combination of resources he can most cheaply buy. This does not mean that he will be free from control; on the contrary, he is the servant of the market, which controls everything that he does. Neither does it limit the scope of planning. For the state can do all the planning it wants by controlling in its turn the market which controls the entrepreneur. The state can plan as much as it wants, but it should plan not by direction but by manipulating the market.'[1]

One of the earliest contributions and one of the most incisive and topically relevant, came in Professor F. W. Paish's two papers on 'Planning and the Price System' and 'Cheap Money Policy' (both 1947). On the current possibilities for policy at that time Professor Paish concluded:

'We have four possible ways in which the present situation may develop—open inflation, increased controls, monetary deflation plus higher interest rates, and a reduction in Government expenditure coupled with increased or maintained indirect taxation, leading to a Budget surplus.'[2]

Regarding controls, he argued:

'No really large-scale extension of controls is now practicable, both because a revival of labour control would be unacceptable to public opinion, and because the recruitment of the great new Government staffs needed to adminster them would still further reduce the already inadequate supply of labour available for production.'[3]

As regards monetary deflation and a rise in interest rates, Professor Paish maintained:

'Such a policy . . . would acutely embarrass the Government's

[1] *The Principles of Economic Planning,* 1949, pp. 18-20.
[2] *The Post-War Financial Problem and Other Essays,* 1950, p. 34.
[3] *Op cit.,* p. 46.

financial arrangements; and it might easily lead to a major financial crisis and severe, if temporary, unemployment. Further, it would almost certainly achieve the desired balance between demand and supply at existing prices only by compelling the postponement of many of the plans which the Government holds necessary for the rehabilitation of the country's productive efficiency."[1]

Professor Paish favoured 'a policy of reductions in subsidies, increased indirect taxation, and Budget surpluses', with an extension of children's allowances. He concluded:

'The popular antithesis between planning and the absence of planning is essentially unreal. The true choice is not between plan and no plan, but between planning through the price system and planning against it.'[2]

A thoroughly realistic, empirical and sceptically unprejudiced approach was expressed by Sir Hubert Henderson (1947-8). Starting from the completely different political assumptions valid in wartime, as contrasted with those relevant in peace, Sir Hubert foresaw 'an indefinitely continuing need for quantitative programmes of import restrictions'.[3] But he expressed somewhat caustic scepticism regarding the more elaborate types of quantitative planning and 'the so-called "model" type of comprehensive forecast'. Sir Hubert was particularly critical of Mr Kaldor's rather optimistic projections.[4] Perhaps Sir Hubert did not sufficiently distinguish between the merits of experimenting with new techniques, and the naiveté of taking seriously, as 'scientific' predictions or as reliable bases for policy, the fruits of such techniques:

'The intellectual ingenuity which goes to this work is often impressive; but for any practical purpose in the sphere of central

[1] *Op cit.*, p. 47.
[2] *Op. cit.*, pp. 49-50.
[3] See Sir Hubert's papers on 'The Uses and Abuses of Economic Planning' (1947), and on 'The Price System' (1948), reprinted in *The Inter-War Years*, 1955; see pp. 338-40.
[4] See Mr Kaldor's Appendix C, in *Full Employment in a Free Society*, by W. H. Beveridge, 1944, p. 344.

economic policy, the method has the serious defect that the factors which are of dominating importance are often quite unpredictable, though the consequent unreliability of the final result is hidden from spectators by the massive bulk of the apparatus employed. Moreover, in the process of guessing the key factors, the sort of Gresham's Law is apt to operate, under which wishful thinking drives out commonsense. . . . If used as instruments of central economic policy, calculations of the "model" type, are unlikely in my view to do more than provide model dwellings for a Fools' Paradise.'[1]

Sir Hubert argued that:

'Disillusionment, following attempts to apply muddled notions about planning, may cause a reaction towards *laissez-faire* doctrine and practice which might prove unfortunate in the extreme. In overcoming our many difficulties, we may derive real help from planned arrangements of various sorts.'[2]

He concluded:

'A century ago economists were laughed at as the practitioners of the dismal science. They scarcely deserve that taunt, or should I say that compliment, today. I feel it must be recorded that during a period in which the British people have been faced with most formidable economic difficulties, to surmount which it is important above all else to appreciate the magnitude of the effort required, the most extravagant propagandist of go-easy illusions, the most pushing salesmen of enervating Fools' Paradises, have been found among economists of diverse schools of thought. We have now, I hope, done with the illusion that a much better time could be had quite easily by all if only industry were mobilized for national purposes, as it was to produce Fido, and Pluto, and Mulberry. It would be no improvement to replace this by the illusion that our present austerities are unnecessary, and would vanish like the snow if the sun of the price system were allowed to shine.'[3]

[1] *The Inter-War Years*, 1955, p. 339.
[2] *Op. cit.*, p. 341.
[3] *Op. cit.*, p. 356.

Much of what Sir Hubert said could have been well said again in the early sixties. But he seems to have underestimated contemporary economists' capacity for generating gloom, when the, usually highly probable, assumption was being realized of their particular nostrum *not* being implemented.

In the course of this debate, as in many other economic policy debates, the examples of other countries were held up with varying relevance, as horrible portents on the one hand or as shining paragons on the other. By 1950, Germany, led by its Economics Minister Dr Erhardt, was about to launch out on free-market policies. The most appalling consequences, both for Germany herself and for the rest of the world, were predicted by Dr Thomas Balogh of Oxford (1950). Dr Balogh denounced 'the terrible limitations of the obsolete economic philosophy held by the present rulers of Germany', that is by Professor Erhardt and his 'experts', and 'satellite economists', who were trying to discredit 'enlightened Keynesian economic policy'.[1] Dr Balogh complained:

'The currency reform helped to weaken the trade unions. They cannot and do not press with decisive force for more decent working and social conditions. Their weakness may even inhibit increases in productivity, since large scale investment at high interest does not pay at the present low relative level of wages.'[2]

According to Dr Balogh:

'In order to enforce efficiency and to prevent cumulative speculative price movements in a tight situation, it will probably prove necessary to restore price supervision if not statutory controls. . . . In the same way some physical control of investment will also prove inevitable.'[3]

Dr Balogh predicted the most dangerous political consequences:

'Nothing but fast reform by free men can prevent the Western

[1] *Germany: An Experiment in 'Planning' by the 'Free' Price Mechanism*, 1950, pp. 67-9.
[2] *Op. cit.*, p. 7.
[3] *Op. cit.*, pp. 62-3.

Germans from deserting political moderation for the militant extremes of right and left. . . . There is a final warning in the gain which the Soviet Zone of Germany has been able to record. With reparations relaxed the Eastern gain is likely to accelerate.'[1]

Dr Balogh's conclusion for the Allied Governments was:

'Having given birth to an iniquitous new German economic and social system they are now condemned to observing the consequences of their actions, actions the import of which most of the actors in Germany and their "masters" in London never comprehended.'[2]

In a further statement of his conclusions on the subject, Dr Balogh maintained:

'The German Government tried to apply to real life an abstract obsolescent and internally inconsistent economic theory; and certainly did not succeed. . . .

The danger of the present policy is that it will first provoke dangerous extremes of political temper and will then be abandoned for internal or international reasons.'[3]

[1] *Op. cit.*, p. 65.

[2] *Op. cit.*, p. 72.

[3] *Banca Nazionale di Lavoro, Quarterly Review*, April 1950, pp. 95 and 97.

By 1956 and 1957, however (with Dr Erhardt and his obsolete experts still in charge, and still without 'statutory controls'), Dr Balogh was noting the 'vast increase in investment and production as in West Germany'. He was pointing out that 'between 1950 and 1955 she (West Germany) invested more than twice as much as Britain', and that 'real wages in England rose only 12·3 per cent since 1950 against 24 per cent in the US and 39 per cent in Germany'. By 1960 (still under Dr Erhardt) it was noted that 'Germany in the period between 1949 and 1958 had established itself as the unchallenged economic leader in Europe'. In 1963 (with Dr Erhardt and his obsolete economic philosophy still prevailing) Dr Balogh set out a League Table of Growth rates (1950-60) for sixteen major countries, with the German Federal Republic well ahead of all others except Japan. He pointed out that in spite (or because) of the 'weakness' of German trade unions (which 'inhibited increases in productivity'): 'The fact stands out that in Germany, France and Japan, the improvement in workers' earnings and social benefits was at a rate two to three times as high—despite a worsening of the distribution of income'—than in Britain. See *New Statesman and Nation*, April 14, 1956, p. 361; December 1, 1956, p. 689; and November 9, 1957, p. 598; *The Free Trade Proposals* (edited by G. D. N. Worswick), 1960, p. 123; and *Planning for Progress*, 1963, p. 3.

(4) FROM DEVALUATION TO KOREA

The possibility of devaluation had been discussed by a number of economists in the years just after the war. As we have seen, Keynes had mentioned (1946) 'exchange variations' as one of the 'quicker and less painful aids' which might be needed to supplement 'the classical medicine'.[1] Professor Robbins (1947) contemplated:

'If, in the long run, we are still unable to balance our international accounts without quantitative regulation, there would be a strong argument for altering the rate of exchange; the extent to which we are in the habit of discussing international equilibrium nowadays without mentioning the rate of exchange is a disgrace to economic thinking.'[2]

Dr J. R. Hicks advocated devaluation at the time of the convertibility crisis of August 1947:

'It cannot be denied that the pound is overvalued, not perhaps in relation to price-levels but relatively to the work which (now that we have lost our foreign assets) it has to do. And now, of the two arguments which have universally been advanced to still the voices of the devaluationists, both are losing their force. Devaluation would stimulate internal inflation; we know that, but at last it has been agreed among sensible people that strong steps against internal inflation must be taken in any case. Devaluation would turn the terms of trade against us; but what turns the terms of trade against us is not devaluation as such, but the stoppage of the gap in the balance of payments—if the gap is to be filled (as we all want it to be filled) by increasing exports. The more exports we push on the world, the less favourable will our terms of trade be, as compared with what they might have been otherwise. We do not now want to reduce imports in order to turn the terms of trade in our favour—the old (and admittedly defensible) protectionist argument. We want all the imports we are likely to get, even if we have to get them on unfavourable terms.'[3]

[1] *Economic Journal*, June 1946, p. 186.
[2] *The Economic Problem in Peace and War*, 1947, p. 65.
[3] *The Economist*, August 16, 1947, p. 276.

Professor Meade (1948), also, cautiously broached the subject:

'Loose talk about an exchange depreciation which may never prove necessary is to be deprecated in view of the foreigners' hesitation to purchase our goods or to hold our money which would result from any expectation that our goods and our money were just about to be cheapened in terms of foreign currency by a depreciation of the pound. Nevertheless it is important to consider whether, in the hypothetical case of our being unable to find sufficient remunerative markets to sell all the exports necessary to finance unrestricted imports, we should be wise to choose import restrictions or exchange depreciation.'

Professor Meade, of course, came down fairly strongly, at least in 'the hypothetical case', in favour of adjusting the exchange rate.[1]

Professor Arthur Lewis (1948) wanted to wait. He thought that the elasticities were not then right. But the time might well come:

'As things sort themselves out in the fifties, and if world trade begins to expand again, we may want to devalue. But to do so in 1948 would seem to be a grave error.'[2]

On the other side, Sir Hubert Henderson was, as usual, sceptical. In his powerful paper 'The Function of Exchange Rates' (January 1949), he noted the 'astonishing vogue among British academic economists', and especially among the more 'liberal' champions of market mechanisms, of

'the idea that variations in foreign exchange rates can serve as an efficient regulator of the freely working international economic system'.

He emphasized the contrasting 'ins' and 'outs' of fashion, as compared with the thirties, when the fixity of exchange rates had been regarded as a condition of international economic health, particularly by the enthusiasts for free-market mechanisms:

[1] *Planning and the Price Mechanism*, 1948, p. 93.
[2] *Manchester School*, May 1948, p. 144.

'A Rip Van Winkle familiar with the controversies of the last decade might, therefore, be startled if he were to wake up today to find that exchange-rate variations have been assigned a high constructive rôle in the ultra-liberal philosophy as the regulating spring of the future international mechanism, and the true alternative to the hated quantitative regulation.'[1]

Of course in the meantime a considerably more refined taxonomic analysis had been developed of exchange-rate variation, in terms of elasticities of demand and supply. But Sir Hubert would probably have considered this analysis, by itself, as of somewhat limited assistance with regard to actual policy decisions. His main concern was with the inflationary wage and price movements which devaluation would set up in full-employment Britain:

'If it were not for the dynamic quality of inflationary movements, it would no doubt be arguable that the rise in internal prices and costs ought to be less than proportionate to the exchange depreciation; and attempts were, I think, made at one time to calculate the degree of inflation that would represent an appropriate adjustment on the basis of an assumed rigidity of certain prices and incomes. In practice, however, the extent of an inflationary movement, once it has been set going, cannot be forecast. The process is apt to be self-perpetuating, and indeed to gather momentum, unless and until it is checked by some obstacle or counter-force, for which there is no provision in the technique of exchange depreciation. There can be no assurance therefore that the rise of internal prices would be stopped at any theoretically appropriate points. It would be a happy accident if it did. . . . If it may be necessary, after exchange rates have been lowered, to use the traditional deflationary instruments to establish a certain degree of undervaluation, why not use them in the first instance to establish the undervaluation at the original parities?'[2]

Sir Hubert proceeded to turn Professor Meade's own admissions regarding the dangers of wage-push inflation under full

[1] *The Inter-war Years*, 1955, pp. 357-8.
[2] *Op. cit.*, pp. 365-6.

employment, against his case for exchange-rate adjustments:

'He is perturbed at the possibility that a high aggregate demand may lead to excessive wage rates, and he has a particular dislike for the practice of raising wages to meet increases in the cost of living. He refers to the danger that this practice may lead to a loss of export trade. . . . It seems reasonable to infer that exchange depreciation would be a most dangerous remedy for a balance of payments deficit. . . . Professor Meade may perhaps suppose that having urged that wages should not rise because the cost of living rises, he is entitled to assume that they will not do so. . . . To prevent substantial wage increases following a sharp increase in the cost of living, it is probable that a drastic restriction of credit, involving heavy unemployment, would be required. A policy of this sort would differ radically from anything that has hitherto been thought of as a policy of full employment, however qualified.'[1]

Sir Hubert went on to examine the rôle of exchange rates in the international economy:

'The idea that exchange-rate variations might be used systematically to correct maladjustments in the balance of payments is not only, as I have argued above, fundamentally impracticable. It misconceives the attributes of exchange rates; it overlooks their special fitness for a function of real importance. They are one of the few things in the economy which can be definitely fixed; and it is well that something should be fixed. The true function of exchange rates is to provide a constant factor round which the more variable elements may move, and by reference to which they can be adjusted; in other words, to provide a focus of stability in an orderly price system. . . .'

However, Sir Hubert agreed that:

'In the meantime, uncertainty upon this matter would suffice to forbid the idea of attaching to modern exchange parities the sacrosanctity which they possessed in the heyday of the gold standard. The possibility of modifying these parities, as a *pis*

[1] *Op. cit.*, pp. 370-1.

aller, must be left open, though it must not be supposed that a new and more orderly international system can be built upon this basis. . . . To suggest, as is sometimes done, that, though import restrictions are necessary now, they may become superfluous comparatively soon if an improved price system is given freer play, is to nurse illusions.'[1]

Explicit discussion of devaluation was fairly restricted and restrained. But shortly before the actual step was taken, Professor D. H. Robertson (July 1949) came out in favour, on similar grounds to those which were apparently moving the United States authorities, that is, that an essential condition for the success of the recovery programme

'is a systematic revaluation of the West European currencies in terms of one another and of the United States and Canadian dollars'.[2]

Professor Robertson was moved by a certain terms-of-trade pessimism. Europe's balance of payments difficulties were not 'simply due to the war'. But, impressed perhaps by Sir Hubert Henderson's arguments, Professor Robertson admitted

'a deep-seated doubt, based on painful experience in France and elsewhere, whether under modern political conditions, the results even of the most clear-cut and deliberate devaluation can be relied upon to stand fast against the erosive action of mounting money incomes and swelling demands for subsidies'.[3]

When devaluation came in September 1949 from 4·03 to 2·80 dollars to the pound throughout most of the Sterling Area and, on a smaller scale, in Western Europe, it was welcomed, if somewhat coolly, by a number of economists.

[1] *Op. cit.*, pp. 373-5. In a further comment of June 1949 Sir Hubert argued: 'So long as inflation is at work in our own economy, devaluation would be a most dangerous remedy threatening a cumulative process. . . . The right policy is to try to avert this contingency by ending the inflationary trend at home; and the idea of devaluation should in my view be ruled out until this has been definitely accomplished.' (*Oxford Economic Papers*, June 1949, p. 157).
[2] *Lloyds Bank Review*, July 1949, p. 12.
[3] *Op. cit.*, p. 12.

Professor Robbins (October 1949), for example, believed, subject to reservations, 'this decision to be sound'. He went on:

'If I were to criticize anything in this connection, it would not be the decision to devalue, but the delay in coming to that decision, which must have cost us many millions of our all-too-scanty reserves. . . . I think it is right too that once this decision was made, it was decided that the cut should be of sufficient magnitude to give reasonable assurance that, provided always that certain other measures are taken and the advantage is not frittered away, the new rate can be held.'[1]

But Professor Robbins had some very important provisos:

(i) that there should be disinflationary action in the form of 'reductions both in the volume of investment and in the volume of public expenditure'—housing being especially emphasized; and
(ii) he urged that 'we cannot afford to dispense with the mechanism of the structure of interest rates'. He went on:

'Many of us who listened to the Chancellor announce the most drastic devaluation in our history must have confidently expected that, before the end of his speech, there would be announced an increase in Bank Rate—a sign to the rest of the world that we had not only decided on a new value for the pound but that we were prepared to defend it.'[2]

(iii) Professor Robbins urged that the problem of the sterling balances should be dealt with, concluding that

'Although there should be no question of repudiation, there can be no obligation to repay at a rate which endangers our general stability.'[3]

Professor D. H. Robertson, for his part, also subsequently

[1] *Lloyds Bank Review*, October 1949, pp. 17-18.
[2] *Op. cit.*, p. 21.
[3] *Op. cit.*, p. 26. See above p. 51.

commented on the devaluation simply as being 'about nine months too late'.[1]

Dr Hicks, writing soon after (December 1949), was very cautiously hopeful that devaluation was 'a step which may possibly go some way towards helping us out of our troubles', though this was far from certain. Above all, disinflation was necessary:

'If there were no disinflation at all in any of the devaluating countries, and no import restrictions . . . , then it is quite certain that devaluation would be abortive, and that the 1949 crisis would repeat itself after no long interval. . . . If the devaluation is to help us out of our troubles, imports into the Sterling Region (in this wider sense) have got to be diminished, but a corresponding rise in spending on "home" products has got to be avoided.'[2]

By 1953 however, in his lecture 'The Long-Run Dollar Problem', Professor Hicks had concluded that the experiment of devaluation had failed for reasons that should preclude its being attempted again:

'The change in relative wages, however it is brought about (whether directly, or by some monetary trick such as devaluation), must be expected to mean a real loss for the British consumer. This, of course, is the real reason why the devaluation of 1949 was a failure. It was put over as a trick which would enable the balance of payments to be righted without real sacrifice. Thus when the sterling prices of imported commodities began to rise in order to enforce a real sacrifice, wages chased after the rising prices, and the rise in wages made the devaluation largely ineffective. If we devalue again in the same delusion, the same thing will doubtless happen again, and may happen even more quickly. Along that road there is no way out.'[3]

Professor Hicks attacked 'a continuing policy of depreciation

[1] *Britain in the World Economy*, 1954, p. 42.
[2] See *Essays in World Economics*, 1959, p. 31.
[3] *Op. cit.*, p. 82.

to deal with a continuing failure of competitive power', and concluded:

'We may be put to great straits in order to maintain the exchange value of sterling (at least to the outsider); but I doubt if we have any alternative but to bear our cross.'[1]

The two most forthright critics of the 1949 devaluation—and also in the main of devaluation proposals in later years—were the two Oxford experts, Mr R. F. Harrod and Dr T. Balogh.[2] In both cases their views underwent considerable evolution and are worth tracing out as exemplifications of some of the problems of topical comment on economic policy issues.

Early in 1949 Mr Harrod wrote of 'the inevitability of a slump', and in May he attacked the controls maintained by the Labour Government:

'There ought to be the greatest vigilance for signs that the post-war boom in the demand for producer goods is coming to an end. . . . We are moving out of the inflationary period. . . . What, then, is the justification for the maintenance of the controls? Their defence, purveyed for the consumption of the intelligent critics, has been the need to preserve our economy from the evils of inflation. That need is now over.'[3]

In fact, the greatest post-war boom of all, on a world scale, was, of course, just about to break out, and might well have done so even without any Korean war. However, in November 1949, shortly after the devaluation, Mr Harrod maintained:

'It is, I think, a fallacy to suppose that devaluation can possibly produce a deterioration on our dollar account. At the worst, all

[1] *Op. cit.*, p. 83n, Professor Hicks reasserted the point in his paper 'A World Inflation?' (1958): 'I am not saying that devaluations of national money may not, on occasion, be necessary, but what is necessary is that they should be regarded with aversion—that the duty of national governments to maintain, at least in the long run, the international value of their currencies should be regarded as being among the first of their duties.' (*Op. cit.*, p. 156).
[2] Sir Ralph Hawtrey was also a persistent critic of the 1949 devaluation as a source of subsequent inflation, and a recommender of an up-valuation of the pound. See his 'Towards the Rescue of Sterling', 1954, particularly pp. 114-118.
[3] *And So It Goes On, further thoughts on present mismanagement*, 1951, p. 134, and *The Listener*, January 13, 1949, p. 52.

will be as before. . . . Devaluation must help the dollar balance a little.'[1]

Returning to the problem of the sterling balances, Mr Harrod argued:

'This big and bold measure of devaluation—the magnitude of the change was probably a mark of wisdom—should have been made the occasion for the clearing up of the whole sterling situation. There, too, an opportunity has been lost.'[2]

Subsequently in 1951 Mr Harrod was doubting if the sum total of changes amounted to a real improvement on balance since 'favourable factors are more than offset by the worsening of the UK's terms of trade, since devaluation'.[3]

However, by February 1952, in his essay *The Pound Sterling* Mr Harrod was maintaining that the relevant elasticities were 'perverse', and that:

'I judge devaluation to have been a disaster of the first magnitude. . . . Devaluation caused a colossal and unnatural rise in the volume of exports . . . a very heavy strain on the manufacturing capacity of Britain. . . . Devaluation has worsened Britain's balance of trade.'[4]

Though admitting that 'it is not easy to interpret the consequences of the British devaluation', Mr Harrod concluded that it was 'adding fuel to the flames of inflation' (which flames he had, in May 1949, proclaimed extinguished). He proceeded to call for 'an upward revaluation of sterling',[5] thus joining with Sir Ralph Hawtrey, the former Treasury expert, who strongly urged this policy. Finally however, in 1958, Mr Harrod took the view that the 1949 devaluation was inevitable:

'In 1949 it was humanly speaking impossible not to have a devaluation when all the world had to come to think that sterling ought to be devalued.'[6]

[1] *Op. cit.*, pp. 141-2.
[2] *Op. cit.*, p. 148.
[3] *Op. cit.*, pp. 190-1.
[4] *The Pound Sterling*, February 1952, pp. 29-30 and 34.
[5] *Op. cit.*, pp. 30 and 38.
[6] *The Director*, February 1958, p. 284.

Dr Balogh's views went through even more vicissitudes. Shortly before the devaluation he had opposed any such measure.[1] But in a Memorandum for a British Cabinet Minister written in September 1949, just after the devaluation, commenting on a series of measures headed, of course, by the massive devaluation, he maintained:

'This is an impressive list of new efforts calculated to redress the dollar balance. If it is firmly borne in mind that the policy advocated by the deflationary school, i.e. a sharp cut in Government expenditure, was the only practical alternative, the Government must be congratulated on their success in devising a programme, which, in the short run, is far less inimical to welfare in this country and, at the same time, gives more hope of overcoming the *immediate* dollar crisis. . . . It is at least not unlikely also, that this policy will have a substantial enough success *in the short run* to vindicate its protagonists.'[2]

However, Dr Balogh in an explanatory note added at a later date to this Memorandum explained:

'I opposed devaluation both in my book *The Dollar Crisis* (Blackwell): and in an article 'Should Sterling be Devalued?' in *Bulletin of the Oxford University Institute of Statistics* (1949). The reasons for my opposition were fully borne out in the history of 1950-51 crisis.'[3]

Certainly in his report to the Fabian Society, *The Dollar Crisis, Causes and Cure* (1949), Dr Balogh was much more critical of the Government's policy than in his Memorandum to a British Cabinet Minister. He listed a closely similar set of measures, with devaluation at the head, as in the Memorandum, but refrained from congratulating the Government or predicting short-run vindication.[4] Furthermore, whereas the Cabinet Minister had been assured that devaluation was, as we have seen, 'the only practical alternative' to deflation, it was suggested to the Fabian Society that:

[1] See his article 'Should Sterling be Devalued?', *Bulletin of the Oxford University Institute of Statistics*, August 1949, p. 228.
[2] *Unequal Partners*, Vol. II, 1963, p. 174.
[3] *Op. cit.*, p. 173n.
[4] *The Dollar Crisis, Causes and Cure*, 1949, p. xxii.

'On the other hand there was, at any rate last year, another alternative to devaluation, far superior from the point of view of non-American living standards. This was a selective control of US imports buttressed by reciprocal purchase agreements between non-dollar countries and a selective stimulus—through pressure on home sales and/or subsidies—to the most favourable exports.'[1]

Possibly the British Cabinet Minister would have been less receptive to this suggestion of extensive further controls in view of Mr Harold Wilson's 'bonfire of controls' in November 1948. However, in 1950 Dr Balogh noted:

'Some, including the present writer, held that a devaluation had become inevitable because of the breakdown of controls. . . . In the circumstances, devaluation was clearly preferable to a (futile and politically dangerous) attempt at a deflationary readjustment advocated by the orthodox. Yet others thought that devaluation was a measure to be welcomed because it gave a chance to restore the competitive position of European countries in third markets, e.g. Mr R. F. Kahn. . . . There is no difference in principle between these two schools of thought.'[2]

Apparently, therefore, Dr Balogh (a) considered devaluation inevitable; (b) opposed it; (c) congratulated the Government on its policy; (d) did not differ in principle with the school of thought which welcomed it. But the difficult and unpredictable events of 1950-51 were still to come.

In June 1950, less than nine months after the devaluation, the war in Korea started, and the effects became very difficult to trace. As Mr Dow describes events:

'Europe had hardly congratulated itself on its "remarkably successful attack" on the problems left over from the 1939-45 war, when the outbreak of war in Korea imposed a wholly new set of strains. In a world heading for a boom, this caused the sharpest burst of inflation in the post-war period, and world-wide shortage

[1] *Op. cit.*, p. xxiv. Mr Harold Wilson's subsequent support of the devaluation decision may be noted: 'Looking back on 1949 one might regard the devaluation of sterling as a realistic reappraisal of the value of the pound in the post-war world, in contrast to the excessive value placed upon it in 1945.' (*Post-War Economic Policies in Britain*, Fabian Society, 1957, p. 6.)

[2] *Unequal Partners*, Vol. II, 1963, p. 201n.

of materials. To the United Kingdom it brought rising prices; a major increase in defence spending; and, within a year, balance of payments crisis. The remaining year of the Labour Government's term of office was preoccupied with the complex series of adjustments that this entailed for the British economy. The inflationary strain was, however, to prove as short-lived as it had been rapid. The years 1950-51 saw a temporary and partial return to a war economics of shortages and controls. But, paradoxically, they also marked another transition. By the end of 1951, the economy had arrived at a state where under-employment was a possibility never far below the surface, and inflation no longer, year in year out, the sole problem. The world boom of 1950-51 was not primarily due to the impact of the Korean War, though this added fuel to the fire. Between 1949 and 1950, world industrial production rose by 13 per cent—almost a record, certainly a post-war one. . . . Commodity prices rose astronomically.'[1]

However, Dr Balogh (February 1951) set out the effects in 1950 of the devaluation as follows:

'The changes in the balance of Britain's international payments in the first half of 1950 shown in the recent White Paper constitute a major event in our post-war economic development. . . . For the first time since before the Great Depression of 1929-33 a favourable overall balance at an annual rate of over £100m. is recorded. . . . The shock effect of devaluation seems to have had the expected result of worsening the balance of trade. Since June 1950, however, the visible balance has shown continuous and rapid improvement. . . . Not since the early 1870s has a comparable position been attained. . . . There can be little doubt that the total (visible and invisible) current surplus in the balance of payments attained in the second half of 1950 an annual rate of somewhere between £300m.-£400m. This is a staggering figure.'[2]

Dr Balogh went on:

'The timing of the improvement in our balance of payments was

[1] *The Management of the British Economy 1945-60*, 1964, pp. 54-5.
[2] *Bulletin of the Oxford University Institute of Statistics*, February, 1951, p. 55.

as important as its extent. It occurred already *before* the Korean crisis. It must have been considerably accelerated since.'[1]

Dr Balogh noted that the recovery in the United States

'lately, as the Korean incident unfolded, assumed the proportions of an inflationary rearmament boom. . . . The "effectiveness" of the devaluation of European currencies is mainly due to this overwhelming factor. Indeed, one might maintain that the readjustment of balances of payments was affected *despite* rather than *as a result* of devaluation.'

He denied, however, the suggestion

'that the balance of payments crisis of UK continues and has assumed the new form of a crisis of our relations with the sterling area. This view, which was very forcibly expressed by *The Economist*, has little to support it.'[2]

Dr Balogh went on to add a military hint (which, in fact, the Government was following):

'In view of the international political outlook the establishment of stocks is in any case urgently required. Britain is far more vulnerable than the US to air and under-sea attack.'[3]

Soon after, in May 1951, at the height of the Korean crisis, Dr Balogh was claiming that 'the present world tension has given the Western world a breathing space'.[4] But in November, just after the Conservatives had taken over, he was bitterly complaining, regarding the policies of Mr Gaitskell and the Labour Government, 'how near to ruin military lunacy and economic wish-dreaming have brought the country', adding:

'The cause of Labour will not really be advanced by attributing

[1] *Op. cit.*, p. 58.
[2] *Op. cit.*, p. 59.
[3] *Op. cit.*, p. 62. As Mr Dow emphasizes: 'Balance-of-payments-wise, our strategic stockpiling must have been as costly as defence production proper.' *The Management of the British Economy 1945-1960*, 1964, p. 64n.
[4] *Bulletin of the Oxford University Institution of Statistics*, May 1951, p. 161.

all ills to the Tory Government, which inherited a grave crisis from the Labour administration.'[1]

On the other hand, in 1955, when it was Mr Butler's turn to be attacked, Dr Balogh maintained that he

'was confronted on taking office in 1951 not with the grave economic disaster which the Labour cabinet feared, but with a temporary balance of payments setback which cured itself automatically once the immediate crisis had passed. A sharp increase in interest rates was enough to stop the drain on the gold reserves, and no further devaluation was needed.'[2]

Much later (1963) Dr Balogh again comprehensively denounced the policies of Sir Stafford Cripps and Mr Gaitskell in 1949-51:

'The failure of analysis lead to a failure of policy.'[3]

Certainly the speed of economic events in 1950-51 was unprecedented in 'peace' time.[4] But if wrong predictions were more than usually excusable, unfair criticisms were less so. As Mr Dow concludes:

'The crisis must, in any obvious sense, be blamed on international fluctuations of a scale and rapidity not likely to be paralleled. If, in part, British policy is to be blamed, it must be for errors of judgment on matters which can never be more than matters of opinion. The 1951 *Survey* was undoubtedly an intelligent analysis of a highly complex situation. . . . It can be argued . . . that rearmament was too rapid: for the defence programme contributed to the balance of payments strain, and it was calculated to be about the limit of what the balance of payments could bear, if all went as expected. . . . It could well be argued that when embarking on the defence programme (in addition to an understanding about sharing the cost of defence), we should have

[1] *New Statesman and Nation*, November 17, 1951, pp. 562-3.
[2] *New Statesman and Nation*, December 31, 1955, p. 872.
[3] *Unequal Partners*, Vol. II, 1963, p. 179.
[4] *The British Economy in the Nineteen-Fifties*, edited by G. D. N. Worswick and P. Ady, 1962. p. 14.

sought an advance undertaking from the United States of temporary support, should the strain on sterling prove too great. But the last word should not lie with such criticisms, since criticisms can always be made.'[1]

(5) THE LABOUR RECORD

The contrasts between politician's words and their actions work in either direction. Usually one tends to think first of magnificent words contrasting with inadequate actions. But sometimes the contrast is rather between politicians' nebulous, even nonsensical, oratory, for the benefit of their political clientele, or of a section of it, and in fact, quite sober, sensible actions into which they find themselves more or less canalized by the sheer logic and pressure of real events.

The Labour Government's economic policy was launched and continued amid a haze of variegated and inconsistent pronouncements about 'socialistic' or 'democratic' planning. But as regards the Labour Government's actual deeds, at any rate from the end of 1947 onwards, Mr Dow has concluded:

'The policy followed was essentially that originally proposed in the "reconstruction" plans of the war days: that of sitting on the post-war boom till it blew itself out. This took far longer, and required immensely more determination, than all but a few had then foreseen. The Government's handling of many important, but in the last resort subsidiary, issues, is certainly debatable: but on the broadest questions of economic policy there is much less room for doubt. Only greater austerity could have greatly shortened the period of disinflation and control; and for the policy itself it is difficult to imagine a sensible alternative.'[2]

That is, it was simply not possible, on the whole, to lift controls sooner without more austerity, or more inequality, or both. To have cut down on capital investment would have been a very dubious way out. Something might possibly have been done in the way of funding, or regulating the release of, the sterling balances, but any major alleviation here might well have had

[1] *The Management of the British Economy 1945-1960*, 1964, pp. 64-5. On this episode see also Joan Mitchell's *Crisis in Britain 1951*, 1963.
[2] *The Management of the British Economy 1945-1960*, 1964, p. 54.

unpleasant political costs, and almost inevitably would have caused hardship to countries much poorer than Britain.

On the one hand, the Labour Government and Party had started on its tremendous and unpredictable tasks with its array of not very clearly thought out ideas about 'socialist planning'. On the other hand, it inherited the extremely comprehensive system of wartime controls and regulations. It also was eager to implement the new agreed Governmental responsibility for a high and stable level of employment; and it was faced with an immensely difficult balance of payments situation and massive inflationary potential internally.

As regards the Labour Government's treatment of controls, Sir Roy Harrod has subsequently (1963) well described the problem:

'We have to consider how the maintenance of the régime of controls has to be interpreted in relation to the socialism of the government of the day. Did the Labour Government regard the controls as temporary expedients that would, in due course, be dismantled, or did it regard them as part of the permanent machinery of regulation in a socialist State? Who knows? Probably different individual Ministers looked at the matter in different ways. . . . Before the end of the term of socialist government, a good many controls were in fact relaxed. . . . The fact is that no one knows how far a Labour Government, if returned to power in the autumn of 1951, would have gone towards liberalization within the private enterprise sector of the economy. *Since it is unlikely that a Conservative Government would have taken a different attitude towards the régime of controls in the 1940s, and, indeed, on its assumption of power (1951) it actually intensified certain restrictions, this aspect of socialism, if it is right so to regard it, cannot be said to have made any lasting imprint on the British economy.*'[1]

Perhaps this passage leans somewhat towards understatement. Nevertheless, much of the contemporary criticism of the Labour Government by economists, the gist of which has been cited in the foregoing sections, seems to have been of doubtful relevance and fairness and not to have taken just account of the ineluctable difficulties of Britain's post-war condition. At times, in writing

[1] *The British Economy*, 1963, p. 48 (italics added).

about 'dwindling production' in 1947-48, even the basic facts and figures seem to have been disregarded.[1] Mr Harrod (September 1948) seemed to suggest that the whole problem was really quite simple:

'I am convinced that if we made it an immediate objective to get rid of the central controls with the utmost speed, and if we became more clear-headed on the question of capital outlay, we could make a good recovery in a very short period.'[2]

In February 1950 (apparently at an election meeting), Mr Harrod proclaimed:

'The post-war unemployment problem lay still in front of us. . . . The Socialists had put everything out of balance and had prepared the ground for the worst slump in history.'[3]

Subsequently however (1963), Mr Harrod agreed that from the end of the war:

'production mounted uninterruptedly until the winter of 1951-52'.[4]

Certainly there was the far from uncriticizable policy of nationalization. But on this subject also, Mr Harrod's subseqent assessment may be cited:

'If we take the whole picture, it appears that the Labour Government from 1945 to 1951 did not take the country much further towards the national ownership and control of industry than might have been thought expedient by middle-of-the-road people who were not deeply wedded to the doctrine of *laissez faire*.'[5]

Regarding the vital problem of raising exports Professor E. A. G. Robinson (1950) stated:

[1] See J. Jewkes, *Ordeal by Planning*, 1948, p. 77.
[2] *District Bank Review*, September 1948, p 9.
[3] *The Times*, February 16, 1950, p. 4.
[4] *The British Economy*, 1963, p. 19.
[5] *Op. cit.*, p. 61. In 1950 Mr Harrod had complained: 'The planned economy we have had since 1945 is most un-Keynesian in spirit because it pays scant regard to the self-interest of the individual.' (*And So It Goes On*, 1951, p. 156.)

'Up to a point it would be no exaggeration to say that we made progress beyond the wildest dreams of those who perforce contemplated these problems of the future during the war years. The seemingly impossible task of raising the volume of exports to 150 per cent of the 1938 level had been achieved by the first quarter of 1949.'[1]

However, even Labour supporters have, in some cases, somehow found it difficult to do justice to the achievements of Sir Stafford Cripps and Mr Gaitskell.

At least at an earlier stage (1952) Dr T. Balogh had recognized that as regards the vital export achievement:

'If the basic difficulties facing Britain are taken into account the success of British post-war international economic policy in this respect must be considered remarkable. . . . The period of 1945-50 viewed as a whole shows a remarkable effort at reconstruction.'[2]

Later, however (1963), Dr Balogh took a remarkably different view:

'Sir Stafford Cripps continued his thoughtless policy, weakening the power of resistance of Britain. Under the influence of the Bank and the Treasury, the fleeting breathing space gained by devaluation was used to relax further controls and renounce further receipts under Marshall Aid. His short-sightedness stands out even in the post-war British annals of failure. Never was a high reputation so little earned by excellence of policy.'[3]

A more balanced interim criticism of Labour's record was provided by Professor Arthur Lewis (1949). He insisted:

'It is not the case that bad planning has hindered the recovery of this country, and caused us to fare worse than unplanned countries. For we have not in fact fared worse than unplanned countries; on the contrary we have done as well and better.'

[1] *London and Cambridge Economic Bulletin*, May 1950, p. 38.
[2] *The British Economy 1945-1950*, edited by G. D. N. Worswick and P. Ady, 1952, pp. 491-4.
[3] *Unequal Partners*, Vol. II, 1963, p. 22.

However, Professor Lewis diagnosed three serious errors in the Labour Government's approach to economic policy:

'To socialists in the past, planning has been concerned principally with the distribution of income and with the nationalization of industry; . . . Socialist planning has had no principles for dealing with money, investment, foreign trade, mobility, or private enterprise. . . . Unfortunately for the Government, the standard of living of the workers is much more intimately affected by these other matters; they ought to have a much greater priority in socialist planning than either income distribution or nationalization, and the fact that a Labour Government always neglects them (exactly the same thing happened in 1929-31) is a tragedy both for the country and for Labour Governments, who are always defeated by just those economic matters that they neglect. . . . The greatest lessons that planners have to learn are that nationalization and the distribution of income are only a small part of the matters that claim their attention; and that when we cannot do everything we must put first things first.'[1]

These 'greatest lessons' still did not seem to have been very thoroughly mastered when Labour, in the end, returned to office in 1964. Nor was what Mr Shonfield has well described as the 'doctrinal confusion at the centre of its thinking'[2] about 'planning', very clearly resolved (at any rate not when, in the autumn of 1966, the wages 'freeze' was simultaneously claimed as a great 'break-through' for 'Socialist planning' and as a regrettable but inevitable temporary expedient). Nevertheless, it is fair in conclusion to emphasize that no British government since the Labour Government of 1945-51 has more unswervingly carried through, in its economic policies, what it thought rightly or wrongly to be its duty, without regard to electoral popularity (even, perhaps, if only because it possessed less awareness as to what electoral popularity implied or precluded). The economic difficulties which confronted the Conservatives on their return to power in October 1951 were primarily the result of a sudden international economic upheaval well beyond the control or responsibilities of their Labour predecessors. Certainly the

[1] *The Principles of Economic Planning*, 1949, pp. 112-14.
[2] *British Economic Policy since the War*, 1958, p. 168.

first two changes of party in power (in 1951 and 1964) both took place amid economic crises, and it was to become a political platitude, with the advent of more sophisticated electoral-economic management after 1955, that no party could hope to oust its rivals and return to power except amid serious economic difficulties at least for the short term. But in 1951-2 the difficulties could not be ascribed to the collapse of a primarily domestic boom which had gathered excessive momentum around the time of an election as in 1964 (and, for that matter, in 1955 and 1959). In 1951 sophistication, at any rate as far as Mr Attlee and Mr Gaitskell were concerned, had not gone that far. Perhaps the only consideration which may possibly have occurred to Mr Attlee when in the autumn of 1951 he declared his innings closed only eighteen months after the previous election, was that if the other side *did* get in they would find themselves on a very difficult economic wicket. This difficulty was, in fact, implied by the predictions of many economists, of varying political colour, especially with regard to the adverse prospects for Britain's terms of trade.[1] These predictions or prophecies proved misleading. After a brief nasty interval the wicket began to play much more easily than predicted, for a time at any rate, and the Conservatives proceeded to build up a lengthy innings.

[1] Dr Balogh has maintained that it was these gloomy predictions (which, incidentally, he supported at the time) which were so influential 'in persuading Mr Attlee to dissolve Parliament'. See *New Statesman and Nation*, January 11, 1963, and below II (1) p. 96n.

2. 1951-1955

DIARY OF EVENTS

(1) Britain and Sterling Strong and Free

(2) The New Monetary Policy

DIARY OF EVENTS
(Dates in some cases approximate)

1951	April 10	Budget: tax increases and Health Service charges
	April 18	Agreement signed on European Iron and Steel Community
	April 22	Mr Bevan and Mr Wilson resign
	July 26	Bank credit restrictions: price controls; dollar imports cut
	October 25	General Election: Cons. 321; Lab. 295
	October 27	Mr Butler becomes Chancellor
	November 7	Economy measures: Bank rate raised from 2 to 2½ per cent—(first post-war increase)
1952	March 11	Budget; Bank rate raised to 4 per cent: Convertibility rumours
	August 10	European Iron and Steel Community starts operations
	November 4	Mr Eisenhower elected President of USA
1953	January 14	Consultative Assembly of Council of Europe meets in Strasbourg to draft constitution for European Political Community
	April 14	Budget: 6d off income tax
	September 17	Bank rate reduced to 3½ per cent
1954	April 6	Budget: new investment allowances
	May 13	Bank rate reduced to 3 per cent
	July 3	End of food rationing
	November 10	End of building licensing
1955	January 27	Bank rate raised from 3 to 3½ per cent
	February 20	'*De facto*' convertibility
	February 24	Bank rate raised to 4½ per cent: hire purchase controls

April 5	Retirement of Sir Winston Churchill: Sir Anthony Eden becomes Prime Minister
April 19	Budget: 6d off income tax
May 26	General Election: Cons. 344; Lab. 277
June 1	Messina Conference on European economic integration: Britain declines invitation
July 25	Credit restrictions
October 26	Supplementary budget: cuts in investment: credit squeeze
December 20	Mr Macmillan Chancellor in place of Mr Butler

2. 1951-1955

(1) BRITAIN AND STERLING STRONG AND FREE

The Korean spasm was as short as it was sharp, and recovery from the following recession, aided by the favourable switch in the terms of trade, was comparatively rapid. The years 1953 and 1954 were the brief, 'bright morning' of post-war Toryism, in some ways the economically most blissful years (though, of course, ignorantly blissful) in many decades. 1953 was the first odd-number year since the war without a severe crisis. In 1954 the British upswing proceeded smoothly in spite of an American 'recession'. The first faint whiffs of a kind of 'affluence' were beginning to be detectable, in place of the long years of 'austerity'. Britain's initial recovery from the war had been more rapid than that of most European countries, and there was little, as yet, in the way of significant, comparable economic growth-rates from other countries, or 'League Tables', to mar complacency. As regards Britain's rôle in the world, Churchill was Prime Minister and a New Elizabethan Era was being proclaimed. It was true that 'foreigners' in places like Strasbourg and Luxembourg were indulging in some very odd talk about economic (and political) unions. But that was, and should remain, their worry—as many British economists agreed. In Britain, there was much spacious confidence in empirically under-scrutinized free-market processes, comparable with the confidence in some nebulous form of 'planning' in the early years of the Labour Government. The new monetary policy, and the 'freeing' of interest rates, was hailed as highly significant. The 'freeing' of wages from Sir Stafford Cripps's 'restraint', seems to have been treated with the same expansive confidence, in spite of all the warnings which economists of different political tendencies had delivered, less than a decade before, about the dangers of wage-push inflation with unemployment at less than 2-3 per cent. Though Dr Balogh had predicted (1949) that 'the coming election will be decided on the issue of full employment and social security',[1] in fact, unemployment rates under the Conservatives remained at about the same average level as under Labour, and in 1952 there was the first significant example of the new type of high-employment recession. The abortive convertibility manoeuvres of 1952 were a further example of the new optimistic free-market expansiveness. However, regarding the relaxation of controls, the Conservatives 'followed a Fabian policy'.[2] There were cuts in food subsidies but not significantly in social services. Writing on Mr Butler's 'carry-on' budget of 1954, Professor Tress observed:

'It was official recognition that the "transition period" after World War II is over. Defence is burdensome, there is too little coal, but what he and his colleagues best hope for as "normalcy" seems at last to have arrived. . . . We have now arrived at that state of "full employment in a free society" which was so much talked about . . . some ten years ago.'[3]

Professor Tress noted 'inescapable signs of prosperity', that the gold and dollar reserves were higher, that exports 'were the highest in their history', with 'industrial production at a record height', and the terms of trade 'continuing to move in Britain's favour'. He concluded:

'In spite of much talk of crises, the system has been for most people by no means an unpleasant one in which to live.'[4]

Though in 1952 he had complained of 'the present hopeless drift towards open inflation';[5] and, in 1953, that 'the world is rapidly returning to the inter-war "normalcy" of deflation'[6] by 1955, even Dr Balogh was prepared to recognize the advance which had been made. But, as we have seen, he maintained that Mr Butler had had it all too easy. Far from inheriting 'a grave crisis' and an economy brought 'near to ruin' (as Dr Balogh had described the situation in 1951), Mr Butler had had only a

[1] *The Dollar Crisis, Causes and Cure*, 1949, p. xiii.
[2] J. C. R. Dow, *The Management of the British Economy 1945-60*, 1964, p. 77. See also the view of Sir Roy Harrod quoted above, I (5), p. 83.
[3] *London and Cambridge Economic Bulletin*, June 1954, p. IV.
[4] *Op. cit.*, p. VI.
[5] *The Economist*, May 3, 1952.
[6] *The New Statesman and Nation*, July 4, 1953, p. 23.

'temporary setback' to cope with which 'cured itself automatically once the immediate crisis had passed'. Manufacturing output, Dr Balogh maintained, was at a level (1955):

'now one-fifth higher than the peak level reached under Labour ... "brimful" employment became the rule; all during 1953 and 1954 the balance of payments steadily improved.... The increase in consumption after 1952 was one of the most rapid in our economic history.'[1]

Of the period 1947-1955 Dr Balogh subsequently noted:

'For sustained growth at a high level the period until 1955 (apart from 1951-2) has hardly a parallel in Britain in this century.... It was indeed a remarkable performance.'[2]

But of course there was plenty to be quite validly pessimistic about. Pessimism can usually, in this world, find some justification somewhere. At most moments some kind of case can usually be made out either that a dangerous inflation or a damaging deflation is in the offing. But it is important, of course, to get them the right way round and to discern and distinguish the empirically valid justifications for pessimism from those devoid of empirical support.

Three reasons for pessimism in these years which turned out to be unfounded were as follows:

(i) First, there was terms-of-trade pessimism, that is that the prices of food and raw materials were going to rise much more rapidly than those of manufactures. This was a widely held and quite reasonable view in the circumstances, but as it happened, at any rate regarding the next decade or so, pretty completely wrong. This prediction was propagated by such authorities as Mr Colin Clark and Professor D. H. Robertson and also by supporters of the Labour Party such as Mr Crosland and Dr Balogh.[3]

[1] *The New Statesman and Nation*, December 31, 1955. (Contrast, *New Statesman and Nation*, November 17, 1951, pp. 562-3.)

[2] *Oxford Economic Papers*, June 1958, p. 220.

[3] Mr Colin Clark had predicted this long-term trend in the terms of trade in his book *The Economics of 1960* (1942). He reasserted the prediction in an

(ii) Secondly, there was the old standby of the imminence of a great American slump, regarding which there were further alarms in 1953-54.[1]

(iii) Thirdly, there were the rather contrasting forebodings about America's relatively more rapidly increasing productivity. In a general restatement of the dollar shortage doctrine, Dr Balogh maintained (1953):

'The dollar shortage originates in the productive capacity of the United States. Her increasing productivity enables America to undersell both manufacturing and primary producing countries simultaneously, despite the high cost of wages. Thus, periodically the rest of the world is denuded of its gold and is forced either to deflate (as in 1951) or to devalue (as in 1949).

article in *Lloyds Bank Review*, April 1952, pp. 2-5. See also Professor D. H. Robertson, *Lloyds Bank Review*, July 1949, p. 2: 'How strong and persistent are the forces making it progressively more difficult for the manufacturing populations of Western Europe, however correct their monetary arrangements, to earn from overseas the requisite fodder alike for their fastidious stomachs and for their insatiable machines.' Professor E. A. G. Robinson, calling for import saving, remarked that 'the terms of trade are moving against us'. *Three Banks Review*, March 1953, p. 3.

With regard to the Labour Party, Mr Shonfield notes: 'The myth which emerged on the Left and held its own for a number of years was that 1951 really presented a foretaste of a secular trend, which put the industrial countries at a permanent disadvantage against the primary producing countries. In this, Mr Harold Wilson, another economist on the Labour side, played as large a part as anybody. The new doctrine was based on a theory of shortages for ever.' (*British Economic Policy since the War*, 1958, p. 76.) See also Mr Crosland's views discussed below and Dr Balogh's review of Mr Crosland's *Britain's Economic Problem* in the *New Statesman and Nation*, July 4, 1953, p. 23. Though in that review Dr Balogh commended Mr Crosland's gloomy predictions regarding the terms of trade, ten years' later he referred to it as having been 'so influential', in 1951, 'in persuading Mr Attlee to dissolve Parliament, thus ending all post-war chances for steady and continuous social advance in Britain' (*New Statesman and Nation*, January 11, 1963).

It may be noted, on the other hand, that in March 1952 the *London and Cambridge Economic Bulletin* was arguing that 'during 1952 we may continue to hope for some small favourable movement of the terms of trade as a whole'. Of course, by the end of the decade the trend was towards a new doctrine of a long-run secular movement in the terms of trade *against* the primary producing countries.

[1] See, for example, Mr Colin Clark on 'Danger Signs of Slump', *Manchester Guardian*, November 16-17, 1953. This particular date was perhaps the one at which forebodings regarding an American depression were more justified than at any other.

This periodic tendency to unbalance would recur even if we were not haunted by the short-term problem—the instability of the United States."[1]

It was the argument from the effects of the allegedly permanent higher rate of technical progress in the United States which, at this juncture, made most of the running. The analysis was coherently developed by Professor Hicks (1953). But it emerged that predictions of a long-run dollar problem, based on this argument, depended on an assumption that American technical progress would be specially biased towards competing with imports into the United States from the rest of the world—empirically a highly questionable hypothesis—which does not so far seem to have been confirmed by subsequent events.[2]

Fundamental and intractable difficulties, in plenty, were soon to be encountered. But except to some extent for the third for a few more years, these three problems were not among them.

Three books, from contrasting points of view, dealing with Britain's economic position in the world, appeared in these years (1953-4) discussing the above and other problems: Mr C. A. R. Crosland's *Britain's Economic Problem* (1953), Professor D. H. Robertson's *Britain in the World Economy* (1954) and Mr A. C. L. Day's *The Future of Sterling* (1954).

Mr Crosland's sombre view of Britain's 'problem' was based, almost entirely and precisely, on the three predictions listed above. He claimed:

'Three major problems are already in the foreground, and compel attention.

(1) The world shortage of food and raw materials.

[1] *New Statesman and Nation*, July 4, 1953, p. 23.

[2] See Professor Hicks's lecture, 'The Long-Run Dollar Problem' (1953) reprinted in *Essays in World Economics*, 1959, (p. 66) and Supplementary Note B (pp. 257-9), in which regarding policy conclusions, Professor Hicks made 'what is mainly a withdrawal'. See T. Balogh 'The Dollar Crisis Revisited', *Oxford Economic Papers*, September 1954, p. 243. See also, F. Machlup, 'Dollar Shortage and Disparities in the Growth of Productivity', *Scottish Journal of Political Economy*, October 1954, p. 250, and Dr Balogh's reply in the same Journal for June 1955, p. 149; also E. J. Mishan, *Oxford Economic Papers*, June 1955, p. 215. For a vigorous contemporary attack on 'this bogy of a centre of superior productivity elsewhere' see L. C. Robbins, *Lloyds Bank Review*, January 1953, p. 5.

(2) The disequilibrium between the dollar and non-dollar worlds.
(3) The instability of the American economy.'[1]

As regards (1) Mr Crosland concluded:

'Alike for food and raw materials, the prospect is thus one of scarcity and a sharp rise in prices relative to manufactured goods.' . . .

'The weight of the evidence, indecisive though it must necessarily be, is definitely on the side of those who expect high primary prices and scarcities, to such an extent that only a very rash person would act on the opposite assumption.'[2]

As regard (2), Mr Crosland did not invoke the factor of superior technical 'dynamism' as the ground for predicting 'dollar scarcity', which he claimed simply and somewhat vaguely

'has its fundamental origin in the natural creditor status of a country which constitutes overwhelmingly the world's largest producing unit'.[3]

Looking to the future Mr Crosland maintained:

'There is no reason to expect American private investment to rise much above its average post-war figure of 1-1½ billion dollars. . . . The conclusion is that nowhere can developments be detected which of themselves will close the gap.'[4]

As regards the third problem, that of American recession, Mr Crosland held

'that cyclical changes would continue, with the recession of 1937-38 perhaps providing an approximate norm. . . . A recession of this magnitude would deprive the world of 10 billion dollars over the whole period of recession and recovery.'[5]

Mr Crosland called for 'a major structural change in the pattern

[1] *Britain's Economic Problem*, 1953, p. 76.
[2] *Op. cit.*, pp. 82 and 84.
[3] *Op. cit.*, p. 125.
[4] *Op cit.*, pp. 132-3.
[5] *Op. cit.*, p. 183.

of British industry', which 'does not come easily or automatically on a deflationary policy'. He was particularly concerned (1953) about the supply of labour to coal-mining:

'What is needed is therefore a wages policy in the limited sense of an agreement first to raise, then to stabilize, the ratio of mining to other wages.'[1]

He concluded that a courageous government should 'steer resources out of consumer goods into the capital goods sector', and, therefore:

'There can thus be no loosening of belts for the next five years.'[2]

Professor Robertson took, on the whole, a considerably less tense view than Mr Crosland. One domestic point which concerned him—as to which there was, in fact, to be much improvement in the subsequent decade—was that of individual saving. He observed that for some years this had been running 'at a substantial negative figure', and expressed himself

'strongly of the opinion that our present pattern of saving is fraught with danger for the future'.[3]

Turning to the outside world, Professor Robertson noted certain tendencies, at once schizophrenic and megalomaniac, regarding colonial investment:

'Those who are the most eloquent both about the limitless resources of the Colonial Empire and about the deplorably low standards of living of many of its 70 million inhabitants are often apt to be the least alive to the essential condition for exploiting the former and remedying the latter· That condition is the development, by increased production or reduced consumption at home, of a persistently favourable balance of payments by the mother-country. A somewhat belated discovery that, on a world scale of reckoning, the Western urban trade unionist belongs to

[1] *Op. cit.*, p. 216.
[2] *Op. cit.*, p. 221.
[3] *Britain in the World Economy*, 1954, p. 28.

the over-privileged rather than the under-privileged classes is apt to fuse, in certain breasts, with an extreme unwillingness to surrender any improvement of standards once secured, and to generate a peculiarly woolly form of semi-philanthropic, semi-predatory pseudo-imperial mystique.'[1]

Regarding 'dollar shortage' Professor Robertson maintained that the original reasons for the phenomenon were obvious enough:

'There is no mystery about why such a state of affairs should have prevailed in Western Europe, including Britain, for some years after the war. Immense destruction had to be made good, disorganization overcome, hunger and lassitude recuperated from. Primarily the dollar shortage was but one facet of a general shortage of productive power.'[2]

Why then was 'dollar shortage' persisting in 1953? Professor Robertson thought there was 'an immense amount of truth' in the accusation that 'dollar shortage' resulted from

'kicking against the pricks by adhering obstinately to occupational immobility and utopian social policy, buttressed by monetary inflation and an over-valued exchange'.[3]

But he did not think that this was the whole truth or anything like it. Professor Robertson gave considerable weight to the argument from the superior technical dynamism of North America with the disparity of endowment

'increasing through the cumulative mutual interaction of capital accumulation and technological progress'.[4]

Professor Robertson maintained that it was America's international duty as far as possible to keep her economy on an even keel, to liberalize her tariff policies and to

[1] *Op. cit.*, p. 51.
[2] *Op. cit.*, p. 54.
[3] *Op. cit.*, p. 56.
[4] *Op. cit.*, p. 58.

'continue and expand her efforts to re-create the stream of private long-term overseas investment'.[1]

We shall be mentioning elsewhere Professor Robertson's unenthusiastic attitude to a European Customs Union. On the other hand he held:

'As a congeries of countries between which business contacts are close, means of payment easy and exchange stability probable if not assured, the Sterling Area seems to me to have a great and innocuous future; as a candidate for a permanent ring-fence I think its claims are low.'[2]

Professor Robertson also asked from America, in connection with the Sterling Area, for

'a more explicitly good-humoured and tolerant—a less theological—attitude towards such differentiations in commercial treatment as may yet remain. . . . I would not myself care to talk in terms which suggest that the day of complete and irreversible non-discrimination is much, if any, nearer than the day of complete free trade.'[3]

Finally, regarding convertibility and the removal of import restrictions, Professor Robertson saw these as, to some extent, alternatives:

'The plain truth is that while technical convertibility and the removal of import restrictions may both be important ultimate objects of policy, they may of necessity be in the meantime to some extent alternative or rival lines of advance, in the sense that if there is to be a larger move along one of them, there will have to be a smaller move along the other. And I fancy that in giving, as it becomes possible, the relaxation of import restrictions parity with or even priority over a progressive movement towards technical "convertibility", Britain would be meeting America's true desires as well as following her own best interests.'[4]

[1] *Op. cit.*, p. 67.
[2] *Op. cit.*, p. 75.
[3] *Op. cit.*, p. 81.
[4] *Op. cit.*, p. 90.

The third book, *The Future of Sterling*, concentrating on a narrower front than the others, was perhaps the most penetrating and far-sighted of the three. Mr Day managed to be incisive without being dogmatic and to keep his predictions comparatively free from ideological bias. He began by urging that it was

'unwise to base policies on any clear conceptions about the future of the dollar problem'.[1]

Mr Day's main argument was that

'a general use of sterling as an international currency can involve the British economy in costs that are not commensurate with the advantages. . . . Whether or not a liberal system is re-established, there are strong grounds for considering that the strains which a pivot must undergo are larger than Britain is likely to be able to endure.'[2]

Reserves of international liquidity would probably prove inadequate to meet inevitable disturbances:

'Exactly what reserves of international liquidity would be needed to absorb likely shocks is perhaps impossible to predict; what can be said with confidence is that the reserves in existence at present are quite inadequate for making a liberal system operate with confidence and stability.'[3]

As regards the Sterling Area it was likely to prove less satisfactory as a stabilizing instrument than in the thirties, and it was argued that

'the inconveniences and strains the system imposed on the centre country, Britain, were likely to grow. . . . There are strong arguments against abandoning the advantages to Britain of a discriminatory system by introducing convertibility and at the same time continuing to carry the burdens of the Area.'[4]

[1] *The Future of Sterling*, 1954, p. 4.
[2] *Op. cit.*, p. 6.
[3] *Op. cit.*, p. 9.
[4] *Op. cit.*, p. 95 and pp. 112-3.

Looking back on the problem of the sterling balances after the war Mr Day concluded:

'It is hard to avoid the conclusion that too much emphasis was laid on the possibility of blocking. . . . It can reasonably be asked whether it is a satisfactory way of re-establishing the usefulness of sterling as an international currency to make a large part of overseas countries' holdings of sterling less useful. Banking confidence depends on ability to pay up, however great may have been the *force majeure* which has made matters difficult for the banker.'[1]

As regards exchange-rate stability, Mr Day maintained that the hopes that major alterations would be infrequent did not look like being fulfilled:

'It may not be possible to absorb all change in the economic relations between countries over longish periods of time by measures other than changing exchange rates.'[2]

On the subject of technique Mr Day recommended holding 'the rate stable for long periods together and then, when change does become necessary, to let the rate free for a short period perhaps of a week or two'.[3]

Mr Day concluded by recommending an extension of the European Payments Union as a possible basis for a world payments system.

(2) THE NEW MONETARY POLICY

In 1952 the new monetary policy was, at home, the economic question of the hour. As Mr Dow points out, Mr Gaitskell had allotted monetary policy 'some rôle: if it remained nevertheless a distinctly subsidiary one', when he welcomed the rise in long-term rates (July 1951) as likely 'to exercise some check on investment'.[4] However, Mr Butler's raising of Bank rate, the first since 1932 except for a brief period at the outbreak of the war, seemed to be a significant new departure. Immediately after the change

[1] *Op. cit.*, pp. 162-3.
[2] *Op cit.*, p. 196.
[3] *Op. cit.*, p. 208.
[4] *The Management of the British Economy* 1945-1960, 1964, p. 60.

of Government in November, along with other monetary changes, Bank rate was raised from 2 to 2½ per cent, Mr Butler explaining that this 'can do much to support other measures to combat inflation'. The Economic Survey for 1952 hailed this, in fact, as 'the most significant change in monetary policy since the beginning of the war'.[1] In March 1952, simultaneously with the Budget, there was another larger rise to 4 per cent.

The *locus classicus* in the way of a theoretical manifesto for the new monetary policy was Professor Robbins's lecture *The Balance of Payments* (November 1951). He insisted that:

'The persistence of external disequilibrium can always be attributed to a failure of financial policy.'[2]

Fiscal policy, Professor Robbins complained, was 'clumsy and inadequate', and he went on:

'We have thrown overboard, as old-fashioned scrap, all the delicate mechanism of financial control which the experience of ages was gradually fashioning. In a situation where there is an obvious scarcity of capital, we have more or less frozen the interest structure.'[3]

For Professor Robbins:

'The obvious course was to revive a monetary policy which is conducted with a full regard to the external balance. When in surplus expand, when in deficit contract. . . . That is a rule which we must adopt ourselves, if the pound is not to drop still further. . . . Stop the inflation, stop it at all costs: that is the paramount need of the moment in the economic sphere.'[4]

The whole question of monetary policy was reviewed from almost every angle, and with disagreement on most significant points, normative and positive, in a Symposium (in two instalments with fourteen contributors) in *The Bulletin of the Oxford University Institute of Statistics*, April-August 1952.

[1] Paragraph 104: quoted by Dow, *op. cit.*, p. 72.
[2] *The Balance of Payments*, Stamp Memorial Lecture 1951, 1952, p. 13.
[3] *Op. cit.*, p. 21.
[4] *Op. cit.*, pp. 27 and 32.

The working of the new policy was first explained in fairly critical terms by Mr H. G. Johnson and Mr C. M. Kennedy.

Mr Johnson emphasized:

'It is important to note that the new policy has operated so far mainly by reducing the willingness of the banks to lend, rather than by choking off the desire of borrowers to borrow. . . . It must be emphasized that the method works, *not* by the adjustment of demand to supply through the raising of advances rates to the competitive equilibrium level, but by the rationing out of the supply by the banks, according to their own standards of soundness and considerations of goodwill and competitive advantage, to the demand at whatever level of rates is established by the combination of official policy and banking conventions. While there might be a case for the rationing of credit by price—and the case for orthodox measures is usually conducted in these terms—that case is largely irrelevant; and there is no good reason to presume that the results of credit-rationing by the banks correspond either to the equilibrium of a competitive market, or (more important) to the requirements of the national interest.'[1]

Mr Kennedy stressed the psychological effects of changes in interest rates:

'The effects on the economy of higher interest rates are not easy to forecast with any degree of confidence, especially since . . . the most important influences are likely to be psychological rather than strictly economic in their working.'[2]

Mr Kennedy felt, in 1952, that speculating on the value of the pound being maintained 'must surely be considered as a "bad risk".' But he was prepared to concede that,

'on this occasion, however, the raising of Bank rate has apparently done much to restore confidence in the currency, at any rate temporarily, and its success in this respect must be regarded as providing in itself the justification of the Government's

[1] *Bulletin of the Oxford University Institute of Statistics*, April-August 1952, pp. 128-9.
[2] *Op. cit.*, p. 132.

policy, in view of the overriding importance of preventing or at least postponing the collapse of sterling'.

However, he concluded:

'The initial success of the Government's policy in this direction can hardly be overestimated, but it would be unwise to count on a repetition of this success should the drain on the reserves once again be resumed. And it would be even more foolish, on the evidence of success in this one particular sphere, to draw the conclusion that the use of orthodox monetary policies will provide the solution to the less immediate, but no less formidable problems which the British economy is facing in the world today.'[1]

Broadly in favour, with varying degrees of intensity, of the new monetary policy, were Mr F. W. Paish, Professor D. H. Robertson, Dr J. R. Hicks, Professor E. V. Morgan and Mr R. F. Harrod.

Mr Paish argued against controls on investment:

'To attempt to reduce investment by physical controls alone would inevitably lead to investment which might or might not be reduced, but would certainly be unbalanced. This is partly because the effectiveness of physical controls varies greatly between different parts of the system; for instance, it is reasonably effective over new building, less so over repairs and alterations, and hardly effective at all over most types of plant and machinery. It is also because control through physical shortages induces a desire to hoard. Firms tend to seize any opportunity to acquire stocks of any raw material or component which may conceivably be scarce in future, even though their existing stocks of it are fully adequate for current needs.'[2]

Professor D. H. Robertson was content to counter fears that monetary policy would bring deflation:

'I do not think that history warrants the view that, given fair treatment in taxation policy and freedom from punitive legislation or administration, a free enterprise system is so lacking

[1] *Op. cit.*, pp. 139 and 140.
[2] *Op. cit.*, p. 142.

in vitality as to be thrown into chronic doldrums by the workings of a mobile bank rate.'[1]

Dr Hicks emphasized that the return to monetary policy was not simply a matter of the change of government in Britain, since there had been similar developments in a large number of other countries. It was because the 'new' fiscal policies and controls had not worked satisfactorily:

'We have to face the fact that the "new" policies have not done all that was expected from them; it is because of the deficiences of the new policies that it has been necessary to resurrect the old. Just what was it that went wrong with the "new" policies? I do not myself think that the main trouble lay in the economic analysis behind them, for that has really stood up pretty well; nor even on the high demands which were made on statistical prognosis, which has stood up fairly well in this country, at least so far; the real trouble was, it seems to me, political. But it was not the sort of political trouble which economists have any right to complain about; it was a trouble which they ought to have foreseen. Taxation, in a democratic country of Western type, is always a central political issue.'[2]

Dr Hicks concluded:

'We are prepared to give the new régime a chance to see what it can do, but we do not want, or expect, to put the clock back to 1640 or 1789.'

But he feared that with bank rate policy now, 'for good or ill, a part of Government policy', this was bound to make for a 'financial bias in favour of Cheap Money'.[3] (But the bias of

[1] *Op. cit.*, p. 155.
[2] *Op. cit.*, p. 157.
[3] *Op. cit.*, pp. 268-9. Contrast, however, J. C. R. Dow, *The Management of the British Economy* 1945-1960, 1964, p. 258: 'Monetary policy was indeed invested with many of the properties of magic. It was often employed as if it, and it alone, would cure inflation, or alternatively, right the balance of payments; and as if it would do so without impinging openly or painfully on any specific class of demand. It is scarcely surprising that Chancellors of the Exchequer grasped at monetary policy as a heaven-sent alternative to budgetary policy.' (As was done of course with electorally, though not economically, very successful results in the spring of 1955.)

governments in favour both of low taxes and low unemployment is far more powerful even than that in favour of low interest rates. Already in the spring of 1955, at the first test of the 'new' policy, it was to be seen which was the less unpopular weapon politically.)

Professor Morgan made the admirable, if unusual, admission 'of my ignorance of what is in "the national interest" ', adding however that 'I think there are reasons why rationing by bankers should conform reasonably well to it'. As regards investment controls Professor Morgan concluded:

'Wartime experience suggests that this sort of control works very well when dealing with all-or-nothing decisions and matters of absolute priority, and very clumsily when dealing with marginal adjustments and matters of relative priority. It is certain that we cannot get out of our present difficulties by giving absolute priority to a few forms of economic activity. On the contrary, any tolerable solution must involve an immense number of delicate marginal adjustments. When it comes to adapting credit policy to this sort of change I am convinced that the banks, under the general control of the central bank, are equipped to do the job far better than it could be done by any other machinery that could be created in the foreseeable future.'[1]

Mr Harrod viewed the new policy in the light of his persisting preoccupations with the need first, to curb investment, secondly, for a settlement of the sterling balances and thirdly, for convertibility.

As regards monetary policy and the curbing of investment Mr Harrod held that 'theory insists that it can make some contribution and reports suggest that it is in fact making a sizeable one'.[2]

[1] *Op. cit.*, pp. 276-7.

[2] Mr Harrod was also much concerned at this time with the 'disorders which are inevitably entailed by inflation', and urged that 'we should announce that we are absolutely determined at all costs to maintain the purchasing power over commodities at a roughly steady level'. (*The Director*, October 1951, p. 50.) During the 1952 recession Mr Harrod continued to maintain that 'a drastic curtailment of industrial investment expenditure must be the main weapon for restoring solvency'. He argued that 'there is a danger of creating excess manufacturing capacity', and that 'policy should be based on the rough assumption that our manufacturing population will not increase'. (*Financial Times*, February 2 and May 24, 1952).

He regarded a settlement of the sterling balances as a 'prerequisite for the successful outcome of the new policy'.[1] As regards the balance of payments he called for an *upward* revaluation:

'I still hold that we could and should improve our balance of trade by some upward revaluation of sterling. . . . It is surely correct that the main method for getting a balance would be to curtail consumption and/or investment internally, with a consequential effect on exports and imports, rather than to curtail imports and let the devil take the hindmost in the internal struggle for the aggregate of goods in short supply.'[2]

As regards long-run prospects, Mr Harrod maintained:

'I have no doubt that vast capital investments in Britain could be profitably undertaken in the long run. We should think in terms of raising the real standard of living by this and other means by 50 or 100 per cent in a generation.'[3]

But Mr Harrod added that 'lack of competitive efficiency has not been the root cause of our recent troubles', He concluded therefore:

'We can thus safely contemplate, without any lasting injury to the body economic, a large reduction in the volume of "widening" investment.'[4]

The case against monetary policy came from Professor R. F. Kahn, Dr Balogh and Mrs Robinson. (At least this Symposium suggested that even if economic events cannot be predicted very accurately, this does not apply to the views of economists on issues of economic policy.)

Professor Kahn seemed to come down in favour of civil servants rather than bankers as the allocators of scarce investment resources (which may or may not have been gratifying to the civil servants of Whitehall, so heavily blamed by some academics for Britain's economic inadequacies):

[1] *Bulletin of the Oxford University Institute of Statistics*, April-August 1952, pp. 166-7.
[2] *Op. cit.*, pp. 168-9.
[3] *Op. cit.*, pp. 170-1.
[4] *Op. cit.*, p. 172.

'Whether reliance is being placed on the decisions of bank managers or on the operation of various rates of interest—both depending, the former entirely, the latter quite largely, on the highly arbitrary distribution of liquidity between firms—the question is whether civil servants could not do better. I do not claim that they could give us anything near the "ideal" distribution; but they could fall far short of the ideal and still do much better.'[1]

However, this pronouncement falls carefully short of saying that civil servants *actually would* do much better. Professor Kahn added that he would

'feel less apprehensive of the new "policy" if there was not such extraordinary divergence of views as to mechanisms and objective'.[2]

Professor Kahn concluded safely that we 'need much more empirical research'.

Mrs Robinson summarized the issue as follows:

'The claim that bank-rate policy is a delicate impersonal instrument which frees us from reliance on "commissars" who take a view about national investment requirements reduces to the claim that the judgment of bankers is the best guide to what schemes of investment should be encouraged and what curtailed. But since the bankers themselves receive instructions from the Government the whole distinction between orthodox monetary policy and unorthodox interventionism wears very thin.'[3]

Mr H. G. Johnson, replying to the debate, observed:

'Practically the only agreement on basic principles to emerge from the Symposium seems to be a general acceptance of the effectiveness of orthodox monetary weapons (i.e. Bank rate and

[1] *Op. cit.*, p. 149.

[2] *Op. cit.*, p. 150. Elsewhere Professor Kahn maintained: 'A combination of balance of payments difficulties and large-scale unemployment . . . is a feature which is likely to recur.' 'Monetary Policy and the Balance of Payments', *Political Quarterly*, Vol. 23, 1952, p. 250.

[3] *Op. cit.*, p. 282.

open market operations, but not qualitative credit controls) as a means of restricting aggregate effective demand. . . . Monetary policy is once more regarded as a potent restrictive instrument, though far less because of its influence on the interest-cost of borrowing than for its effects in generating uncertainty and the expectation of lower future interest rates among borrowers and lenders. . . . But while there is agreement on the *effectiveness* of monetary policy, there is fundamental disagreement over its *efficiency* as an instrument of economic policy.'[1]

As regards the fundamental political issue running through the debate, Mr Johnson concluded:

'Set up in such general terms, the argument can only lead to an affirmation of personal preferences as between the imperfections of monetary restraint and the imperfections of controls. This solution, while in the best tradition of modern welfare economics, seems to me an unsatisfactory one. . . . A more useful approach, I think, is to regard monetary policy and direct controls as both substitutes and complements. . . . This implies that monetary policy should be used as a supplement to budgetary and direct measures of control. As such, it can play a useful subordinate part in reinforcing and lightening more discriminatory methods of control.'[2]

Monetary policy, of course, met its first serious test in 1955, after the two, if not golden at least gilt-edged, years of '53 and '54. By 1956 the Economic Survey which in 1952 had held the new policy to be so 'significant', was conceding that 'monetary policy was not operating as rapidly as had been expected'.[3] On the other hand monetary policy at least remained as a stand-by to be called upon in the not infrequent crises of confidence in sterling. What is noteworthy about this Symposium, as with other subsequent debates on the same or similar questions, is that the more technical points are comparatively peripheral and subordinate, while the main issue amounted largely to an ideological confrontation between the champions of 'planning', on the one

[1] *Op. cit.*, p. 304.
[2] *Op. cit.*, p. 305.
[3] Para. 68: quoted by J. C. R. Dow, *The Management of the British Economy 1945-1960*, p. 79.

hand, and the price mechanism, on the other, without very clear and explicit value-judgments, that is, without precise policy preferences and objectives getting at all fully stated. Regarding the main 'positive' questions in dispute, these were inevitably to a large extent a matter of speculation and guesswork, the answers to which, in fact, tended to be shaped and biased ideologically (for example, regarding the comparative merits as allocators of scarce resources, of bankers and civil servants).

This Part II, headed 1951-1955, has impinged marginally on the difficult year of 1951 at one end and on the crucial 'climacteric' year of 1955 at the other end. But 1951 was dealt with mainly in Part I and we are leaving 1955 to Part III. This much briefer part has centred round the interlude of the, in themselves, apparently quite successful years of 1952, '53 and '54.

3. 1955-1960

DIARY OF EVENTS

(1) Climacteric: an End of Innocence

(2) The Development of Growth Consciousness

(3) The Pushes and Pulls of Inflation

(4) Losing an Empire and not Finding a Balance of Payments

DIARY OF EVENTS

(Dates in some cases approximate)

1955	January 27	Bank rate raised from 3 to 3½ per cent
	February 20	*De facto* convertibility
	February 24	Bank rate raised to 4½ per cent: hire purchase controls
	April 5	Retirement of Sir Winston Churchill
	April 6	Sir Anthony Eden becomes Prime Minister
	April 19	Budget: 6d off income tax
	May 26	General Election: Cons. 344; Lab. 277
	June 1	Messina Conference on European economic integration: Britain declines invitation
	July 25	Credit restrictions
	October 26	Supplementary budget: cuts in investment: credit squeeze
	December 20	Mr Macmillan becomes Chancellor in place of Mr Butler
1956	February 16	Bank rate raised to 5½ per cent: restrictions on investment and hire purchase
	April 17	Budget: premium bonds
	May 11	European Coal and Steel Community adopts resolution on European Common Market and Euratom
	July 17	Mr Macmillan proposes investigation of Free Trade Area
	September 17	End of bread subsidy after fifteen years
	October 31	Britain and France wage war on Egypt
	November 6	President Eisenhower re-elected
1957	January 9	Sir Anthony Eden resigns
	January 10	Mr Macmillan Prime Minister
	January 13	Mr Thorneycroft Chancellor
	March 25	Treaty of Rome signed setting up EEC
	April 9	Budget: Surtax relief: Radcliffe Committee on Working of Monetary System set up.
	July 6	Rent Act

	August 12	Council on Prices, Productivity and Incomes appointed
	September 19	Bank rate raised from 5 to 7 per cent
1958	January 6	Mr Thorneycroft resigns: Mr Heathcoat Amory becomes Chancellor
	February 21	First Report of Council on Prices, Productivity and Incomes
	March 20	Bank rate reduced to 6 per cent
	April 15	Budget: purchase tax reliefs
	May 29	Charles de Gaulle forms government in France
	July 3	'Special deposit' scheme announced: end of credit squeeze
	December 15	Negotiations for Free Trade Area break down
	December 27	Convertibility for external sterling: EPU replaced by European Monetary Agreement
1959	January 1	EEC's first tariff reductions
	April 8	Budget: 9d off income tax: Reductions in purchase tax
	August 20	Report of Radcliffe Committee on the Working of the Monetary System
	October 8	General Election: Cons. 366; Lab. 258
	November 20	EFTA Treaty signed
1960	January 12	First EFTA ministerial meeting
	January 21	Bank rate raised from 4 to 5 per cent
	April 4	Neutral budget
	June 23	Bank rate raised to 6 per cent: credit squeeze
	July 27	Mr Heathcoat Amory resigns: Mr Selwyn Lloyd becomes Chancellor
	November 8	Mr Kennedy elected President of USA
	December 8	Bank rate reduced to 5 per cent

3. 1955-1960

(1) CLIMACTERIC: AN END OF INNOCENCE

At home the year 1955 saw the end of the fleeting interlude of comparative innocence regarding the management of the economy, and 1956 brought the traumatic puncturing of political complacency regarding Britain's position in the world, in the fiasco of Suez. The processes of disinflation, both in domestic economic terms and in world political terms, were somewhat painful. Furthermore, in the next year or two, disquieting comparisons were just beginning to emerge regarding the progress of Britain's Western European neighbours, while collectively these neighbours were going ahead with plans for economic unification, to which a shrug of the shoulders was hardly any longer an adequate answer from Britain.

With the boom mounting, 1955 opened with two increases in Bank rate totalling 1½ per cent. In the April Budget 6d was taken off income tax, and at the election five weeks later the Conservatives won a notable increase in their majority—at that time a rare political achievement. From then on, for the rest of the year, continuing efforts, monetary and fiscal, were made to bring the boom under control, culminating in an autumn Budget of additional taxation, restrictions and investment cuts, and soon after, the resignation of Mr Butler.

Perhaps the Chancellor in the spring of 1955 really was relying, to get the boom under control, in full sincere confidence on a 1½ per cent change in Bank rate, that is, on 'the delicate mechanism of financial control which the experience of ages was gradually fashioning'.[1] But then 'the experience of ages' had not had to cater for the newly acquired national taste for a 98½ per cent level of employment and for the Government's ability and electorally stimulated eagerness to meet this new taste.

Certainly Mr Butler would have been encouraged, in his hopeful reliance on a 1½ per cent rise in Bank rate, by Mr Harrod, who immediately championed the economic management

[1] See above II (2), p. 104.

and political rectitude of his Budget. Regarding any possible political calculations—five weeks before an election—on the part of the shrewd Mr Butler, Mr Harrod wrote:

'Perhaps he did have it in mind in thinking that the voters would best like the man who did not deviate one inch from the course that the economic circumstances suggested is right. . . .

It is to be observed that the recent inflationary symptoms have only been mild. It is reasonable to believe that monetary policy may bring them to an end in a fairly short period—and considerably before next Budget day.'[1]

In June Mr Harrod proclaimed:

'There have been some vapourings about the Chancellor's modest concessions tending to intensify inflation and being inconsistent with the monetary policy that is now being pursued. These are largely doctrinaire and abstract, and quite out of relation to any analysis of the situation as it is at present.'[2]

However, already Mr Harrod found it 'highly relevant' to refer to:

'a well-established dictum that the only way to cure slumps was to prevent antecedent booms going too far'.[3]

Only two months later Mr Harrod was expressing misgivings regarding Mr Butler's monetary 'correctives' of January and February:

'It may be that they were a little too late and a little too mild.'

He complained that, unfortunately,

'parts of the business world . . . did not react appropriately'.[4]

Mr Harrod was concerned regarding

'a credit squeeze of remarkable persistence and duration. We need

[1] *Financial Times*, April 23, 1955, p. 8.
[2] *The Director*, June 1955, p. 446
[3] *Financial Times*, June 24, 1955.
[4] *Financial Times*, August 11, 1955.

have no doubt that this squeeze will eventually do its work and take inflation out of the system. But events are moving with disappointing slowness.'[1]

By September, only four and a half months after the Budget he had praised so enthusiastically, Mr Harrod was complaining of how 'severely' and 'grievously' we were suffering from inflationary symptoms. Foreign confidence in sterling was showing signs of weakness. But Mr Harrod was opposed to import restrictions and an autumn Budget, though he conceded that the latter might have a ritualistic effect on 'the all-important foreigner':

'It would be most misplaced to impose import restrictions. The imports are useful and help to mitigate inflationary pressure.... Furthermore it would have a disastrous effect on foreign confidence.... Equally foolish is the proposal that there should be an autumn Budget.'[2]

When, a few weeks later, Mr Butler duly brought in his autumn Budget, Mr Harrod found the additional taxes on household goods to be 'right' and 'abundantly justified'.[3]

A main source of trouble, according to Mr Harrod seemed to be that:

'Of course, foreigners cannot diagnose our situation accurately.'[4]

or that they 'do not understand us'. Again, 'the foreigner' cannot 'make a close diagnosis'.[5] Of course these defects of the (admittedly 'all-important') 'foreigner' were especially irksome for a vigorous champion of the convertibility of sterling, who had 'uttered a loud whoop of joy'[6] when *de facto* convertibility had been declared the previous February.

[1] *The Director*, August 1955, p. 791.
[2] *Financial Times*, September 10, 1955.
[3] *Financial Times*, October 28, 1955.
[4] *The Director*, December 1955, p. 460.
[5] *Financial Times*, September 10, 1955 and *The Director*, October, 1955, p. 65.
[6] *Topical Comment*, 1961, p. 85. Incidentally, this move to convertibility was also approved by Mr H. Wilson as a 'useful' one, the effect of which was 'temporarily to strengthen confidence in sterling'. See *Post-War Economic Policies in Britain*, Fabian Society, 1957, p. 10.

Professor Tress took a very different view, in spite of his observation that the 'economy has learnt the taste of 1½ per cent unemployment', and his rather optimistic cost estimate:

'For the present winter at least, Mr Butler and his colleagues are not wrong if they count the costs of enforcing a change too great for any long-run stability which they might purchase.'[1]

Professor Tress also maintained regarding the Budget changes that:

'their immediate contribution to any inflationary tendencies can still be accounted small'.

But of course it was rather irrelevant that the addition to inflationary tendencies was only a small one, if what was urgently called for was a reduction. As Professor Tress warned:

'It is difficult to share Mr Butler's confidence that . . . there will be enough room in the balance of the economy for the whole extra volume of exports needed in 1955.'[2]

Even more seriously, Professor Tress suggested:

'The great danger is that what began as a temporary and so bearable deficiency in the balance of payments might turn into a loss of confidence in sterling which would be far more costly.'[3]

Professor Tress concluded:

'Mr Butler appears to have decided to drive hard and to take a chance on the outcome.'[4]

Professor E. A. G. Robinson maintained in December (in what, for the *London and Cambridge Bulletin*, were quite severe terms):

'It is difficult to resist in retrospect the impression that the April Budget left too much to be done too quickly by the operation of interest rates and put too little onus on the direct restraint of

[1] *London and Cambridge Economic Bulletin*, June 1955, p. iv.
[2] *Op. cit.*
[3] *Op. cit.*
[4] *Op. cit.*

consumption in a situation which had acquired an expansionary momentum of its own. . . .

It is difficult for the moment to know whether to admire Mr Butler's nerve or to question his determination."[1]

In the same month Mr Butler resigned from the Chancellorship.

We would suggest that the April Budget of 1955 was a very serious portent and landmark. Of course, vote-catching measures are as old as democracy, and not, as such, necessarily reprehensible. But this was the first time that the immensely heightened post-war economic power of government had been operated, with such successful timing, in harmony with electoral considerations. No one, on either political side, could have made such a claim for, or such a charge against, Mr Attlee, Sir Stafford Cripps or Mr Gaitskell in 1950 or 1951.

Of course, at the time, the prospects did not seem as clear-cut as they do with hindsight. Some kind of case can usually be made out for a more optimistic view, justifying a more lenient or expansive budget. There are always arguable alternatives *ex ante*. But to allow that when *any* doubts can be justified the electorally more promising policy may be adopted, is almost to concede that it may *always* be adopted. 1955 provided a demonstration of two main economic components of electoral success (or what seem to be believed to be such), in combination inevitably rather dangerous. Not only must a boom have got nicely under way some time before the election, but, on top of that, nearer, or as near as possible, to the actual date (in 1955 only five weeks before), popular concessions in taxation are thought desirable, stepping on the accelerator, that is, just when, of course, on normal economic criteria, an unpopular application of the brake might be required.

There had, after the very severe Korean spasm, been no undue prolongation of the 'stop' phrase in 1953 (in contrast with what was to occur in 1958, and similarly in 1962). Eased forward by the favourable switch in the terms of trade, Mr Butler's boom had come to a head about eighteen months before the next election was ultimately due (which was not until October 1956). In the absence of a convincing reason, electors do not usually like to be consulted, nor sitting MPs to forego their seats, much

[1] *London and Cambridge Economic Bulletin*, December 1955.

earlier than is necessary. Fortunately Sir Winston's retirement provided excellent grounds for an election around the peak of the boom. Otherwise with the boom collapsing into crisis, or near-crisis, the Government might have been caught short electorally.

Indeed the succeeding three to four years of rather prolonged recession—as most would agree excessively prolonged—can also, by cynics or realists, be interpreted in terms of the influence of the electoral cycle on economic management. As the mid-term recession proceeds, the question of the timing of re-expansion arises. There are usually impressive grounds for cautious restraint or for prolonging 'convalescence', particularly if, as in 1957 (or 1966), there had been a major sterling crisis. For the mass media, verbalizations in terms of 'laying firm foundations' or 'steady as we go' will be in order. Though such prolongations of the 'stop' phase will not improve the opinion poll ratings at the time, they will, of course, probably help to leave, and indeed be *essential* for leaving, a sufficient margin for an impressive re-expansion and popular budgeting in the crucial pre-election year or two. If a boom that is to have a sharp impact on electoral mood and opinion *can* only last for a short time, it is electorally important not to bring it on (with its swiftly succeeding crisis and cuts) too soon. The second half of the fifties saw the first, exquisitely timed, example of the political business cycle, bringing to the Conservatives a third electoral success running, almost unique in modern British political history.[1]

Apart from this political development, the difficulties of 1955 suggested the end of comfortable assumptions regarding the easy

[1] Mr Samuel Brittan (*The Treasury under the Tories*, 1964, pp. 198-203), though not hinting at any such interpretation as that sketched above, nevertheless gives an account of the 1958 and '59 Budgets which perfectly fits such an interpretation. He quotes Mr Heathcoat Amory, in his 1958 Budget, predicting a further fall in production and rising unemployment, but maintaining that 'we are not yet strong enough to give the economy more than a minor stimulus'. On the other hand, in 1959: 'Mr Amory was told by his colleagues that he was the one man who could lose the Conservatives the election.' Nine-pence was taken off income tax, and, of course, 'orthodox economists and officials have ever since regarded the 1959 Budget as an object lesson in the dangers of trying to go too fast'. Mr Brittan quotes Mr Gaitskell's criticisms in the Budget debate (1959): 'A year ago during the middle of the most favourable six months for the balance of payments there was far less danger of expansion involving us in a balance of payments crisis than there is now.' Mr Brittan insists (in italics): *'The real error of the 1959 Budget is surely not that it gave away too much, but that it came too late.'* This is, of course, according to an economist's simplified point of view. *Politically*, far from being

harmonization, through monetary policy, of the 'full' employment objective with free wage bargaining, as, of course, many economists had predicted in the preceding decade. But at the same time as this fundamental problem was brusquely reasserting itself, that is, the problem of reconciling 'full' employment with something not too remote from price stability and a reasonable balance of payments, the Government felt impelled to take on another fundamental responsibility, or at least began to edge towards it: that of encouraging a higher rate of growth. Hardly capable of juggling with two plates, the Government now felt impelled to try to keep a third in the air. In the White Paper (1956) on 'The Economic Implications of Full Employment', the Government was 'pledged to foster conditions in which the nation can, if it so wills, realize its full potentialities for growth in terms of production and living standards'.[1]

Meanwhile, the Chancellorship not surprisingly became something of a hot-seat, a post which might bring some initial bonus of prestige, but one in which it was politically unhealthy to linger (like the Foreign Secretaryship in the later thirties). In place of Sir Stafford Cripps and Mr Butler, carrying through reasonably coherent lines of medium-term policy for three or four years, there came now a succession of birds of passage; there for a season, to do their turn, go through the time-honoured motions of the traditional Budget-day rituals, hold aloft the battered dispatch-box for the press photographers, produce some gimmick, gadget or 'talking point', and then to be rushed off stage (or to rush themselves off). Successive occupants found themselves hopelessly

'too late', the timing was perfect—and in any case highly successful. When Mr Brittan goes on to point out that 'the Treasury made the very same error in delaying re-expansion all over again in 1962', the same question of criteria and interpretation arises. That the electoral results were, this time (only very narrowly) unsuccessful may be attributable to the upsetting of the timing, in the crucial year 1963, by a coincidence of random exogenous shocks from such directions as General de Gaulle, the winter weather, Miss Keeler, and Mr Macmillan's indisposition. Economists (perhaps because it involves handing over one of their central problems, short-run aggregate fluctuations, or a half share in the problem, to the political science department), do not give the electoral business cycle very detailed attention. Of course, 'stops' and 'goes' are more or less unavoidable, but it is obvious that the four-five year electoral interval has had a major rôle in shaping the periodicity of the main aggregate fluctuations in the British economy over a decade or so, and that it may remain a rather serious problem.

[1] Cmd. 9725, para. 25.

caught between electoral pressures and their thorough-going ignorance as to how to satisfy (or, indeed the outright impossibility of satisfying) the competing and conflicting criteria and objectives of policy set by the pretensions of the time, pretensions often stimulated by economists.[1]

But while all these dilemmas of internal policy and external rôle, crowded in on policy-makers and their critics and advisers, they largely passed by, during these years at any rate, the mass of the electorate, as indeed was demonstrated in 1959 when the Conservative Government was given yet another increased majority. Many in Britain were experiencing years of comfort and security unprecedented for decades. Paradoxically perhaps, amid these dilemmas, it could reasonably be maintained (November 1959), with much validity, on the crest of another electoral boom:

'We must accept not as a piece of political propaganda but as a fact of history, that this is a period of exceptional economic success. Our difficulty in accepting such an assertion comes in part from the influence of the economists as the professional mourners of society, always eager to find loss and desolation to bewail.'[2]

Approving these views, Mr Alan Day maintained:

'From now on, we can hope that the major problems of the British people will not be problems to which economists can provide the answers, for the simple reason that they have already solved the most serious problems of keeping the economic system working reasonably satisfactorily. . . . This does not imply that it is unimportant to consider whether economic growth should be more or less rapid. Here, economists should be doing more than they are, by demonstrating clearly what the choices are that face the community. . . . But the economist cannot begin to provide the answer to the question of whether we want more rapid growth, because the decision cannot be reduced to primarily

[1] Subsequently, of course, an alternative hot (or, indeed hotter) seat was created in the form of a Department of Economic Affairs, which attracted away some of the heat off the Chancellorship.

[2] C. F. Carter, *Three Banks Review*, December 1959, p. 4.

technical matters. The decision (like that on our future economic relationships with Europe) must depend on one's views of the sort of political and social structure one wants to see in Britain during the final decades of the twentieth century. . . . Everyone except the Blimps now realizes that we cannot group ourselves with the super-powers such as the United States and Russia. Our relative power in the world is declining; what we must do is to prevent it from declining too quickly. It will not be easy to hold on to our rightful place at the top of the Second Division. It will be impossible, if the economic resources of countries such as France and Germany pull ahead of those we can command, as they may well do in the next few years."[1]

(2) THE DEVELOPMENT OF GROWTH CONSCIOUSNESS

Very little or no *distinct and explicit* discussion of economic growth as an objective of policy is to be found in the various debates on British post-war economic policy until about the middle fifties. For example, there is little or no explicit mention of growth in the wide-ranging debate on planning and the price mechanism, discussed above.[2] Of course, *implicitly* the growth objective was present. In the central Keynesian problem of a major rise in the level of activity and employment, raising output significantly in the short run is, of course, included; and the short-run problem of maintaining a high level of activity and output with regard to existing resources leads on logically to the problem of the growth of resources.

Interest in growth rates of GNP obviously depends considerably on reasonably regular and reliable statistics of GNP. Mr Colin Clark's great work, *The Conditions of Economic Progress* (1940), was one major landmark, and, of course, the first National Income White Paper of 1941 was another. But it was not until the early or middle fifties that, with improving statistics, and after the recovery and readjustment from war to peace had been more or less completed, that international comparisons of current, or very recent, growth-rates began to become significant. Since other European countries had inevitably been slower than Britain in

[1] The *Observer*, November 15, 1959.
[2] See above I (3).

recovering immediately after the war, it was only as their recovery advanced in the middle fifties that invidious questions of comparative growth-rates began to emerge (under the stimulus, notably, of reports from ECE and OEEC).

As we have seen, it was the comparative growth-rates, or increases in productivity, between Britain and the US which were first invoked (1953-54), as a new support for the thesis of a long-run dollar shortage (just when a certain sluggishness was settling, for almost a decade, on the American economy). We have already noted Mr Harrod urging that we should think in terms of raising the real standard of living 'by 50 or 100 per cent in a generation'.[1]

In the political arena the Chancellor, Mr Butler (May 1954), did something to arouse a more expansive 'growth consciousness' with his appeal to focus on the 'aim to double the standard of living in the next twenty years' (soon after lowered to twenty-five years, in October 1954).

Early in 1955 appeared another Oxford Symposium, this time on 'Growth and the Balance of Payments'. Again, a very wide range of views was discernible. As Mr Streeten observed with regard to one of the main issues:

'An examination of the literature on the relation between divergent rates of productivity growth and their effects on the balance of trade of the economically progressive country, leaves one somewhat bewildered. There is hardly any conceivable proposition that has not been maintained by somebody.'[2]

Winding up the debate, seventy pages later, Mr P. D. Henderson observed:

'The various contributions disclose a remarkably wide dispersion of opinions.'[3]

The starting point of the Symposium had been an article of May 1954 by Mr Henderson on the Economic Survey for that year, in which he had asked:

[1] See above II (2), p. 109.
[2] *Bulletin of the Oxford University Institute of Statistics*, February 1955, p. 11.
[3] *Op. cit.*, p. 88.

'Is it possible to establish any relationship between the rate of economic growth and the condition of the balance of payments?"[1]

On the one hand, there were 'clear conflicts between economic expansion and the needs of the balance of payments'. On the other hand, progress and growth brought possibly 'immense competitive advantages'. With regard to the conflict between home and foreign demands on productive capacity Mr Henderson urged:

'A reduction in demand may help to increase the supply of goods which can be exported; but it would be preferable to achieve this object by expanding productive capacity in the export trades, and in the industries on which they depend.'[2]

Mr Henderson's apparent assumption of excess capacity seemed to fit in with his judgment (May 1954) that:

'Inflation came to an end at least two years ago.'[3]

As regards the stimulation of economic growth as an objective of policy Mr Henderson observed:

'There is a sense in which it is as reasonable to exhort the Government to stimulate increases in productivity as to expect it to raise the national standard of cooking.'[4]

But Mr Henderson concluded that there was some case for fiscal stimulation of investment and that there were strong arguments for reform of the system of business taxation but that it was difficult to decide on the most efficient method.

Mr H. G. Johnson questioned Mr Henderson's basic assumption regarding the desirability of a high rate of growth:

'Philosophically speaking, there is nothing inherently desirable in a high rate of economic growth: insistence on it as the sole

[1] *Op cit.*, May 1954, p. 162.
[2] *Op. cit.*, *February* 1955, p. 2.
[3] *Op. cit.*, May 1954, p. 170. (This was just when a new upswing was getting under way.)
[4] *Op. cit.*, May 1954, p. 169.

criterion of efficiency for economic systems is a currently fashionable value-judgment less defensible than those economists usually make, amounting in extreme cases to pure fetishism. . . . As a matter of fact there is some doubt whether the recent masochistic tendency to bewail Britain's low rate of growth is justified by the evidence—the rate of increase of British productivity since the war has been quite impressive. . . . It is questionable whether Britain might not be better advised to accept and adjust to a gradual surrender of her place as a leading industrial nation, either by a planned withdrawal from the competitive struggle or by a planned transfer of productive resources (labour and capital) to other countries where the prospects of growth are better, than to attempt to retain her present relative position among the industrial nations by rapid expansion of her productive capacity.'

Mr Johnson reformulated the basic question as follows:

'The basic policy problem arising from economic expansion is whether fixed exchange rates are consistent with British economic structure and policy objectives, and not, as Mr Henderson believes, whether expansion will threaten solvency.'

Mr Johnson pointed out:

'In certain circumstances a country might gain, in terms of the rate of growth of its real income, by having a relatively low rate of growth of productivity, and lose by having a high one. . . . This may well be a reasonable approximation to the long-run prospects of the British economy: above a certain rate of growth, the adverse movement of the terms of trade required to maintain or expand the British share in the world manufacturing market might be so great that most of the benefit from increasing productivity accrued to other countries.'[1]

Professor R. Nurkse maintained:

'There is no doubt that, on the whole, the needs of the balance

[1] *Op. cit.*, February 1955, pp. 8-9 and pp. 4-5. Mr Johnson at this time actually advocated reduction of exports (and subsidies to agriculture): 'There are, in my view, good economic reasons for believing that we are in fact exporting too much rather than too little, and that as a nation we should gain by doing less trade rather than more.' *The Listener*, March 24, 1955.

of payments *have* governed the pace of internal investment in the recent past.'

He criticized Mr Henderson for his belief that output could be expanded under conditions of full employment, and expressed doubts about devaluation as a remedy:

'However favourable the price elasticities, and abstracting from any worsening of the terms of trade, the devaluation will be of no use unless some act of domestic retrenchment is enforced that serves to *make room* for an improvement in the foreign balance.'[1]

Professor Arthur Lewis was doubtful whether investment in the UK was too low:

'It is certainly arguable that the rate of investment is too low in this country, but it is not self-evident.'

But he wanted more exports (contrast Mr Johnson):

'If we could sell more exports, we could have more investment, and in due course our standard of living would rise more rapidly.'[2]

Replying to the debate, Mr Henderson reasserted his view, against Mr Johnson, that though a high rate of growth was 'an essentially subordinate aim of policy', it *did* 'appear to be a desirable objective'. He reasserted, also, the view that the rate of investment had 'probably been too low' and was 'consistent only with an unnecessarily and undesirably low rate of growth'.[3] Finally he called attention to the controversial problem of the 'right' level of aggregate demand:

'The main reason for advocating a more or less permanent state of excess demand, or alternatively the maintenance of a reserve of unemployed labour, is in each case a belief that this will enable a higher rate of growth to be achieved.'[4]

The question of the level of demand, as judged by the level of

[1] *Op. cit.*, pp. 41 and 49.
[2] *Op. cit.*, pp. 57-8.
[3] *Op. cit.*, p. 78.
[4] *Op. cit.*, p. 85.

unemployment, has, of course, remained the persistent normative-*cum*-positive issue of post-war economic policy. As regards the issue as stated by Mr Henderson, regarding the effects of alternative levels of demand on the rate of growth, the essentially very long-run evidence is so indefinite and uncertain, that confidently decisive views must inevitably be based more on ideological bias, or on fashion, than on positive or convincing testing. However, in this Symposium, as contrasted with the earlier debate on Monetary Policy discussed above (II (2)), the many and important disagreements did centre rather more round positive issues, and the element of ideological confrontation was comparatively rather smaller. In the next few years, that is in the later fifties—with the Government gradually accepting after its 1956 declaration, an increasing responsibility with regard to the objective of economic growth and with comparisons with other countries and 'league tables' of growth-rates becoming more significant and disquieting—the discussion of growth policies became more and more prominent and intense, as we shall see in some of the memoranda and evidence submitted by university economists to the Radcliffe Committee on the Working of the Monetary System.

(3) THE PUSHES AND PULLS OF INFLATION

The renewed controversies over monetary and wage policy in these years had several points of departure, notably:

(i) The phenomenon of the long upward 'creep' of prices for the previous decade and a half, and the question as to how harmful and dangerous this might or might not be;
(ii) The nature of the 'crisis' of September 1957;
(iii) The causation of inflation, or different types of it, in particular wage- or cost-push inflation and the problems of its control; and
(iv) The techniques of monetary control, and their possible effectiveness, with regard to much more ambitious policy objectives, and in a changed institutional framework.

Of course, these headings overlap and merge into one another, and some of the discussion we have included under one heading might just as well be included under one of the others.

However, from whichever point they started, these controversies almost invariably seemed to lead, fairly soon, to one question, in which normative and positive elements were blended and seldom sufficiently distinguished as they could and should have been. This question was the perennial, central operational issue of Britain's post-war domestic economic policy: the question as to the level of demand at which the economy should be run, as usually roughly judged by the criterion of the percentage of unemployment.

(i) *Creeping Inflation*

As regards our first point of departure, Professor D. H. Robertson, in his paper 'Creeping Inflation' (March 1955), observed:

'There is a general feeling about that the position is unstable, and that most indices of prices are more likely to go on rising than remain stationary or to fall. . . . A continuous, even if moderate, rise in prices has come to seem an inescapable feature of the modern world.'[1]

As regards causation, Professor Robertson maintained:

'Primacy of place must be given to the tremendous emphasis everywhere placed by public opinion, and hence reflected in Government policy, on the objective of "full employment". . . . Secondly, this buoyancy of demand in fact operates to diminish resistance to pressure from the side of work-people for higher wage rates. . . . Thirdly, the fear of creating pockets of unemployment tends to cut across and to stultify other Government policies directed towards the breaking down of monopolistic practices or barriers to international trade, and so hinder the reduction of costs.'[2]

Professor Robertson's main objection to creeping inflation was its inequity, and the danger that attempts to remedy the inequity, such as 'the insidious philosophy of the sliding scale', would turn the planned orderly fall in the value of money

[1] *Essays in Money and Interest*, selected—with a Memoir—by Sir John Hicks, 1966, pp. 246-7; first published in the *London and Cambridge Economic Bulletin*, March 1955.
[2] *Op. cit.*, p. 248.

'into a landslide, generating not a comfortable condition of "full employment" but a hectic and disorderly muddle, which could only be checked, at the cost of much disemployment and distress, by the re-establishment of drastic monetary discipline'.[1]

He inquired:

'Is it really too late to embark resolutely on the other course and attempt to re-establish in the public consciousness the belief that stability of the price level *means* stability of the price level and not stability in its rate of upcreep?'[2]

Professor Robertson thought that greater activity on the part of the Monopolies Commission might contribute, and concluded:

'In the last resort, over however many dead bodies, the public can doubtless get the monetary policy it desires. It may be that it does *not* desire one which is compatible with genuine long-term stability of the price level. But if it does, from what has been said already it seems to follow that it must be prepared not only to adopt a reasonable interpretation of the concept of "full employment", but to recognize that it may not be wise to regard the attainment even of an employment objective in itself reasonably conceived as in all circumstances the absolutely overriding aim of policy. Experience shows that this is a subject on which it is almost impossible to speak plainly without incurring misunderstanding and obloquy.'[3]

The following year (1956) Professor H. G. Johnson reviewed the revival of monetary policy over the previous five years. He conceded two effects to monetary policy, on stockholding and on short-term capital movements. Apart from this, his conclusions were severely negative:

'Monetary policy is unlikely to be able to do much towards solving the major long-run monetary problem of the British economy, the tendency for British wages and prices to increase more rapidly than those of Britain's international competitors.'[4]

[1] *Op. cit.*, p. 252.
[2] *Op. cit.*, p. 253.
[3] *Op. cit.*, p. 256
[4] *Three Banks Review*, June 1956, p. 19.

Professor Johnson did not favour the policy of 'damping down demand':

'Substantial unemployment would be required to prevent wages from increasing at an inflationary rate. Given the narrow limits set by current opinion as to what constitutes a tolerable margin of unemployment, this means that neither monetary policy nor alternative methods of controlling aggregate demand offer much prospect of a solution. . . . Nor can we see any hope of success in controlling the wage-price spiral by appealing for the re-introduction of rigid wage and price controls, or by pledges by individual industries not to raise their prices for the next six months, still less by despairing appeals to employers and employees to moderate their greed by self-restraint such as hard-pressed Chancellors tend to make.'[1]

Professor Johnson concluded on a note of resignation:

'Is there any solution? . . . The solution to the overload on the economy seems to be to stagger along under it as we have been doing, meeting crises by a succession of temporary and regrettable expedients. This solution would probably prove much more satisfactory than it sounds.'[2]

Professor A J. Brown (1958) was inclined to dismiss as somewhat alarmist the dangers of creeping inflation. He concluded:

'I see no sign that expectation of continued price-increase has become engrained in the system; there are spasmodic signs of it in the distinct separate booms of the post-war years, but for the period as a whole it seems to be notably absent. There is no sign that saving has been seriously affected by inflation, and by achieving fuller employment and higher real income than before the war, we have increased the proportion of the national product devoted to investment. We have also achieved an accelerated rate of growth, connected with improved technology even more than with the enlargement of the capital stock. The occupational and industrial structure of the economy has apparently been about

[1] *Op. cit.*, p. 19.
[2] *Op. cit.*, p. 20.

as flexible under full employment as it was with a great deal of unemployment, though the price-mechanism has been more patently the servant of demand changes in bringing it about. The key to the positive achievement of this period has been full employment.'[1]

This rather rosy view of the condition of the British economy did not, however, take much account of the 1957 crisis.

(ii) *The 1957 'Crisis'*

The sterling crisis of 1957 probably aroused more heated disagreement than most of the other crises since the war.[2] It occurred when the British balance of payments, on current account, was, fleetingly, in a fairly favourable condition, for the moment at any rate, and this caused considerable division of opinion as to whether there really was a 'crisis' at all. Mr Harrod (1961) wrote of 1957 that 'the sterling crisis that came on in August and September was real enough'.[3] But two years later he held that it, 'of all those that have occurred since the war must be pronounced the most totally bogus'.[4] He firmly maintained (1958) that inflation could not have been a cause of the crisis, because in 1957 there was no inflation in Britain:

'It ought not to have been possible, for instance, for anyone supposed to be knowledgeable and sensible, to have said in September 1957 that inflation was rampant in England. That is not a statement like "I feel depressed", about which only the speaker can be presumed to judge. Rather it is like the statement "it is raining", which may be verified or falsified by certain observations.'[5]

[1] *Economic Journal*, September 1958, p. 462.

[2] 'At the present time, there is more confusion, more division among men of knowledge and goodwill than perhaps at any time in post-war history.' L. C. Robbins, 'Thoughts on the Crisis', *Lloyds Bank Review*, April 1958, p. 1. Four years later, in the middle of the crisis of July 1961, Professor Paish was to make a similar claim: 'There have been few periods in British history when economists have found the situation more perplexing than they do at present, or were more divided in their views.' (*Studies in an Inflationary Economy, The United Kingdom 1948-1961*, 1962, p. 309.) 1966-67 was still to come.

[3] *Topical Comment*, 1961, p. 186.

[4] *The British Economy*, 1963, p. 145.

[5] *Policy against Inflation*, 1958, p. xi. In October 1956, Mr Harrod maintained that 'UK has finally brought its inflation under control'. (*Sydney Morning Herald*, October 30, 1956.)

Mr Harrod maintained that

'Under the Conservative régime, internal inflation has been kept in check.'[1]

On the other hand Mr Harrod accepted that the problem of excess demand had been chronic except for two brief interludes:

'It seems that the periods 1952-3 and 1956-7 are the only occasions since 1946 when Britain has been exempt from the evil of over-full demand.'[2]

Regarding the 1957 sterling 'crisis' Mr Harrod maintained in January 1958:

'It does not all matter very much, because basically the position is not serious. The so-called crisis was the result of a great pile-up of words about trifles.'[3]

Soon afterwards, in an article entitled 'The Last Sterling Crisis?', Mr Harrod was prognosticating:

'It may quite well happen that the crisis of August-September 1957, is the last of this sort that we are destined to have as an aftermath of war.'[4]

By early 1958, according to Mr Harrod, inflation was ceasing to be a problem:

'It is doubtful if inflation is still a problem at all. With a gathering world recession we shall shortly have other and much more serious problems to be concerned with.'[5]

For Professor Robbins the 1957 crisis was certainly a very real one, although he agreed that 'this was not a crisis of the current account'. Nevertheless he maintained:

[1] *The Times*, May 20, 1958.
[2] *Policy Against Inflation*, 1958, p. 230.
[3] *Liverpool Post*, January 21, 1958.
[4] *The Director*, February 1958, p. 284.
[5] *The Director*, April 1958, p. 73.

'The root cause of our weakness, of our failure to accumulate a sufficient reserve and to achieve a position in international trade strong enough to be immune to the impact of international rumour, was the continuation of internal inflation.'[1]

It was 'quite obvious' that monetary policy up to the autumn of 1957 'had not stopped the inflation'.[2] As regards the Government's duties in respect of maintaining employment on the one hand, and restraining inflation on the other hand, Professor Robbins concluded:

'It is not the duty of governments to make the maintenance of employment the be-all and end-all of policy, regardless of what happens to the value of money. It is their duty rather to maintain conditions which will make a high level of employment compatible with a stable value of money. They should not say we guarantee employment whatever demands are made in respect of wage-rates; they should say rather we will try to maintain such a volume of expenditure as, given an income-level rising with productivity, will maintain a high level of employment. If they do this, then in a free society at any rate, it is for trade unionists and all the rest of us to decide how we react as regards the prices we put on our own particular products. This, clearly, is a controversial view. There are many who hold that salvation lies in a much more authoritarian direction. Control of wages from the centre, plus some measure of dividend limitation, is the solution they favour. My solution is in quite conscious opposition to this. I do not think that experience elsewhere suggests that in the absence of deliberate monetary stabilization a general wage control is likely to be successful; and, if monetary stabilization is attempted, such a control seems to me unnecessary.'[3]

Mr R. F. Henderson was also concerned about inflationary trends, and inclined to forebodings regarding 'creeping inflation' and its long-run effect on confidence in sterling:

'What was required—and achieved in September 1957—was to

[1] *Lloyds Bank Review*, April 1958, p. 4.
[2] *Op. cit.*, p. 7.
[3] *Op. cit.*, pp. 23-4.

establish confidence in future price stability. This meant giving it, temporarily at least, first priority among the aims of the Government's economic policy, and establishing such a high rate of interest on gilt-edged that their prices were about the bottom and that they were worth purchasing by investors who had the alternative of buying equities. Until that was done the position was grave. . . . *For a general loss of confidence in the future of currency starts slowly like a snowball, and then builds up very quickly. That in the summer of 1957 it should have produced a balance of payments crisis in spite of a comfortable surplus in the balance of payments on current account is not an indication that it was a 'phoney' crisis, but rather that it was a peculiarly grave one.* It was a real crisis of confidence in the future of sterling, originating in this country.'[1]

(iii) *Prices Productivity and Incomes and the Problems of Wage-Push Inflation*

Reports from two government bodies added considerably to the monetary controversies in the later fifties. There were, in particular, the reports of the Council on Prices, Productivity and Incomes, and of the Committee on the Working of the Monetary System (1959). The former body, The Three Wise Men, reported in all four times. Its first and most controversial utterance came in February 1958, and followed in its main principles the ideas of Professor Robertson's essay on 'Creeping Inflation'. Regarding the cause of the rising trend of prices and incomes, it was maintained:

'Viewing the period as a whole, we incline to think that the main cause has been an abnormally high level of demand for goods and services in general, maintained for an abnormally long stretch of time.'[2]

The two main policy themes of the report were the desirability of stable prices, and the achievement of this by 'damping down demand'. For these themes there may well have been much to be said. But they were presented simply as obviously desirable and agreed, without any explicit estimate being offered of the

[1] Not *Unanimous*, edited by A. Seldon, 1960, p. 44. (Italics added.)
[2] First Report, 1958, p. 24.

opportunity costs involved in terms of the level of employment and the rate of growth, which would be attainable with the strict pursuit of price stability. Positive predictions, or estimates of possibilities, were not always kept clearly separate, as they could and should be, from the recommendation of norms. In other words, policies were being discussed without adequate specification of the objectives envisaged.

This first report of the Council on Prices, Productivity and Incomes (February 1958), was a signal for an outburst of controversy over the distinction, and its significance, between 'cost-push' and 'demand-pull' inflation. First, on the level of pure analysis or taxonomy, this discussion led to some useful distinctions between model processes. But secondly, and empirically, the task of distinguishing which process, or precise blend of processes, was actually, and to what extent, operating in the British economy at particular junctures, was usually much more difficult and controversial. Thirdly, regarding the implications for policy which emerged, there was still more room for controversy. In fact, here again the debate boiled down to or indeed largely amounted to a kind of rationalization of the central normative-*cum*-positive issue of post-war economic policy, that of the level of demand (or target level of unemployment) at which the economy should be run. Those who put great stress on the rôle of cost-push tended to coincide with those who wanted a 'high-pressure' policy; while those who, like Professor Robertson and the Cohen Council, put more stress on demand-pull as the cause of inflation, implied, at the same time, that a lower level of demand was desirable. As Mr Dow pointed out at the time, regarding the infusion of ideological 'colour' in the theorizing on this question:

'Attitudes to inflation are coloured by very general, more or less implicit, assumptions about how the economy works; and in particular about the degree to which it is sensitive to "market forces".'[1]

The debate derived its edge from this element of ideology. In fact, it soon had to be admitted by all but the most dogmatic and exclusivist extremists on either side that often, or usually, there

[1] *Economic Journal*, September 1958, p. 613.

were both processes of 'demand-pull' and 'cost-push' at work in most actual inflationary processes.[1] But the division of views on the policy issue was left much as it had been before.

One economist, who inclined quite markedly to the demand-pull explanation, did also develop a relatively precise thesis about the level of demand, in terms of the level of unemployment, which should be aimed at in order to secure approximate price stability and also a satisfactory balance of payments. This was Professor F. W. Paish, who began by defining the elusive concept of 'full employment' as:

'The level of employment which is consistent with securing, not the maximum rate of current output, but the maximum long-run rate of growth of output.'[2]

This was likely to be below that at which current output is at its maximum, because (among other reasons) of the effects on efficiency of a very high pressure of demand. Professor Paish continued:

'If this accelerated rate of long-term growth is to be maintained, production and employment must always be kept below the level which could be secured in the current year by the creation of additional demand.'[3]

Professor Paish was thus attacking the 'high pressure' thesis that there was a fortunate harmony between keeping unemployment down to a minimum and maximizing the rate of growth, though he did not think the disharmony was very extensive. He then went on to ask what level of unemployment was consistent with stable prices and concluded:

[1] This was pointed out three years later, by the Fourth Report of the Council, July 1961. (The Council had been reconstituted, and its Third and Fourth Reports differed in emphasis from the First): 'The experts . . . were at one time divided into two schools: one laid stress on the pull of demand drawing pay and prices up wherever the flow of current or potential expenditure was rising above present supplies; the other stressed the upward push of negotiated rises in rates of pay, initiating rises in cost. More recently the experts have found more common ground. There is now a wide measure of agreement that both "demand-pull" and "cost-push" have been active, that they have reinforced one another, and that policy has to tackle both.' (p. 15)

[2] 'Progress, Prices and the Pound', *District Bank Review*, March 1958, p. 3.

[3] *Op. cit.*, p. 4.

'The minimum level of total unemployment consistent with stability of prices may not be more than about 2 per cent or not far above the present level.'[1]

Professor Paish attacked the cost-push thesis by calling attention to the extensive wage drift:

'To make a policy of wage control effective would almost certainly require legal action, enforced by severe penalties for infringement both upon employers and employed.'[2]

Finally he inquired whether price stability and a higher rate of growth, even if mutually compatible in a closed system, were also consistent with equilibrium in the balance of payments for a country situated as Britain then was. Again Professor Paish came up with a moderately optimistic answer (providing that a level of about 2 per cent unemployment was acceptable):

'Provided home demand is kept at a level which enables and obliges producers to seek out export markets with efficiency and enthusiasm, there seems to be a very good chance that policies sufficient to maintain stability of prices at home will also be sufficient to ensure an adequate balance of payments surplus.'[3]

On the other side, two papers from Oxford appeared (1958) in favour of the cost-push thesis. In the first, Dr Balogh maintained that there was 'cumulative and overwhelming evidence' in favour of the cost-push explanation, and that 'all available material massively points away from the explanation of the inflationary process as originating in "too much money chasing too few goods" '.[4] Although the evidence may have been described as 'overwhelming' and 'massive', perhaps the thesis which it was alleged to support or refute needed rather more precise definition. Dr Balogh went on to explain:

'There is no need to assume the existence of excess demand in

[1] *Op. cit.*, p. 9. In 1948 his estimate had been 4 per cent. See p. 31n 2.
[2] *Op. cit.*, p. 12.
[3] *Op. cit.*, p. 17.
[4] 'Productivity and Inflation', *Oxford Economic Papers*, June 1958, p. 225 and p. 230.

order to show that trade union claims led to the increase in prices. It would suffice if entrepreneurs thought, as indeed they could not fail to do, that individual wage demands are part of a general wave, likely to be self-justifying.'[1]

As regards 'The Outlines of a Solution', Dr Balogh concluded:

'It is clear that a double-pronged attack on the problem is the only one likely to succeed. Investment must be increased to accelerate the rise in productivity (and thus in the ability to satisfy wage demands) *and wage-demands must be mitigated first to permit an increase in investment and subsequently (and to a much lesser degree) to keep them within the bounds of the increase in productivity achieved.*'[2] (Italics added.)

Such a policy required 'the whole-hearted *co-operation of the trade unions*'. But Dr Balogh conceded:

'I am in no position to judge whether trade union co-operation would immediately be forthcoming if a policy of balanced social justice were adopted.'[3]

Nevertheless:

'Wage restraint will hardly be politically practicable without first plainly demonstrating that social justice will be safeguarded.'[4]

The plain demonstration of the safeguarding of social justice (or the 'adoption' of 'a policy of balanced social justice') together with the raising of investment, required, among others, the following measures: (a) restraint on profits and not merely dividends; (b) taxes on wealth, including capital gains; (c) a conventional budget surplus of perhaps between £900 and £1,200 million; (d) much closer direct control over investment; (e) far more stringent powers of price control.[5]

[1] *Op. cit.*, p. 239.
[2] *Op. cit.*, p. 240.
[3] *Op. cit.*, p. 242.
[4] *Op. cit.*, p. 240.
[5] *Op. cit.*, pp. 240-1.

Dr Balogh maintained that:

'These measures together should enable the country to accelerate the annual increase in physical productivity from the present roughly 1 per cent per annum to something between 2 and 3 per cent.'[1]

This claim was a relatively modest one, for two years before Dr Balogh had described an 'increase in productivity to at least 6 per cent per annum'[2] as having been 'easily' inducible.

Mr G. D. N. Worswick also rejected the demand-pull explanation of inflation, as well as advocating a high level of demand and as high a level as possible of employment for its own sake and for its social benefits. He explained:

'I support very strongly on social grounds the benefits to be derived from a very buoyant demand for labour. I rate very highly as an objective a state of affairs in which a man can leave his present employment and look for other with a hope of success if he finds his work conditions uncongenial in one way or another.'[3]

Fortunately, as Mr Worswick saw it, there was a harmony between very high levels of employment, and efficiency and growth. There was no need to make hard choices at the margin. On the contrary, Mr Worswick maintained that:

'A fairly acute shortage of labour has two strongly beneficial effects upon productivity. The first is to make managements endeavour to adapt their working conditions to get some output from even the least promising employees. . . . Secondly, managements are induced to become more and more machine-minded, to go for automation, and so forth. . . . In so far as the rise in prices is accompanied by a very high level of employment, the effects on productivity, on balance, would seem to be favourable.'[4]

Nor did the external consequences cause Mr Worswick much concern. There was always devaluation:

[1] *Op. cit.*, p. 241.
[2] *New Statesman and Nation*, April 14, 1956, p. 361.
[3] 'Prices, Productivity, and Incomes', *Oxford Economic Papers*, June 1958, p. 248.
[4] *Op. cit.*, pp. 248-9.

'As to the external consequences of price increases in Britain, these matter more or less according as to what is happening to prices elsewhere. We argued that there is always devaluation to correct any significant divergence of British prices from those of competing exporters. Certainly it is wrong to think of a further devaluation as a kind of national disaster.'[1]

Mr Worswick maintained that very high levels of unemployment might be necessary to stop wages from rising:

'While trade union leaders might be deterred from wage demands if unemployment were 10 or 15 per cent, so that the argument that "wage increases cause unemployment" (at best a very doubtful one) might deter them, they would hardly be deterred by a mere 2 or 3 per cent unemployed.'[2]

With regard to creeping inflation in general, Mr Worswick's answer to the question 'whether a continuing upward movement of prices mattered?' was that, as regards the domestic economy, 'it does not matter very much'. But he later insisted that:

'On balance, the present rate of increase of prices is excessive and must be brought under control. I think that at the present time price stability is a sensible objective, though I should not regard it as a permanent one.'[3]

Moreover a main item in his 'Frontal Attack on the Problem' was the stabilization of the cost of living as a precondition for an incomes policy. This measure of stabilization might entail subsidies and price controls, but Mr Worswick did not go nearly as far as Dr Balogh in demanding investment controls, profits taxation, a massive budget surplus, or a demonstration that 'social justice will be safeguarded'. Mr Worswick concluded optimistically that:

'The present economic circumstances are quite exceptionally favourable for securing not merely a temporary stability of the

[1] *Op. cit.*, p. 249.
[2] *Op. cit.*, p. 253.
[3] *Op. cit.*, p. 256.

general level of prices in Britain, but for working out arrangements which will keep the movement of money wages within bounds thereafter."[1]

In the middle fifties a series of empirical and statistical studies appeared on the sources or causes of inflation, and, in particular, on the rôle of wages and trade unions. In 1956 Mr Dow, in explaining inflation in Britain since the war, put the emphasis primarily on rising import prices, attributing a passive rôle to wages as simply following up rises in the cost of living.[2] Though this explanation was relevant in the opening years of the decade, import prices ceased to rise significantly after about 1952-53, while the general price level continued sharply upward. In a subsequent article with Mr Dicks-Mireaux (1959), Mr Dow assigned a greater influence to the aggregate demand for labour, though they also included an element of trade union 'pushfulness'.[3]

A much-discussed pioneer contribution to the debate on the causation of inflation was Professor A. W. Phillips's study 'The Relation Between Unemployment and the Rate of Change of Money Wage Rates in the UK 1861-1957'. Professor Phillips claimed to show that:

'The rate of change of money wage rates can be explained by the level of unemployment and the rate of change of unemployment, except in or immediately after those years in which there is a sufficiently rapid rise in import prices to offset the tendency for increasing productivity to reduce the cost of living.'

The conclusion for policy which Professor Phillips derived was fairly close to that advocated by Professor Paish:

'If aggregate demand was kept at a value which would maintain a stable level of product prices, the associated level of unemployment would be a little under 2½ per cent.'[4]

[1] *Op. cit.*, p. 264.
[2] *Oxford Economic Papers*, October 1956.
[3] 'The Determinants of Wage Inflation in the UK', *Journal of the Royal Statistical Society*, 1959. See also L. A. Dicks-Mireaux, *Oxford Economic Papers*, October 1961.
[4] *Economica*, November 1958, p. 299.

A study by Professor R. G. Lipsey (1960) also found evidence of a fairly close association between changes in the level of demand and changes in wage rates, though not quite as close as that found by Professor Phillips.[1] In a further contribution Professor Lipsey concluded:

'The picture we have arrived at is that the major part of the price and wage rises in the United Kingdom cannot be accounted for by the exercise of trade union power independent of the state of the market. Wages rise mainly as a result of excess demand. . . .
Variations in wage rates are associated significantly with variations in the level of excess demand.'[2]

However, these tentative conclusions may subsequently have been rendered of somewhat doubtful significance by a paper by Mr A. G. Hines (1964), which, using an index of trade union 'pushfulness', concluded:

'Contrary to the prevailing view, trade unions do affect the rate of change of wages *independently* of the demand for labour.'[3]

So the net effect, thus far, of these econometric investigations, seems hardly likely to have swayed any of the more determined supporters of the main alternative policies for countering inflation (except for Mr J. C. R. Dow who had at first been most critical of the emphasis on demand-pull in the first report of the Three Wise Men).[4]

This literature, and the complex problems involved, were reviewed by Sir Donald MacDougall in 1959. Sir Donald began by asserting, perhaps a little optimistically, 'that both major political parties take inflation seriously'. Regarding the recent controversies, Sir Donald maintained again, perhaps, rather optimistically:

'The controversy was so heated partly because surprisingly little

[1] R. G. Lipsey, 'The Relation between Unemployment and the Rate of Change of Money Wage Rates in the United Kingdom, 1862-1957: A Further Analysis', *Economica*, February 1960.
[2] *An Introduction to Positive Economics*, 2nd edition, 1966, pp. 728 and 730.
[3] See 'Trade Unions and Wage Inflation in the UK 1893-1961', in *Review of Economic Studies*, 1964, p. 221.
[4] I am grateful to Professor A. W. Phillips, of the Australian National University, for pointing out this exception.

careful work had been done on these matters so that protagonists on both sides were able to throw rather dubious statistics and arguments into the ring. In the last few years, however, more careful work has been done, and a good deal more has been started, so that in a few years time I am hopeful that we may know much more about the economic relationships involved—and not only because of the research now in progress but also because the events of the next few years seem likely to be revealing.'[1]

However, regarding the central policy issue, Sir Donald was *not* optimistic, and was critical of the view that the pace of inflation was sensitive to, and controllable by, slight adjustments in aggregate demand:

'I am not convinced that, in future, price stability will prove compatible with full employment, high output and rapid growth—at least if we keep our present methods of wage bargaining.'[2]

If trade unions had more than a passive rôle in the inflationary process, then:

'Action to influence the attitude of the trade unions may be an indispensable part of any policy that attempts to achieve price stability without sacrificing employment, output and growth.'[3]

Sir Donald concluded:

'The fundamental problem is how to reduce the level of unemployment required to stop prices rising.'[4]

Measures to reduce frictional and structural unemployment were of key importance, and, initially, making productivity grow faster might help with the inflation problem. However:

'Any kind of "wages policy" for Britain simply bristles with economic, political and administrative difficulties.'[5]

[1] *Economic Record*, December, 1959, p. 372.
[2] *Op. cit.*, p. 380.
[3] *Op. cit.*, p. 384.
[4] *Op. cit.*, p. 384.
[5] *Op. cit.*, p. 388.

As an example of the gradual shift of opinion in some quarters towards an incomes, or wages, policy, Mr Harrod's views may be cited. In 1956 he was doubtful whether in the long run wage-push inflation would be a problem,[1] and in a paper of that year he was sceptical regarding wages policy on grounds of the importance of 'demand-pull':

'We shall probably be drawn to the decision that the national wages policy just would not work in conditions of excessive aggregate demand for labour. . . .

. . . Furthermore, if we could get over our demand-induced inflation, it is not so clear that a national wages policy would be needed after all. . . . There are undoubted disadvantages in a national wages policy. There is the great underlying issue of freedom of bargaining. . . . I regard any idea of a national profit policy as highly dangerous; but without one can we really get agreement for a national wage policy?'[2]

Mr Harrod's diagnosis of inflation was in terms of demand-pull:

'It is probably true to say that the excess of demand over supply has been a more important influence on the upward course of wages than trade union pressure.'[3]

However, by 1958 Mr Harrod was criticizing the second report of the Council on Prices, Productivity and Incomes for its claim that the 'damping down' of demand in 1957 had played a significant part in the reduction of wage increases. According to Mr Harrod, the effect of the slackening of demand on the abatement of wage-push had been only 'a minor one':

'Part, but only part, of this is attributable to the policy of having

[1] 'Some hold that wage-earners are greedy, not to say insatiable, and that, with full employment, they will persistently bid up their wage demands more than the rise in productivity and that we are thereby doomed to a régime of chronic inflation. I regard this as unduly pessimistic.' *Time and Tide*, July 28, 1956, p. 900.

[2] *Topical Comment*, 1961, pp. 158-9. By 1967, one of the two postulates 'of the whole system' of policy, which Sir Roy proposed was 'that we should put the utmost stress on the incomes policy'. *Towards a New Economic Policy*, 1967, p. 67.

[3] *Sydney Morning Herald, Finance Supplement*, October 30, 1956, p. 4.

a slack economy. Something is due also to the campaign of education, to the leadership of a well-trusted Prime Minister, to the sense of responsibility of many trade union officials. . . .[1]

As an institutional support for incomes policy, 'the leadership of a well-trusted Prime Minister', was to prove, perhaps, a little short on mileage. But, after 1959, Sir Roy continued to move towards advocating more drastic measures of wage and income regulation, without, however, entering very far into the institutional and practical difficulties, economic, political and administrative, with which, as Sir Donald MacDougall had observed, any kind of wages policy for Britain 'simply bristled'.

An interesting and timely symposium on Wage Policy and Inflation appeared in June 1958 in *The Scottish Journal of Political Economy*. The case for curbing wage increases by reducing excess demand was cogently stated by Mr J. R. Parkinson who argued:

'We might surmise, therefore, that in UK conditions unemployment of, say, 3 per cent might effectively reduce the annual wage increase to manageable proportions.'[2]

The issue, as he saw it, was whether

'it would be better to attempt to run the economy at a rather less full level of employment in the hope that a more sustained rate of increase in productivity can be maintained, without however, producing the maximum that could be turned out at any one time, or whether it would be better to produce at maximum rates intermittently. . . .

. . . It is possible that minimum unemployment does not give rise to the maximum rate of growth or the maximum production of goods and services over a long period.'[3]

Alternative ideas regarding the reform of wage bargaining were put forward by Mr D. J. Robertson and Mr A. Flanders. Mr Robertson complained that purely advisory bodies (like the

[1] *The Director*, October 1958, p. 70.
[2] *Scottish Journal of Political Economy*, June 1958, p. 95.
[3] *Op. cit.*, p. 97.

Cohen Council) and wage freezes represented temporary expedients. What was needed was a 'permanent remedy', which he sought in the direction of confining national wage negotiations to the settlement of minimum rates, while negotiations about standard rates in particular firms and industries

'should be shifted to the local level and should become much more detailed'.[1]

Mr Flanders, on the other hand, proposed central bargaining over an annual round of increases, with the Government representing the public interest. The process would be voluntary and result in recommendations rather than compulsory rates.[2]

Professor Phelps Brown (as later Professor H. G. Johnson) suggested that neither of these reforms of wage bargaining, nor any others, would be effective without adjusting demand:

'It seems to me probable that national money income will continue to rise faster than national real income so long as proposed rises in pay that will raise unit costs are not generally seen to imperil turnover and employment.'[3]

But Professor Phelps Brown did not

'believe that there is any dependable relation between the rate of change of money incomes and the level of unemployment even when that is considered only as an index of the strength of the forces that bear directly on incomes. Still less do I believe that unemployment is one of those forces itself. It is quite wrong to suppose that unemployment inherently has to be created if costs are to be stopped rising. With greater short-run mobility of labour and an improved personal quality at the margin of the working population, a balanced demand would be compatible with less unemployment. . . .

. . . We should regard it as an integral part of full-employment policy to maintain agencies and apply resources to provide more jobs at particular places and help particular men and women raise their employability.'[4]

[1] *Op. cit.*, pp. 108-9.
[2] *Op. cit.*, p. 121.
[3] *Op. cit.*, p. 146.
[4] *Op. cit.*, p. 147.

Professor H. G. Johnson supported Mr Parkinson's (and the Cohen Council's) thesis that as regards the cause of inflation in Britain since the war,

'the predominant factor has been high demand'.[1]

On the other hand, Professor Johnson did not believe that stopping the inflation, of the kind that had persisted since the war, was worth the costs involved in doing so. As regards the persistent balance of payments difficulties:

'It is true that continuing inflation, in conjunction with our policy of maintaining a fixed exchange rate and preserving London's rôle as a world financial centre, must lead to recurrent trouble. But such trouble is highly unlikely, to say the least, to be as catastrophic as this argument for stopping inflation requires; and it seems unreasonable that the prospect of it should be ascribed solely to inflation, when it might just as well be laid at the door of the country's international financial policy.'[2]

(iv) *The Radcliffe Report and the Means and Ends of Monetary Policy*

In August 1959 the report of the Radcliffe Committee on the Workings of the Monetary System appeared, with extensive Memoranda and Minutes of Evidence following in 1960. The Committee's exposition of monetary theory, with its emphasis on the structure of interest rates rather than the quantity of money as 'the centrepiece of monetary action', aroused considerable theoretical controversy. The theoretical debate took on a sharper edge by reason of the policy implications which the alternative theories, and terminologies, were held to suggest. We are not concerned here with the 'pure' (or at least more abstract) theorizing, nor with the various technical recommendations on such subjects as the relations between the Treasury and the Bank of England; local authority finance; liquidity controls by special deposits or variable ratios; and the guidance of long-term interest rates.

The Committee itself did not go into such broader policy issues as, for example, the continuing controversial question of the right

[1] *Op. cit.*, p. 149.
[2] *Op. cit.*, p. 151.

level of demand, simply suggesting that, whatever this level was, monetary policy could not contribute very much to its achievement or regulation. But the central question of the level of demand, along with problems of wages policy and the objective of economic growth, did figure prominently in some of the Memoranda from university economists. Also, the Committee's generally sceptical attitude to monetary policy, with its stress on the variety of objectives which economic policy should seek to attain, played a part in the broad shift in emphasis of the policies of the Conservative Government, which was to take place in the opening years of the sixties.

In their Memoranda and Evidence the university economists tended to take up fairly predictable attitudes. The new 'growth' motif was exemplified by Dr Kaldor and Dr Balogh. Dr Balogh's statement of policy objectives was not very precise:

'I shall assume that policy should aim at maintaining price stability and full employment and growth at home and at the same time enhance Britain's economic and political influence abroad.'[1]

Just previously Dr Balogh had maintained that the main policy objectives were compatible, and that there was no 'dilemma' or need to choose:

'There is no dilemma between growth, stability and redistribution. In the long run a high rate of growth *promotes* price stability; in the short run demand can be contained through taxation, and a certain rate of wage inflation through redistribution. The compatibility of these goals, obviously says nothing about their political desirability.'[2]

[1] *Committee on the Working of the Monetary System. Principal Memoranda of Evidence*, Vol. 3, HMSO, 1960, p. 40.

[2] P. Streeten and T. Balogh, 'A Reconsideration of Monetary Policy', *Bulletin of the Oxford University Institute of Statistics*, November 1957, p. 339. See also P. Streeten (in *Economic Growth in Britain*, ed. P. D. Henderson, 1966, pp. 42-3): 'There is much more compatibility than is often admitted. . . . It is, as we shall see, possible to combine, for example, the following objectives:

1. Any desired rate of capital accumulation and therefore, with some qualifications, any desired rate of growth of income per head;
2. Full employment without demand inflation; and
3. Greater equality of income and wealth.' (Of course, it depends what you mean by 'possible'.)

His central policy message for the British economy was certainly not lacking in confidence:

'*There is, in my opinion, a perfectly simple and attainable remedy for the recurrent difficulties and embarrassments which have afflicted Britain since the war.* . . . It consists in transforming the country from a relatively low- to a dynamic high-investment economy and thus imparting a decisive bias towards expansion. In my opinion, we could achieve this aim by relatively small sacrifice in a relatively short time and we should in this way be able to solve most of our domestic and international problems.'[1]

Dr Balogh put great stress on raising the level of investment. He maintained:

'An increase of gross investment towards say 25-28 per cent of the national income might, under careful management, accelerate our rate of increase of productivity to between 4 and 6 per cent per annum.'[2]

Dr Kaldor gave his vigorous support to the cost- or wage-push theory of inflation.[3] He rejected the view that a moderate degree of unemployment would suffice to reduce the rate of increase in

[1] *Committee on the Working of the Monetary System. Principal Memoranda of Evidence*, Vol. 3, HMSO, 1960, p. 40. See also *New Statesman and Nation*, February 15, 1958, p. 190: '*There is a clear and definite answer to the economic difficulties of Britain.* We have to change this country from a low- to a high-investment economy. If we could do this, we should automatically solve a number of our most painful domestic and international problems.' See also *New Statesman and Nation*, April 12, 1960, p. 475: '*The problem is essentially simple.* It is only the implementation of an obvious solution which appears to be difficult—and that because the Government has abolished the controls which are necessary for it.

We must increase our investment, especially in our heavy basic industries. If we could devote some 6 to 8 per cent more of our national income to investment we should be safe.' (All italics added.)

On the other hand, an important article at this time by Dr T. Barna, on 'Industrial Investment in Britain and Germany', had stressed that it was not so much in the aggregate level of investment or the investment ratio that Britain had fallen behind Germany, as in the allocation, efficiency or quality of investment: 'We put some of our money on the wrong horse.' (See *The Banker*, January 1958, p. 22.)

[2] *Op. cit.*, p. 40.

[3] *Op. cit.*, p. 150. Mr Kaldor subsequently introduced his own concept or term of 'cost-pull' or 'wage-pull'. See *Essays on Economic Policy*, Vol. I, 1964, p. 194.

money wages to levels consistent with cost and price stability. For Britain, price stability and a brisk rate of growth were *not* compatible objectives. Dr Kaldor maintained:

'It is dangerous for a weakly progressive economy to aim at a régime of stable prices.'[1]

He argued that either restraint (with moderate unemployment) will be broken down by growth, or growth will be frustrated:

'It may not be possible to run a growing economy at half-cock. In the second place, there is the question whether the prospective rate of profit in an economy of stable prices would be attractive enough (relative to the market rate of interest) to keep the process of investment and expansion going.'[2]

Mr Kaldor blamed Britain's slow rate of economic growth on 'the low technical dynamism of those in charge of British industry'. Low investment was only a symptom of

'the historical, sociological or institutional factors which make the majority of British businessmen less alert and more sluggish in their reactions than some of their competitors in other countries'.[3]

Mr Kaldor amplified his analysis in a lecture of 1959.[4] On that occasion he maintained, however, that the low rate of growth of productivity in Britain might be connected with the near stationariness of her industrial working population, since

[1] *Op. cit.*, p. 149.
[2] *Op. cit.*, p. 150. But Mr Kaldor earlier had strongly opposed optimistic views regarding the effects of a high pressure of demand on exports: 'I know that it is urged . . . that a healthy home trade is the foundation of a good export trade, and therefore the purchase taxes which are specially designed to make the home trade unhealthy should be abolished. In my view this is a most pernicious argument: it is the very opposite of the truth. You cannot sell the same commodity twice: if more is sold at home, there is so much less available for export. It is moonshine to think that if only home sales were encouraged, productivity would increase so much that the could have our cake and eat it as well.' *The Listener*, May 11, 1950, p. 817.
[3] *Op. cit.*, p. 151.
[4] *Essays on Economic Policy*, Vol. I, 1964, p. 166.

this made for a low rate of absorption of new equipment and a low rate of obsolescence with weak incentives for improvements in design. But he concluded with an optimistic and activist attitude to growth policy, provided there was 'purposive direction':

'There is no real justification for having a fatalistic attitude concerning the rate of economic growth that could be attained in the British economy, given the proper diagnosis and given a purposive direction.'[1]

Professor R. F. Kahn's theoretical stress on 'the structure of interest rates' rather than the quantity of money, as some kind of essential determinant or 'centrepiece' apparently carried much weight with the Committee. He conceded 'substantial influence on investment' to monetary policy. But this was slow and unpredictable, and it was apt to conflict with 'the outstanding need' to avoid discouraging investment. Professor Kahn urged the Committee to ignore the distinction between demand inflation and cost inflation as 'unhelpful and misleading'.[2] As regards the merits of absolute price stability, Professor Kahn considered their advocacy to be 'highly prejudicial to the country's interests'[3] (of which he was apparently endowed with a very definite conception which he did not further elucidate).

As his main policy weapon for combating inflation, Professor Kahn appealed, in rather general terms, for some kind of wages policy as an institutional *deus ex machina*:

'The more unbridled are the procedures for negotiating wages, the less feasible is it to run the economic system under really full pressure. But in the absence of anything like what might be called a wages policy, it would, I am convinced, be economically expedient, as well as politically inevitable to abandon any idea of stability of the price level. The only relevant question would be

[1] *Op. cit.*, p. 199.
[2] *Committee on the Working of the Monetary System. Principal Memoranda of Evidence*, Vol. 3, 1960, p. 142. On the other hand, Mr Harrod informed the Committee that 'a clear understanding of the vast difference between a demand inflation and a cost inflation is essential for the formulation of monetary policy'. (*Op. cit.*, p. 115.)
[3] *Op. cit.*, p. 144.

in what degree a progressive rise in prices should be tolerated for the sake of avoiding undue restriction of demand.'[1]

As above, with the fortunate harmony between what he considered to be 'economically expedient' and 'politically inevitable', Professor Kahn was inclined to a certain optimism regarding the prospects for a wages policy:

'There has been a considerable improvement in the state of awareness of the importance of restraint over wage increases.'[2]

Professor Kahn held that:

'Negotiation of some kind of national wage structure, conceived in terms of relative wages, at least for the most important sections of labour, is an essential prerequisite to securing over any term of years a tolerable behaviour of the absolute wage level.'[3]

This would call for 'strong central direction' inside the trade union movement. Meanwhile Professor Kahn maintained:

'Adjustment of the exchange rate has, however, to be laid on one side so long as there is so little hold over the wage position.'[4]

Messrs I. M. D. Little, R. Neild and C. R. Ross took a more realistic view of the main policy objectives than some of the other witnesses, and emphasized their probable incompatibility:

'There is no reason why a high level of employment, a satisfactory growth of production, and a stable price level should be capable of achievement at one and the same time.'[5]

[1] *Op. cit.*, p. 143.
[2] *Op. cit.*, p. 143.
[3] *Op. cit.*, p. 144.
[4] *Op. cit.*, p. 141.
[5] *Op. cit.*, p. 161. See also *Bulletin of the Oxford University Institute of Statistics*, November 1957, where Mr Ross states (p. 297) that the main policy objectives were very probably 'irreconcilable' under present arrangements; and Mr Little (p. 315) maintained, very appositely: 'Such widely agreed aims of policy as full employment, price stability, and steady growth, cannot as Mr Ross has said, be simultaneously and satisfactorily achieved—at least, not with our present system of wage determination, and the low level of reserves.

Their views on the effectiveness of monetary policy ran in very similar terms to those of the Committee. Monetary policy had a rôle, but it was a subsidiary one, acting on too small a part of total demand. But it was foolish to neglect it, particularly with regard to crises in sterling.

Mr Alan Day addressed himself to questions of convertibility, international liquidity and the rôle of sterling, the vulnerability of which he was concerned to reduce. He favoured restrictions on capital exports:

'The British economy cannot prosper by investing heavily in factories overseas to produce the things we can no longer hope to export. The better way to prosperity is for us to keep ahead industrially here at home.[1]

Meanwhile he observed that it was:

'Most unwise to regard the present exchange rate between sterling and the dollar (and other major currencies) as immutable.'[2]

Mr J. R. Sargent was also critical of the move towards convertibility, and was also concerned to reduce the vulnerability of sterling. He suggested that this should be attempted by funding sterling balances; by accumulating dollar securities in the hands of government; by the close scrutiny of UK investment in dollar and hard-currency countries; and by negotiating an agreed timetable for withdrawals of sterling balances.[3]

Professor J. R. Hicks examined British inflation in the light of the experiences of other countries and concluded that the British record did not look relatively so bad and that the devaluation of 1949 had been a main cause of inflation in the 1950s:

This means that the best way of operating the monetary system depends upon the relative emphasis put on the aims. The more the Radcliffe Committee commits itself to any particular emphasis, the less generally interesting and acceptable will its report be.' The Radcliffe Committee did not commit itself to 'any particular emphasis' of this kind, but the point is certainly acutely relevant to a number of the leading memoranda from university economists which it received, and indeed to many expert pronouncements on policy before and since.

[1] *Op. cit.*, p. 74.
[2] *Op. cit.*, p. 71.
[3] *Op. cit.*, p. 242.

'It looks, in the light of the British experience, as if there was much to be said for the view which was advanced in 1949 by those economists who opposed devaluation altogether—that devaluation would not stimulate exports, but would *merely* result in an adjustment of internal prices to the (new) external price-level expressed in sterling. It was essential, they maintained, to pay proper attention to the consequences of Full Employment. In a Full Employment economy such as the United Kingdom already was (and still is, with an unemployment index that has rarely risen above 2 per cent ever since that date), it is impossible, just by making export industries temporarily more profitable, to draw resources into the export industries; all that would happen, as a result of an attempt to expand exports in that way, would be a rise in prices and wages throughout the whole economy.'[1]

To the factor of the devaluation, Professor Hicks added the further inflationary forces in the labour market, in the form of a reaction to the rise in the cost of living caused by devaluation, and by the removal of rationing and subsidies.

However, Professor Hicks rejected crude analogies with Germany as nonsense:

'It is really nonsense to suggest that the phenomenal growth in productivity which has been attained in Germany during the 1950s could conceivably have been attained in a country such as Britain, if only our policies (monetary or otherwise) had been different, and (especially) if capital investment had been increased. What has been happening in Germany is that consumption *and* investment *and* exports have all of them been expanding vastly. This has only been possible because the opportunities for expansion were ready made.'[2]

Professor Meade in his lecture 'The Control of Inflation' (submitted as evidence to the Committee), began by stressing the distributive injustice of inflation and the dangers to the balance of payments. Professor Meade made price stability a prime objective of policy, and urged that the Government should 'take the plunge' of committing itself to the stabilization of a price index,

[1] See his paper 'A World Inflation', in *Essays in World Economics*, 1955, p. 136. This paper was submitted as evidence to the Radcliffe Committee.
[2] *Op. cit.*, p. 145n. See below p. 211n.

'which was specially constructed to cover the selling prices of all domestically produced goods and services except those subject to price control, excluding from such prices the import content of home production and indirect taxes.'[1]

Professor Meade wanted an increased rôle for the Council on Prices, Productivity and Incomes and pointed out:

'If it is desired to combine full employment with price stability, it would be well worthwhile applying greater thought and expenditure of resources to such problems as the retraining, removal, and rehousing of unemployed workers and their families.'[2]

Professor Meade proposed attempting to take stabilization policy out of politics by setting up a Stabilization Commission, though he conceded that this would have to be under the ultimate control of the Chancellor. Finally, Professor Meade hoped that if domestic price stability could be approached there would be more scope for variations in the exchange rate, or even for a floating rate.

Professor Robbins took price stabilization as the first objective of policy. In contrast with Mr Kaldor he submitted that:

'There is a greater probability of solid growth on a stable rather than on a depreciating medium.'[3]

With the objective of price stability Professor Robbins, a little vaguely, combined that of 'appropriate levels' of employment:

'I can see nothing inconsistent in urging that the aim of monetary policy must be at once to maintain stability in the value of money and to facilitate the achievement of appropriate levels of activity and employment.'[4]

But it was not quite clear what levels of employment Professor Robbins had in mind as 'appropriate':

[1] *The Control of Inflation*, 1958, p. 19.
[2] *Op. cit.*, p. 29.
[3] *Committee on the Working of the Monetary System. Principal Memoranda of Evidence*, Vol. 3, 1960, p. 212.
[4] *Op. cit.*, p. 213.

'I am bound to say that a good deal of the recent talk about the dangers of under-employment, with an unemployment percentage of under 2·5 seems to me very unrealistic. In the past, I think it would be true to say that percentages of this order have only occurred in circumstances of considerable inflationary pressure. . . . I still think that to frame general financial policy on the assumption that anything more than, say, 1·5 per cent is under-employment is to invite secular inflation in an eventually acute form.'[1]

To help enforce monetary policy Professor Robbins was prepared to envisage some kind of statutory regulation of the growth of the note issue, a proposal also favoured by Professors T. Wilson and E. V. Morgan. In a subsequent essay criticizing the report of the Radcliffe Committee, Professor Robbins argued, in broad general terms, for the potential scope and power of monetary policy. He recognized that a proper and desirable implementation of monetary policy would probably involve more frequent and drastic changes in interest rates:

'I would like to express the view that the correct conduct of policy, far from demanding fewer changes of interest rates as seems to be suggested by the Committee, in fact demands changes which will probably be more frequent and perhaps more vigorous than in the past.'[2]

Professor Victor Morgan, in a subsequent criticism, also thought that the Committee had allowed

'the case for monetary policy as a short-term regulator to go largely by default'.

This was especially serious because of the weakness of democratic governments:

'The diagnosis of inflation in its crucial early stage is a matter not only of information and of judgment, but also of mental attitude and will. . . . At this early stage, however, the evidence is difficult

[1] *Op. cit.*, p. 213.
[2] *Politics and Economics*, 1963, p. 221.

to interpret, and the statistical indicators are unlikely to be unanimous in their verdict. In such circumstances a democratic government, especially if it has an election in the offing, is likely to give itself the benefit of the doubt, avoid unpopular restrictions, and allow inflation to develop in the guise of expansion. This is why it is so important that governments should impose on themselves some kind of external discipline in monetary affairs, but the Committee fails to suggest any sort of way in which this can be done.'[1]

In particular, Professor Morgan was critical of the Committee's

'reluctance, largely unexplained, to see frequent and fairly wide fluctuations in short-term interest rates, and to their equally unexplained reluctance to contemplate a further large-scale funding with the changes in financial habits that such a course would involve'.[2]

In its report the Radcliffe Committee, as we have remarked, did not go into the wider policy issues—involving wages policy and the growth objective— with which some of the Memoranda from university economists had, as we have seen, been concerned. As in the Oxford Symposium of 1952 on monetary policy, and the subsequent debates over the first report of the Council on Prices, Productivity and Incomes, there was an underlying element of ideological confrontation in the various Memoranda. As before, those broadly in favour of monetary policy usually favoured 'demand-pull' explanations of inflation, and usually seemed to be ready to accept rather higher levels of unemployment. But, except for Professor Paish, they were inclined to be somewhat vague as to just how much more unemployment their policies would entail. On the other hand, the 'cost-push' theorists tended broadly to reject monetary policy, gave priority to a very high level of employment, and to the growth objective, and tended to appeal, usually somewhat vaguely, for an incomes or wages policy. Just as the exponents of monetary policy and demand-pull inflation were rather vague about the level of unemployment their policies might involve, so the exponents of cost-

[1] Not *Unanimous*, edited by A. Seldon, 1960, p.22.
[2] *Op. cit.*, p. 35.

push and a full pressure of demand were inclined to be rather vaguely presumptuous (or optimistic) about the practicability, workings, and institutional adjustments, of an incomes policy. In fact, objectives, policy preferences and value-judgments seldom got very clearly or precisely stated when it came to the critical margins of what was possible. With regard to positive possibilities, it was to some extent inevitable that empirical evidence on both sides was apt to be casual and insubstantial, as well as biased by ideological preconceptions and swayed by fashion.

(4) LOSING AN EMPIRE AND NOT FINDING A BALANCE OF PAYMENTS

In the disenchantment or 'climacteric' of 1955-56—as Mr Shonfield has called it[1]—the onset of doubts and difficulties about domestic economic policies, and the failure to regulate the economy by the 'new' monetary methods, coincided with the emergence into more acute prominence of questions about Britain's economic and political position in the world. These external anxieties included firstly, the continuing alleged 'dollar problem'; secondly, developments in Europe which had reached a decisive phase (1955-58); and thirdly according to some economists, the 'challenges' of other countries, notably Russia and China.

(i) Some authorities still (1955-57) continued to regard as one of Britain's main external economic problems that of the dollar shortage, although a somewhat lone Oxford voice proclaimed (1955) that 'the structural reasons for world dollar scarcity are generally subsiding'.[2] But in 1957 came the most thorough and expert treatment of The World Dollar Problem, in one of the major works of applied economics in Britain since the war, in many respects in quite a different class to most of the other literature on the subject. Sir Donald MacDougall emphasized the fundamental importance for policy of a right judgment of the issue:

'It is important to form a judgment on the long-run dollar problem. If it is thought likely to be chronic and serious, there may

[1] *British Economic Policy since the War*, 1958, p. 196.
[2] D. Seers, *Bulletin of the Oxford University Institute of Statistics*, February, 1955, p. 36.

be a case, if not for a permanent bloc of nations that would try to become more independent of America, at least for caution before non-dollar countries finally embark on full currency convertibility and non-discrimination in trade. . . . If, on the other hand, it is thought unlikely that dollar shortage will recur, countries can advance with more confidence to freer trade and payments, and there will be a very strong case against attempts to form a permanent non-dollar bloc, with all the economic and political difficulties and dangers that this would involve.'[1]

Though admitting that dollar difficulties *might* arise from these sources, Sir Donald did not entertain very serious forebodings regarding *either* the instability of the American economy *or*, on the other hand, its faster growth of productivity—the two main alleged causes of a long-run dollar problem which had been so much stressed since 1945. Sir Donald's survey of the statistics

'does not confirm the widely held view that the proportionate growth of productivity is normally substantially greater in the US than it is elsewhere'.[2]

Furthermore:

'The fact that the US is so much richer than other countries generally and can so afford a higher level of saving does not, as is sometimes thought, mean that her productivity must rise more quickly.'[3]

Sir Donald's predictions, prophecies, or forebodings, regarding the world dollar problem, were based rather on structural changes, which, for reasons other than the predicted American instability, or her alleged faster growth of productivity, 'tend to increase the rest of the world's demand for dollars more quickly than the supply'.[4]

Estimating future trends in the balance of trade, Sir Donald suggested that

[1] *The World Dollar Problem*, 1957, p. 27.
[2] *Op. cit.*, p. 143.
[3] *Op. cit.*, p. 144.
[4] *Op. cit.*, p. 28.

'a worsening in the rest of the world's balance is more likely than an improvement.[1]

As regards United States investment abroad, Sir Donald agreed this 'may grow rapidly in the future'. But he held that foreign investment, in its turn, as the earnings from it got 'out of all proportion to trade',

'may help to create dollar shortage so that a necessary price to pay for more rapid development through the aid of US capital may be continuing restrictions on American goods'.[2]

Sir Donald's concluding prediction was nicely timed for the emergence, in the next year, of the dollar into surplus, over the following decade at least:

'Our analysis has suggested that, if price levels in the rest of the world kept in line with that in the US, and both areas maintained a steady level of "full employment without over-employment", structural changes might possibly, on optimistic assumptions, tend to improve the rest of the world's balance of payments with the US; though it is quite likely that, in the circumstances, countries would pursue bolder policies which offset any such favourable tendency. It seems more probable, however, that structural changes will in fact lead to a worsening in the rest of the world's balance and that this will be aggravated by a tendency for prices to rise faster than in the United States. The rest of the world's balance could then well tend to worsen each year by an amount equal to several per cent of its annual trade with the US.

It is, nevertheless, as likely as not that a widespread dollar problem will recur, say, a couple of times during the next twenty years."[3]

In a reappraisal in 1960, Sir Donald restated his conclusion

'that the US balance of payments was more likely to improve than it was to worsen, at least over the following couple of decades'.[4]

[1] *Op. cit.*, p. 237.
[2] *Op. cit.*, p. 278 and p. 279.
[3] *Op. cit.*, p. 342 and p. 343.
[4] *The Dollar Problem, a Reappraisal*, 1960, p. 3.

Dr Balogh was still proclaiming the theme in June 1958:

'The dollar shortage which has been buried with such solemn rites by a large majority of economists has not merely reappeared, but its existence has been accepted by a number of writers who have hitherto been at pains to deny its very possibility. The world in the first half of 1957 has been losing gold to the US at the alarming rate of $2 billion per annum despite a record export of capital by the US amounting to over $3 billion—a rate which will hardly be maintained in a period of declining primary prices.'[1]

However, an end was eventually recognized, and even the Oxford experts were finished with 'the dollar problem'. In a review of the episode (1962) it was claimed:

'If one compares the events of the fifties with the fears and the warnings of the forties, it appears that the movement towards freer multilateral trade has not justified these fears and warnings. They had centred on (1) a drastic fall in demand for Britain's exports—as a result either of a depression in the United States or of her growing competitive strength—and (2) a possible shortage or very high prices of imports. Many forecasts predicted, in the short run, an American slump, and, in the long run, Malthusian perils and American super-salesmanship, both playing havoc with Britain's terms of trade and her balance of payments. These fears turned out to be, on the whole, unjustified. There was no sustained drastic fall in demand for Britain's exports (though her share in an expanding volume of trade shrank and although net invisible earnings fell in the last years of the decade). Imports were short only during the Korean and the Suez crises. The terms of trade worsened between 1949 and 1951, but have improved since then (with a slight setback in 1955). The supply of primary products has risen by more, and the demand by less, than had been anticipated, and technical advance has reduced the dependence of industrial manufacturers on the traditionally imported raw materials. Most spectacularly, the dollar situation has been reversed, and the United States has been losing gold since 1958. The dollar shortage had turned into a dollar glut.'[2]

[1] *Oxford Economic Papers*, June 1958, p. 235.
[2] P. Streeten, in *The British Economy in the Nineteen-Fifties*, edited by G. D. N. Worswick and P. H. Ady, 1962, p. 108.

However, if one were to conclude that any mistaken predictions had been made, this would, of course, involve a very crude and naïve misunderstanding:

'But this does not mean that the optimists were right. The solution of the problems was partly the result of the attention paid to the warnings. Korea stimulated the production of primary products, and, more importantly, American aid to Europe and European discrimination against the dollar greatly contributed to Europe's recovery and subsequent vitality. The theorists of the dollar shortage are in the same position as the prophet Jonah who, by predicting the destruction of Nineveh, prevented it.'[1]

In fact, we have here an expression of what might be called the Principle of the Economist as an Infallible Prophet of Disaster. If disaster comes, of course he is right. But if it does not come, then it was thanks to the warnings of the prophet, working through such phenomena as the initiative of General Marshall, Far Eastern warmongers, a great economic revival in Western Europe, or fundamental movements in primary prices. But it might well be asked whether, if *no* mistaken predictions were made, in fact *any* empirically falsifiable predictions were made at all. Or was it simply that portentous prophetic forebodings were being expressed as a persuasive technique for influencing policy in a particular direction desired by the prophets anyway on other grounds, irrespective of whether there was going to be a dollar shortage or not? A reasonably disciplined (not to say 'scientific') prediction requires *some* attempt at stating its conditions reasonably precisely, as contrasted with the prophecies of the ideologue.

(ii) Meanwhile in Europe, not only was the rate of growth of leading Western European countries apparently beginning to stand out as markedly faster than Britain's, but fundamental developments were taking place in European economic cooperation. However, most English economists in the fifties, right across the political spectrum from Professor Robbins to Dr Balogh, remained somewhat unenthusiastic about what was going ahead in Western Europe. Doubtless they were ready enough for 'cooperation' in some sense or other, provided it was along the lines

[1] *Op. cit.*, p. 109.

of their particular, favourite policies. But not much interest, sympathy or confidence was expressed in what the Western European countries were actually wanting to do, and to a significant extent succeeding in achieving. This attitude in Britain can be traced right along since the early post-war years.

One of the first great achievements of Western European economic co-operation in which, apparently after much hesitation, Britain took part, was the European Payments Union (1950). As Mr Dow has said, this

'should rank as one of the major achievements of post-war European economic co-operation'.[1]

The Union lasted as long as it was needed, until it was supplanted by the European Monetary Agreement (1958). However, even this initiative was greeted with scepticism in Britain. For example, Professor R. F. Kahn (1950) predicted:

'One doubts, in the light of such considerations, whether the EPU is seriously intended to survive the end of Marshall Aid on the 30th June, 1952.'[2]

In the same year (1950), Professor Robbins noted little progress in European economic co-operation in the three years since the Marshall initiative and the creation of OEEC. As an explanation of this failure, he laid down the proposition:

'The main forms of European economic co-operation, which have been proposed in this connection, involve, if they are to be carried any length, European political union as well.'[3]

Regarding the proposed Coal and Steel Union Professor Robbins was also somewhat reserved:

'The most that can be said is that, *if* such a plan were to solve the age-long problem of Franco-German relations without

[1] *The Management of the British Economy 1945-60*, 1964, p. 52.
[2] *Economica*, August 1950, p. 310.
[3] See a paper 'Towards the Atlantic Community' first published in July 1950, reprinted in *The Economist in the Twentieth Century*, 1954, p. 171.

jeopardizing the successful defence of the West in general, it would be worth its probable cost; but that the onus of proof that it would do so still rests wholly with its proposers.'[1]

The argumentative ploy of demanding 'proof' of the effects of new political and economic measures, was frequently used subsequently to justify negative British attitudes to Europe in the next decades. Professor Robbins held that there could be little possibility of Britain joining Europe, in terms very similar to those used by President de Gaulle nearly fifteen years later:

'Although the island on which we live is undoubtedly part of Europe, united to Europe by geography and history, it is also part of an extra-European complex of associations and linked to it by historical, cultural and legal ties. The structure of the Commonwealth of Nations is not capable of easy definition.'[2]

The possibility of Western European union without Britain 'though not to be ruled out as quite impossible', in fact seemed 'not very probable':

'It is unlikely that the immediate neighbours of Germany, whose populations were starved and tortured by Germans, are really very anxious to be joined to Germany in indissoluble political wedlock, with a clear prospect that policy would come more and more to be made by the numerically preponderant partner.'[3]

Professor D. H. Robertson (1953-54) also saw little future in a European Customs Union:

'It has become pretty clear that this concept of a Customs Union is not really a very helpful one. Great difficulties have been found in giving real economic content to the Customs Union which has now for five years been in nominal existence between Holland and Belgium. . . . Complete economic union between the countries of Western Europe is not achievable in advance of a political

[1] *Op. cit.*, p. 174.
[2] *Op. cit.*, p. 179.
[3] *Op. cit.*, p. 182. In a paper of 1960 Lord Robbins stated: 'I am in favour of our application to join the Common Market and I accept the further political implications which this may have.' See *Politics & Economics*, 1963, p. 155.

union which is not yet above the horizon. . . . Fundamentally, it would seem, the nations of Western Europe are doomed to a high degree of mutual competition. . . . There is a certain risk . . . of the countries of Europe developing into a lot of old flower-women, each pestering the others to buy her early violets and all finding themselves without the means to buy their daily bread. All things considered, I am not sure that on general economic grounds Western Europe is really a much stronger candidate than the British Commonwealth or the Sterling Area for the new-found American tolerance towards preferential groupings.'[1]

A severely reserved attitude was supported by four Oxford economists (Messrs Balogh, Seers, Streeten, and Worswick) regarding the projected European Coal and Steel Community:

'The British Government are surely right on both economic and political grounds to treat the whole proposal with reserve.'

The Oxford experts were prepared to agree

'that "something ought to be done" to "integrate" or "co-ordinate" the European economic system is a safe enough proposition'.

However, their political attitude to co-operating towards new European arrangements was summed up as follows:

'It is rather naïve, however, to hope that the present proposals are worth more than the "Ruhr Statute", the Potsdam Agreement, or the Treaty of Versailles. So long as the allies are capable of enforcing their will nothing much matters. Once we lose control no agreement is worth the paper it is written on.'[2]

[1] *Britain in the World Economy*, 1954, pp. 76-79.

[2] See *The Times*, June 6, 1950. The attitude expressed seems to foreshadow somewhat that subsequently developed by the Earl of Ullin: 'If there's one thing certain in this uncertain world, it's this. You can't trust foreigners. . . . I'm all for going into Europe. But as I told Wilson, Heath and Asquith only the other day, it must be on our own terms. And that means getting rid of all the foreigners who now seem to be running the place. Once we'd put paid to those chaps, we wouldn't have to bother about whether Europe wanted us or not. We could go in anyhow and have Europe all to ourselves' (as reported in *Daily Telegraph*, May 25, 1967, p. 18).

Dr Balogh had been (1949) even more condemnatory of Customs Unions:

'The establishment of monetary or customs unions would, as we have seen, inevitably cause large-scale dislocation, bankruptcy and unemployment without any immediate tangible advantage.'[1]

Certainly Dr Balogh, over the years, frequently called for some kind of 'integration' or 'co-ordination' of the Western European economy and/or the Commonwealth, or some kind of full employment bloc to counter what he called the 'US menace':

'We need the creation of a potentially viable area, outside the United States, which can provide a solid basis for the planning of a burst of re-equipment sufficient to raise the proportion of our total resources devoted to the growth of productivity to at least 25 per cent of the national income'.[2]

However, writing at the time of the signature of the Rome Treaty (March 1957) under the title 'The New Utopia', Dr Balogh was highly sceptical:

'All these considerations suggest that the New Utopia is unlikely to benefit economically any country in Europe except West Germany.'[3]

Later he maintained:

'As a Socialist I have always disliked and distrusted the so-called "Common Market" concept of uniting Europe. I dislike it because I feel doubtful whether such a negative approach to unifying such different societies can do anything but make the strong richer and the weak poorer. . . . Even within well-integrated national entities the fierce forces of the freely competitive system make for cumulatively increasing inequality and insecurity. Only

[1] *The Dollar Crisis, Causes and Cure*, 1949, p. 180.
[2] *New Statesman and Nation*, July 4, 1953, p. 23. See also *Unequal Partners*, Vol. I, 1963, p. 110.
[3] *New Statesman and Nation*, March 30, 1957, p. 402; also *Unequal Partners*, Vol. II, 1963, p. 260.

the majestic power of a modern state, armed with elaborate administrative apparatus can stem this tide.'[1]

On the eve of the signing of the Rome Treaty, Mr R. F. Harrod (January 1957) recalled:

'I was at The Hague in the spring of 1948 when Sir Winston Churchill, against the background of a great thunderstorm, called upon the nations of Western Europe to unite. There was plenty of ardour and enthusiasm at that meeting.'[2]

However, on the British side the 'ardour and enthusiasm' was hardly sustained. In fact, as Mr Harrod put it, a 'Commonwealth alibi' developed:

'In view of her traditions, so strongly rooted in free trade, Britain should not have been more reluctant than other European countries to contemplate such a revolution. But one great difficulty stood out from the beginning—her relation to the rest of the Commonwealth. In the early days the existence of the Commonwealth may have served as an excuse for lazy-mindedness, for not considering carefully the various obstacles to the abolition of tariffs and whether they could be surmounted. The Commonwealth may have provided a sort of alibi against the duty of hard and painful thinking about this matter.'[3]

Mr Harrod suggested an explanation of the current (1957) revival of British concern in very suitably cynical terms:

'It may be said that Britain for the first time believes that the continental countries mean business, and that she feels that it would be gravely to her disadvantage to have a common market formed on the Continent while she was left out in the cold.'[4]

In contrast with much of the foregoing record, there is one authority whose timely general warnings stand out from this

[1] *New Statesman and Nation*, February 7, 1959, p. 177. See *Unequal Partners*, Vol. II, 1963, p. 262.
[2] *Foreign Affairs*, January 1957, p. 225.
[3] *Op. cit.*, p. 230.
[4] *Op. cit.*, p. 237.

period: Sir Oliver Franks. In his Reith lectures (1954) he emphasized how little understanding there was in Britain regarding the magnitude of the changes going forward in Europe:

'There is no subject of absolutely first-class importance to Britain on which the great majority of the British people have thought less and cared less.'[1]

He warned (1954):

'We have to make a choice in the next ten, perhaps in the next fifteen, years. We can live half in a dream and behave as if the world had not changed greatly or our position in it. We can live as if we need not bestir ourselves; as if the British Commonwealth was sure to go on of its own accord; as if it did not matter whether we get the Americans wrong or they misunderstand us; as if Europe was still the Europe we used to know. . . . Or we can live wide-awake to the changes round us and take our opportunity.'[2]

By the opening of 1957 discussion was centring on proposals for a Free Trade Area, including, of course, Britain, linked with the six 'Common Market' countries then about to sign the Rome Treaty (March 1957). This was the occasion for another Symposium.

Mr J. Black opened by setting out a series of basic statistics and concluding:

'Provided that reasonable time for adjustment is allowed, as is in fact proposed, and provided that proper measures are taken to even out any dislocation in the balance of payments which occurs while we are converting to freer trade, joining in the scheme rather than staying out provides better hopes of progress both for Britain and for the other countries of Western Europe.'[3]

Professor H. G. Johnson held that Mr Black had not provided the relevant statistical material and 'implicitly accepts the popular terms of the debate much too readily'. Arguing that 'the likeli-

[1] *Britain and the Tide of World Affairs*, 1955, p. 38.
[2] *Op. cit.*, p. 61.
[3] *The Free Trade Proposals*, 1960, p. 29 (Part I of the book being a reprint from the *Bulletin of the Oxford University Institute of Statistics*, February 1957).

hood of economies of scale as such is extremely small', Professor Johnson offered the judgment:

'It is extremely difficult to believe that British industry offers substantial potential savings in cost which cannot be exploited in a densely-populated market of 51 million people with a GNP of £18 billion.'[1]

However, Professor Johnson concluded:

'Whether the economic advantages outweigh the disadvantages, and if so by how much, is a question whose answer could only be approached by a detailed calculation.'[2]

Dr Balogh certainly believed, as for some time past, in closer European economic 'co-operation' in the form of 'a regional bloc' in accordance with his specifications:

'Only a large regional bloc comprising at least the Sterling Area and possibly Western Europe and its dependencies would offer a chance of creating conditions for large productive units to arise spontaneously which would be capable of meeting US competition on equal terms.'[3]

But disliking strongly the forms of integration which were actually being proposed in Europe, and believing that 'Britain's effective power to bargain is still strong', Dr Balogh maintained:

'We can and should insist on a modification of the scheme which would render it less risky and more hopeful for a full development of European productivity and competitive power.'[4]

Mr R. F. Harrod seemed, at this stage, to be contemplating with equanimity Britain's entry into a European Common Market and suggested a very high estimate of the opportunities for economies of scale therein:

[1] *Op. cit.*, p. 33.
[2] *Op. cit.*, p. 36.
[3] *Op. cit.*, p. 37.
[4] *Op. cit.*, p. 42.

'Having the United States in mind, we may ask how many main types of motor car should be produced in Europe. It is true that the population of the proposed common market is slightly greater than that of the United States, but, whatever benefits flow from the common market, it will be a very long time before its population can afford to buy so many cars per head. To say that there should be four different types of car—aside from specialities—is probably to admit a wholly uneconomic level of diversification. Yet this would mean that, at the most, Britain should not be producing more than one type of car. That is the kind of problem we are called upon to think about.'[1]

Professor R. F. Kahn began by stating his position as follows:

'I see no reason for questioning the view, which seems to be fairly generally accepted, that if *in any case* there is going to be a European Customs Union, comprising the six Schumann plan countries, it is better for this country that we should join the projected free trade area rather than that we should stay out—at any rate if we can confine our participation to non-agricultural products. The interesting question is not that one but whether, from the point of view of this country, we should welcome and encourage the scheme as a development which is likely to work out positively in our own economic interests or whether it is really most unfortunate and awkward that the issue has arisen at all.'[2]

Professor Kahn was prepared, somewhat grudgingly perhaps, to give a positive answer, because of his pessimism regarding the alternatives to closer Western Europe integration:

'If there were reason to think that something might still be made of the Commonwealth and the sterling area, a closer affiliation with Europe, even though unavoidable, might be regretted on account of consequent losses elsewhere. But the tide has turned strongly against closer affiliation with Commonwealth and sterling area countries.'[3]

[1] *Op. cit.*, p. 51.
[2] *Op. cit.*, p. 61. See also *The Listener*, February 28, 1957, p. 331.
[3] *Op. cit.*, p. 61. Contrast Professor Kaldor's view quoted below p. 206.

Furthermore, Professor Kahn hoped that since 'free trade is not such a very popular idea',[1] the freedom of trade, in the proposed free trade area, might in practice be closely restricted. On the other hand:

'It has to be recognized that on the whole those who supply the positive impetus towards the free trade area—those who really believe in it as opposed to sceptics who regard it as an inescapable but sad necessity—are those who hanker after the free operation of economic forces and are unable to see the need or feasibility of tempering influences.'[2]

Professor Kahn insisted:

'In the European context, it is easy to exaggerate the importance of the economies of division of labour and of specialization, of the spur to efficiency provided by extra competition and of the erosion of profit margins.'[3]

But Professor Kahn was hopeful about the 'trade-diverting' effect of the formation of a free trade area:

'The formation of a free trade area means an improvement—compared with what would otherwise, at the same point of time (we are of course looking ten years and more ahead!), be the situation—in the balance of payments position of the area, and therefore of most, if not of all, its members. Unless this country turns out to be especially vulnerable to European competition in its domestic market, it can hope to enjoy a reasonable share of that improvement.'[4]

(iii) Anxieties as to Britain somehow getting 'left out in the cold', or left behind, were no longer aroused, as in the past, only by comparisions with the United States or by contemporary comparisons with Western Europe in the later fifties. Admiration for the Russian economic system, and the lessons for British

[1] *Op. cit.*, p. 61.
[2] *Op. cit.*, p. 62.
[3] *Op. cit.*, p. 63.
[4] *Op. cit.*, p. 64.

policy that should be drawn from it, had long been a favourite theme of some British economists.

Regarding the lessons for economic policy, Dr Balogh repeatedly emphasized Russian achievements and 'the Soviet challenge':

'Soviet output *per head* considerably surpasses that of Italy, and is likely to catch up with the present level of French output per head in 1955. At the same rate of progress, the British output *per head* of 1951 will be overtaken by Russian between 1960 and 1962. This means—since the population of Russia is over 200 million—that Russia will enjoy in a decade an *absolute* preponderance economically over Western Europe unless energetic action is taken.'[1]

In 1956 Dr Balogh was emphasizing 'the present rapid drift towards economic inferiority in relation to the Soviet world'.[2] By 1959 Russia was even being outstripped by China:

'The fact that the original claims which the Chinese were making for their industrial and agricultural growth were grossly exaggerated should not blind anyone to the fact that an unparalleled revolution has taken place in the Chinese productive framework and that Chinese production, and more particularly agricultural production, is increasing at a rate which far outstrips the Russian.'[3]

Even the United States was being overtaken:

'The Soviet Union has made gigantic strides and is within striking distance of making good its claim of catching up Europe and then the US—even without the "leap forward" of China.'[4]

Thus, for many prominent British economists of varying points on the political spectrum, it seemed, as regards Britain's relative position in the world, a case of change and decay in all around

[1] *New Statesman and Nation*, August 15, 1953, p. 173.
[2] *Op. cit.*, May 19, 1956, p. 558.
[3] *Op. cit.*, December 12, 1959, p. 846.
[4] *New Statesman and Nation*, January 3, 1959, p. 21. See *Unequal Partners*, Volume I, 1963, p. 135.

they saw. However, amid the encircling gloom, Mr R. F. Harrod remained resolutely optimisitic. On the eve of the Suez campaign (October 30, 1956), an operation he heartily supported in the columns of *The Times* as a 'notable act of courage and statesmanship',[1] Mr Harrod was calling for a reduction in Bank rate:

'I now hold that the Bank rate should be reduced. The credit squeeze has done its work. The economy has been shaken down.'[2]

Of course, in the closing months of 1956, with the economy 'shaken' up rather than down, there was something of a run on the pound, followed by the imposition of petrol rationing. But by July 1957, shortly before the famous September crisis, Mr Harrod maintained:

'In fact, our economy, on both internal and external accounts, has never been so healthy as it is now. It is through bad presentation that sterling is being sold.'[3]

In March 1958, Mr Harrod discovered further encouragement, rather curiously, in respect of population prospects which, as we have seen, a decade before had caused him extreme alarm as 'a major crisis'. (Fortunately or unfortunately, the new optimism at the prospect of a stationary population was approximately as well- or ill-founded as the previous pessimism and alarm at the prospect of a falling population):

'In the long run we are in a very strong position on our balance of trade, because the rest of the world will increase in population and, we hope, in buying power per head, while our population will remain stationary.'[4]

On the basis of the prediction of a roughly stationary popu-

[1] *The Times*, November 6, 1956: At the time of the Suez Campaign, Mr Harrod regarded it as 'especially incumbent on the more level-headed British, whom I believe to be in the majority though not the most vocal, to express their support and admiration for the British Government in its notable act of courage and statesmanship'.
[2] *Topical Comment*, 1961, p. 143.
[3] *Op. cit.*, p. 170.
[4] *The Economist*, March 29, 1958, p. 1125. See above, I(i), p. 27.

lation, Mr Harrod (August 1959) repeated his call for low interest rates to facilitate foreign lending:

'The British population is due to be roughly stationary in the period ahead. . . . Britain, a mature, high-saving country with a stationary population, ought to have low interest rates, and thus to put herself in the position of being able to be a lender on favourable terms to the outer Commonwealth and other parts.'[1]

Generally Mr Harrod maintained:

'We are too modest in Europe; we do not realize our importance in the world. We are more important in some ways than the United States.'[2]

[1] *Topical Comment*, 1961, p. 236.
[2] *The Times*, May 9, 1958.

4. 1960-1966

DIARY OF EVENTS

(1) A Great Reappraisal

(2) In or Out of Europe

(3) Going for Growth

DIARY OF EVENTS
(Dates in some cases approximate)

1960	January 12	First EFTA ministerial meeting
	January 21	Bank rate raised from 4 to 5 per cent
	April 4	Neutral Budget
	April 28	H.P. restrictions. Special deposits required for first time
	June 23	Bank rate raised to 6 per cent: credit squeeze
	July 27	Mr Heathcoat Amory resigns: Mr Selwyn Lloyd becomes Chancellor
	November 8	Mr Kennedy elected President of USA
	November 24-26	FBI Conference at Brighton on 'The Next Five Years'
1961	April 17	Budget: surtax limit raised to £4,000
	July 20	Plowden Report on Control of Public Expenditure
	July 25	Emergency Budget: Bank rate raised to 7 per cent: pay pause announced
	August 8	Employers and TUC invited to join NEDC
	August 10	Britain applies for membership of EEC
	November 8	EEC negotiations begin
	November 17	OECD agrees on 50 per cent growth target for 1960-70
	December 8	Bank rate reduced to 5 per cent
1962	February 2	'Guiding light' of 2-2½ per cent for incomes
	March 2	Britain applies to join European Coal and Steel Community
	March 31	End of pay pause
	April 9	Budget: short term capital gains tax
	July 13	Seven Cabinet Ministers dismissed: Mr Maudling becomes Chancellor in place of Mr Selwyn Lloyd
	July 26	National Incomes Commission announced
	October 1	Reorganization of the Treasury
	November 5	Increased investment allowances: purchase tax on cars reduced

1963	January 14	President de Gaulle opposes Britain's entry into EEC
	January 18	Death of Mr Gaitskell
	February 6	NEDC approves 4 per cent growth target
	February 14	Mr Wilson elected leader of Labour Party
	April 3	Expansionary Budget: regional reliefs
	October 18	Resignation of Mr Macmillan
	October 19	Lord Home becomes Prime Minister
	November 22	Assassination of President Kennedy: Mr Johnson becomes President
1964	February 27	Bank rate raised from 4 to 5 per cent
	April 14	Budget: slight increase in taxation
	July 6	Resale Prices Act comes into force
	October 15	General Election: Lab. 317; Cons. 304
	October 16	Mr Wilson Prime Minister; Mr Callaghan Chancellor; Mr Brown Secretary of State for Economic Affairs
	October 26	Import surcharge of 15 per cent
	November 3	President Johnson re-elected
	November 11	Emergency Budget. Income tax and pensions to be raised in following year
	November 23	Bank rate raised to 7 per cent
	November 26	Loan of 3,000 million dollars to save pound
	December 16	Joint Statement of Intent on Productivity, Prices and Incomes
1965	February 11	Machinery for National Board for Prices and Incomes announced
	March 17	Mr Aubrey Jones appointed Chairman of National Board for Prices and Incomes
	April 6	Budget: Capital gains tax: corporation tax: measures to restrict overseas investment
	April 27	Import surcharge reduced from 15 to 10 per cent
	June 3	Bank rate reduced from 7 to 6 per cent
	July 27	Restrictions on public and private investment: tighter hire purchase restrictions

	September 16	National Plan proclaimed, based on economic growth of 25 per cent, 1964-1970
1966	March 31	General Election: Lab. 363; Cons. 253
	May 3	Budget: Selective Employment Tax
	July 14	Bank rate raised from 6 to 7 per cent
	July 20	Mr Harold Wilson announces cuts and restrictions. Foreign travel allowance reduced to £50. Six months' standstill proposed for incomes, prices and dividends, followed by six months' severe restraint
		Secretary of State for Economic Affairs tenders, but subsequently withdraws, his resignation

4. 1960-1966

(1) A GREAT REAPPRAISAL: 'PLANNING' AGAIN

We have noticed above how the 1959 Budget, with its ninepence off income tax, its reductions in purchase tax and reintroduction of investment allowances was, presumably, an important factor in the third successive Conservative electoral victory with an increased majority, an extraordinary political phenomenon.[1] As in 1955, the pre-electoral Budget was overstimulating an upswing already under way. In 1955 a rather slighter stimulus was given to an already strong upswing. In 1959 a stronger stimulus was given to a less powerful upswing. In both cases the timing was nicely effective, in electoral terms.

The 1959 boom has been described as an 'object lesson in the dangers of trying to go too fast';[2] and Mr Dow has remarked how 'the expansion induced in 1958 and 1959 had to be severely checked, barely fifteen months after it had got under way'.[3] In fact, by April 1960 the Chancellor, in his Budget speech, was already noting the signs of 'incipient overstrain',[4] and soon after he reintroduced hire purchase restrictions and a credit squeeze, with the first call for special deposits. In June Bank rate was raised from 4 to 5 per cent.

Professor E. A. G. Robinson had in fact warned (June 1958):

'In the present situation unilateral action to re-expand the British economy, quite apart from any effects it might have on prices and wages, might be thought likely to run Britain quickly into difficulties with regard to the balance of payments and reserves.'[5]

A year later (June 1959) Professor Tress, in a carefully balanced assessment of the Budget, on the one hand observed:

[1] See above I.3, pp. 117-24.
[2] See S. Brittan, *The Treasury under the Tories*, 1964, p. 203.
[3] *The Management of the British Economy 1945-60*, 1964, p. 111.
[4] J. C. R. Dow, *op. cit.*, p. 110.
[5] *London and Cambridge Economic Bulletin*, June 1958, p. iv.

'The main criticism as far as 1959 is concerned, therefore, is that the measures taken ought to have been taken a year earlier, and that by this delay a year's opportunity has been lost for little other than the saving of political face.'[1]

On the other hand, Professor Tress went on to warn:

'Certainly one wishes to avoid a repetition of the excessive boom in private investment demand which characterized 1955. . . . Looking back now, for example, it is easy to see that some of Mr Butler's taxation reliefs in April 1955 were misjudged because they lagged behind the situation they were intended to prescribe for. And their effect, so different from the intention, was that they added to an overloaded demand instead of supplementing a shortfall.'[2]

Sir Roy Harrod, on the other hand, during 1959 was demanding further expansion. In June he called for more stimulus for the economy, especially on the side of investment, and in November he called for a reduction in interest rates:

'Recent British expansion is to be welcomed, but it has not gone far enough.'[3]

In December Sir Roy maintained:

'The British economy has been proceeding at a moderate pace. There need be no fear that it will soon develop so powerfully as to need official curbing.'[4]

Sir Roy repeated his call for expansion in July 1960.[5] Later in that year, though agreeing that 'a substantial excess of aggregate demand, such as we had in 1955 must be avoided', Sir Roy complained:

'It is beginning to look as if the restraining measures undertaken earlier in the year were overdone. . . . It seems that some relaxation here is called for.'[6]

[1] *Op. cit.*, June 1959, p. iv.
[2] *Op. cit.*, June 1959, p. iv.
[3] *The Times*, November 18, 1959. See also *District Bank Review*, June 1959.
[4] *Birmingham Post*, December 8, 1959.
[5] *The Times*, July 5, 1960.
[6] *The Director*, October 1960, p. 85.

Sir Roy's views continued, of course, strongly expansionist:

'It may be that our modern maxim should be—quite the opposite of that now current—that we should always strive to offset any forces making for inflation, by ensuring as much growth as possible.'[1]

To ward off the obvious dangers of a buoyant demand becoming over-buoyant, Sir Roy urged reliance on an incomes policy (which, as we have seen, he had strongly opposed in 1956) combined with 'the shield of temporary import restrictions', as and when required.[2]

However, it was against this background of the need for an early application of the brakes after a brief, spasmodic (though electorally nicely-timed) 'go', that in 1960 what Mr Brittan has called 'The Great Reappraisal' took place. At any rate in this 'year in which everything happened', as Mr Brittan, again, has described it, an attempt was made at a major re-charting of Britain's economic policies.[3]

If one tried to characterize the four phases into which the two decades 1946-1966 divide, in one word for each, the first (1946-51) could obviously be called 'Recovering', the second (1951-55) perhaps 'Relaxing', and the third (1955-60) might be called 'Dithering'. The fourth phase (1960-66) might, if one followed initial intentions, be described as 'Planning' or, alternatively and perhaps more realistically, as 'Dreaming'.

Apparently much of the running in this move towards 'planning for growth' was made initially by, or within, the Federation of British Industries, whose Brighton Conference of November 24-26, 1960, called for a kind of indicative planning, in the form of 'assessments of possibilities and expectations', which 'should be approached by Government and industry together'. The idea was that 'the main aim should be economic growth'.[4] There was some to-ing and fro-ing across the Channel, and 'French planning', or 'indicative planning', became the

[1] *The Director*, February 1961, p. 259.
[2] *The Director*, April 1962, p. 97, and October 1962, p. 99.
[3] *The Treasury under the Tories*, 1964, p. 204.
[4] See *The Times*, November 28, 1960.

trendy new idea for the 'experts'.[1] If growth was to be 'the main aim' of planning, an incomes policy was to be an essential means. The eventual well-known result was the setting up of NEDC, the crucial step in which was the agreement to serve of the TUC (January 24, 1962), the first meeting following in March. The other planning organ, the short-lived National Incomes Commission (which, of course, was boycotted by the trade unions), followed in July 1962 (just after the overnight sacking of nearly half the Cabinet, including the Chancellor).

Sir Roy Harrod was quick to express the trend, while devoting rather more attention to the incomes-policy aspect of the new departures, than to 'something in the nature of a planned economy'. In an article on 'The Significance of "Planning"' he wrote:

'According to spokesmen of varying levels of responsibility on the labour side, something more than an assurance about profit is demanded. It has been suggested that before agreement could be secured in sufficiently wide circles among workers for anything like a more rational wages policy, it would be necessary to have something in the nature of a planned economy. It is hoped that this would not mean detailed direction and control. Rather it might be sufficient to have something in the nature of the French plan, which has been having some influence on thinking here, the implementation of which is largely on a voluntary basis. Some compromise of this sort might not be too far from the ideology of a Conservative Government, and yet go far enough to make those called upon to implement a more rational wages policy feel that the whole economic effort of the country had a more rational guidance.'[2]

Sir Roy however (without appealing this time to the institu-

[1] 'French planning was held up as a model in many British discussions. However, French planning as visualized in the discussions was a process by which the government and the two sides of industry, meeting as equals, arrive at a target for future output and a sketch of a path to the target. This target and sketch, serving as an indication of what was possible, motivated the spontaneous efforts of individuals and firms. . . . This is a caricature of the French planning process.' See *Great Britain: Quiet Revolution in Planning*, by E. E. Hagen and S. F. T. White, 1966, p. 124.

[2] *District Bank Review*, December 1961, p. 15.

tional bulwark of 'a well-trusted Prime Minister') emphasized that:

'The freedom pertaining to collective bargaining must be maintained.'[1]

He added:

'Any attempt to get a more rational wages policy must be simultaneously linked with the inception of a policy of growth, quite different from anything we have had so far. . . .
'It would be better to have a directive from the very top, to the effect that the planners *must* plan for a growth rate far in excess of what we have been achieving lately. . . . The idea of overtaking the Americans in their level of productivity is by no means chimerical.'[2]

A more sceptical view of 'The Uses of Nick and Neddy' was expressed by Professor C. F. Carter:

'The economist is treated by the public rather like a quack doctor, or like a priest of an ancient religion surviving into an age of scepticism. Generally, he can be treated with amused contempt, as an unscientific person who talks in mysteries, or who (if he ventures to make a clear, definite statement) will at once be contradicted by a fellow-economist. But when people can find no relief from the pains of economic life, and the fears of the unknown gather round, they return to the economist as Expert, invest him with authority in a Council or a Committee or a government office, and wait for a report which will ease the pains and remove the fears.

This is a misuse of experts. It discredits what is valuable in their work by expecting them to find ways of avoiding the inevitable. It is the equivalent of expecting doctors to make their patients immortal. Economic life necessarily sets before us difficult choices; the expert can make clear the nature of these choices, but he cannot spare the politicians and the electorate the pains of decision. It is necessary to set down this rather obvious point,

[1] *Op. cit.*, p. 17.
[2] *Op. cit.*, p. 16 and p. 21.

because there are signs that the National Economic Development Council and the National Incomes Commission are being loaded with a burden of expectations which they cannot possibly bear. The little orphan Neddy and the infant Nick can both, over the years, achieve a modest usefulness, but they represent no addition to the intellectual resources of the country, and offer no assurance that unpleasant decisions will be easier to take. The wise will keep their hopes small.'[1]

One would only venture the comment on these sane observations that some economists were far from shrinking from the proffered rôle of 'expert' and were ready to claim, if not that they would make their patients immortal, at least that they had the secret of rapid, painless growth.

Regarding the basic question of the compatibility of objectives, Professor Carter—unlike, for example, Dr Balogh and Mr Streeten—insisted:

'The essence of the British economic problem is that the desired purposes cannot simultaneously be attained within the limited area available for manoeuvre.'[2]

Professor Carter complained:

'It is not easy to obtain a clear non-platitudinous statement of what Neddy is supposed to do. It appears, however, to have two functions. One is to find out and to study the consequences of a desirably rapid rate of growth. The other is to alter the thinking of industry by "talking growth"—to induce in British business, by a kind of psychological warfare, an expansionist frame of mind.'[3]

As regards the problem of co-ordinating industrial plans Professor Carter maintained:

'I see no evidence that the failure of industries to co-ordinate their plans has been an obstacle to growth; it is a hypothetical danger for the future, and (given freedom to import) perhaps not a very serious one.'[4]

[1] *District Bank Review*, September 1962, p. 3.
[2] *Op. cit.*, p. 4.
[3] *Op. cit.*, p. 8.
[4] *Op. cit.*, p. 9.

Professor Carter concluded that both Nick and Neddy

'have a logical and potentially useful part to play in changing the institutions and loosening the assumptions which bind the British economy; but that in both cases (and perhaps especially for Neddy) the task set is exceedingly difficult and the prospect of outstanding success correspondingly limited'.[1]

On the political left, the move towards 'planning' was taken, of course, as a final admission that 'conservative freedom did not work', while it was naturally held that only a Labour Government could introduce 'effective' planning, which would really bring into play what Dr Balogh called 'the majestic power of a modern state, armed with elaborate administrative apparatus'.[2] Commenting approvingly on Mr Harold Wilson's highly ambitious Four Year Plan (April 1961), Dr Balogh maintained:

'It is, of course, quite possible to expand production by well over 10 per cent in the first two years of a well-prepared plan. And GATT provides perfectly adequate means of dealing with any resultant balance of payments problem.'[3]

Meanwhile, the great 'challenge' of the centrally planned economies, notably that of Russia, continued to receive stress (right down, oddly enough, until 1963, when the Russians had at last begun to attempt some decentralizing reforms of their over-centralized economy). For example, Dr Balogh emphasized:

'The terrible potential threat to the decentralized manufacturing economies of the relentless increase in Russian industrial capacity cannot be doubted.'[4]

In the *Economic Journal*, Mrs Robinson had maintained regarding the economic growth of China:

'Even upon cautious estimates, the rate of growth of industrial capacity is probably the most rapid the world has ever known.'[5]

[1] *Op. cit.*, p. 16.
[2] *Unequal Partners*, Vol. II, 1963, p. 262.
[3] *New Statesman and Nation*, April 28, 1961, p. 662.
[4] *Unequal Partners*, Vol. II, 1963, p. 140.
[5] *Economic Journal*, June 1960, p. 410.

Subsequently she emphasized the dilemma of the 'Western industrial Nations':

'They are now rivalled by socialist nations which have installed modern industry far more rapidly than they did themselves.'[1]

Meanwhile, the European issue had become more important and inescapable than ever. In fact, entering Europe had been an important component of the 'grand design' resulting from the Great Reappraisal of 1960, and to this issue we must now again return.

(2) IN OR OUT OF EUROPE

The negotiations for linking a Free Trade area, including Britain, with the European Economic Community broke down in November 1958. A separate EFTA of the 'Outer Seven' was achieved, and the first ministerial meeting held on January 12, 1960. Shortly before the completion of the EFTA arrangements a 'Further Appraisal' was made of the Free Trade Proposals in a further Symposium composed in the summer of 1959.

Professor H. G. Johnson, in a brief contribution, sought to give an estimate of the gains from freer trade with Europe, based on predictions of the values of trade between this country and Europe in 1970 for eight major industries.[2] These gains consisted first, of those on the export side from selling products on better terms and, secondly, of the gains on the import side, from the opportunities provided to consume imported goods in place of more expensive domestically produced goods, to which the purchaser had been directed by the tariff. In addition there would be the effects of freer trade with Europe on the value of trade with the rest of the world, and so on the amount of tariff revenue collected on that trade. Professor Johnson finally arrived at a 'very rough' estimate of a total gain of about 1 per cent of GNP in 1970.[3]

Next, Mr A. C. L. Day delivered a cogently argued case for

[1] *Economics: An Awkward Corner*, 1966, p. 14.
[2] These predictions had been worked out in the Economist Intelligence Unit's study *Britain and Europe*, London, 1957.
[3] *The Free Trade Proposals*, edited by G. D. N. Worswick, 1960, pp. 102-8.

British entry into the European Economic Community. He began by recognizing that:

'In its fundamentals, the case for British initiative to enter the Common Market must rest on political judgments.'[1]

Moreover, Mr Day recognized the need to consider what, in fact, was negotiable with the Common Market countries, and the limits thereof, which was in complete and refreshing contrast with those who seemed to be possessed by quite deluded notions regarding Britain's bargaining power, or seemed to assume that European governments would at once be ready to overturn their complicated and arduously worked out arrangements at the behest of some British university economist.

Holding that it was probably no longer possible to negotiate a Free Trade Area covering the whole of Europe, Mr Day observed:

'Inevitably outsiders cannot reasonably expect to be allowed into the club on their own terms. There has always been a clash of basic conception between the ideas of the Six, based on twentieth-century ideas of conscious economic integration and the ideas of Whitehall, based on an idealized version of nineteenth-century free trade and national sovereignty.

Beyond the purely economic points, there lies the ultimate fact that the aim of the Rome Treaty is to establish a high degree of political integration in Europe. Reasonably enough, the view is held in the Six that the countries which are not willing to accept this political involvement cannot expect to be able to demand the benefits of membership of the Community.'[2]

Turning to the economic arguments, Mr Day stressed the view that:

'There are big potentialities for developing mutually advantageous trade between industrial countries which are, broadly speaking, competitive rather than complementary in their present trade.'[3]

Mr Day predicted:

[1] *Op. cit.*, p. 109.
[2] *Op. cit.*, p. 111.
[3] *Op. cit.*, p. 113.

'There can be no doubt that Commonwealth Preference is an asset which will waste away steadily over the next ten or fifteen years. The danger for our industry is that this will happen, at the same time as we are being excluded from many European markets by the customs union of the Six.'[1]

Mr Day concluded:

'The choice, then, that faces Britain is a real challenge to our imagination. Either we drift, and find ourselves excluded from free access to European markets, while coming to enjoy less and less in the way of favours in Commonwealth markets; or we make a great effort of imagination and will, and initiate the complicated bargaining process leading to our entry into the European Community, together with an external association for all the Commonwealth countries that desire it. . . . At the very least, it would be a tragedy if in a few years time, we found we had once again missed a European bus, for want of trying.'[2]

Mr Day continued to prove himself the most lucid and expert of the economist champions of Britain's entry into Europe. Later (March 1961) he was urging:

'Our only hope of reaching a satisfactory European settlement is to accept the framework of that treaty [of Rome] exactly as it stands: that is the only procedure which could hope to outflank French opposition. Within the framework of the treaty it would then be sensible for Britain to bargain as strongly as possible to satisfy Commonwealth interests.'[3]

Dr Balogh, under the title of 'The Way to Nowhere', repeated how he had always 'disliked and distrusted the so-called Common Market concept of uniting Europe'.[4] But in contrast with other opponents of Britain's entry, Dr Balogh held:

'It must be admitted that its treatment of underdeveloped areas is far more enlightened than the British official attitude has ever been.'[5]

[1] *Op. cit.*, p. 116.
[2] *Op. cit.*, p. 118.
[3] *The Times*, March 13, 1961.
[4] *The Free Trade Proposals*, 1960, p. 122.
[5] *Op. cit.*, p. 124n.

For Britain, Dr Balogh argued:

'The real threat consists of exposure to a more dynamic economy having institutionally renounced the right of protecting oneself and without any compensating advantage of receiving organized help to achieve a greater equality of opportunity.'[1]

To ward off this threat Dr Balogh urged that if Britain was to join, the Common Market countries must set up an Investment Equalization Fund.

He maintained:

'It would be essential to obtain a much closer agreement on policy with the Sterling Area countries before attempting to go much further either with the Outer Seven or the Six. . . .

If no Commonwealth agreement could be obtained to our participation in a closer European Trade Organization, the next best solution would be the re-creation of a closely co-ordinated and actively functioning Sterling Area. Even this might now prove impossible—though I believe it ought to be tried. Only if it failed would I think of severing the remaining ties of the Sterling Area—coming to some agreement about Sterling balances—and try entry into a European Trade Organization without the Commonwealth. The least palatable solution would be "to go it alone" or merely with the Outer Seven.'[2]

Soon after (May 1960), Dr Balogh was expressing a strikingly more positive attitude towards British entry. The 'threat' of 'exposure to a more dynamic economy' had been transformed into a possible injection of 'new energy'; and the Commonwealth complications were now an unconvincing 'excuse'. Under the title 'Last Chance in Europe', Dr Balogh now wrote:

'The real issue which will decide British participation, in fact, is not commercial. *It is whether Britain can afford to stay out of a combination which has already proved remarkably dynamic, and which might, if we joined, inject new energy into our lethargic economy. Should we refuse, Britain risks becoming an*

[1] *Op. cit.*, p. 125.
[2] *Op. cit.*, pp. 134-5.

N

economic backwater and eventually losing such political influence as it still retains. This loss of influence might be disastrous for the world as well as ourselves. . . . In the past, Britain has refused to join Europe in order to maintain what we call our "special relationship" with the US. This is now irrelevant. . . . *The Commonwealth complex, our other excuse for rejecting Europe, is even less convincing.*'[1] (Italics added.)

However, Dr Balogh now feared (1959) that while it had still been 'strong' in 1957, 'our bargaining power is weak'. Though Dr Balogh urged Labour supporters to 'make up their minds', he himself in due course swung back to his previous hostile views. By 1963 after setting out a programme (a) to 'transform Britain into a high-investment economy', (b) to 'come to some specific agreement with the trade unions on wages', and (c) for 'showing that a 5 to 6 per cent a year, or even higher rate of growth is consistent with stability and balance in external payments', Dr Balogh concluded regarding the Common Market:

'I have been fundamentally opposed to our joining the Common Market. But the reforms outlined above are essential if we are to stay out. Should these reforms be accomplished the advantages of joining are far outweighed by the grave political and economic risks it entails. The City might benefit (as in 1925) by having a greater scope for its financial operations. Big business might get by at the price of our losing freedom to plan a steady expansion of industry as a whole. In any event the European exclusiveness of the Community is likely to endanger the prosperity of underdeveloped countries on the way to industrialization, and thus help the communists.

Only if all hope of getting on to our feet by our own efforts has been lost would I contemplate any jolt into dynamism which the Common Market would bring from German competition. After all, if we were to be swamped rather than stimulated (as so many areas were, Scotland and Southern Italy, for instance), I rely on the robust commonsense of Parliament (not much in evidence lately) to take us out of the Common Market—Rome treaties or not. By that time, perhaps, there will appear a resolute leader—such as we have not had since Lloyd George—someone

[1] *New Statesman and Nation*, May 21, 1960, p. 742. See above, III (4), p. 169.

strong enough to reform our methods and personnel of decision-making. In all conscience we ought to have learnt, sooner, before the Commonwealth connection has been foolishly permitted to disintegrate completely."[1]

A 'leader'—frequently compared with Lloyd George—was indeed soon to emerge, and somewhat suddenly to seek entry into Europe. Whether, in putting his case, he explained that if Britain *did* get in he would promptly take her out again if this seemed desirable, may perhaps be somewhat doubtful.

The Symposium on the Free Trade Proposals (1960), closed with some trenchant methodological criticism from Professor H. G. Johnson. He began by claiming that his estimate, discussed above, of Britain's gains from freer trade with Europe

'illustrates, in a very rudimentary form, the kind of exercise that needs to be undertaken if economists are to play a professionally, and not merely a ceremonially, adequate rôle in the formation of economic policy'.[2]

Certainly few economists were actually fulfilling their 'professional' obligations in this particular way. Nevertheless, the precise value of Professor Johnson's calculations for the process of practical decision-making was not entirely clear or certain. They seemed to be contributed on the principle that any, or almost any, figures are better than none. He agreed that his estimate was based on incomplete figures, collected by a method that was not altogether clear, and rendered suspect by 'the partisan tone' of the volume in which they were published. Furthermore, they referred to only one of the economic aspects of the issue, leaving out questions of economies of scale and 'the growth-and-efficiency-stimulating effects of competition', which also 'demand an attempt at quantification'. As Professor Johnson explained:

'Much of the argument both for and against freedom of trade is concerned with its influence on the rate of economic growth, a subject on which there seems to be no clear-cut empirical evidence.'[3]

[1] *Unequal Partners*, Volume II, 1963, p. 270.
[2] *The Free Trade Proposals*, 1960, p. 135.
[3] *Op. cit.*, p. 137n.

Professor Johnson, therefore, although going notably further than his colleagues in the way of at least a 'professional', if dubiously based, gesture of quantification, almost inevitably and excusably stopped short of attempting quantitative, empirical answers on what were, arguably, the most important of the economic questions.

In a general methodological criticism of his colleagues Professor Johnson maintained:

'A re-reading of the first round of this symposium leaves me with a strong impression that the contributions were both predictable, and predictably unsatisfying as a guide to the economics of the policy problem. . . .

All contributors faced with the problem of evaluating a scheme whose effects would be far-reaching changes in economic structure of a sort easy enough to predict in direction but extremely difficult to predict in magnitude, were under a strong inducement either to exaggerate the relevance of the knowledge they were sure of, or to form and use judgments as to the magnitudes of various economic effects based necessarily on one degree or another of sheer speculation. In this respect the contributors were in no different a position than the general body of British economists, faced with an urgent policy problem on which an economist would naturally be expected to have some sort of opinion.'[1]

While agreeing with this not excessively sceptical analysis, one wonders just where it leaves, with its *necessity* for 'sheer speculation', the 'professionally, and not merely ceremonially adequate rôle' of the economist, mentioned earlier by Professor Johnson.

Turning to the politics of the issue Professor Johnson remarked:

'The most striking characteristic of the reactions of British economists to the Common Market and Free Trade Area Schemes . . . was the solidary Britishness they displayed. . . .

The fact that Britain has been trying to muscle in on a scheme whose earlier development she had formerly been steadily resisting, has been conveniently forgotten.'[2]

[1] *Op. cit.*, p. 138.
[2] *Op. cit.*, p. 139.

Professor Johnson emphasized:

'The insularity of the reactions of British economists, and the grudgingness with which they tend to recognize the Continental viewpoint. . . . The presumption that Britain gives the lead.'[1]

Returning to his methodological criticisms, Professor Johnson criticized 'the tendency to use descriptive statistics as if they were arguments', and 'the Gestalt, analogue, and psychic methods of arriving at quantitative appraisals of economical significance', which he attributed to Sir Roy Harrod, Professor Kahn and Dr Balogh, particularly with regard to

'Mr Harrod's ability, simply by "having the United States in mind", to arrive at the conclusion that "at the most, Britain should not be producing more than one type of car". Professor Kahn's view that "in the European context it is easy to exaggerate the importance of the economies of division of labour and of specialization". . . . Dr Balogh's psychic dismissal of economies of scale—"I wonder, however, whether the merely negative act of opening national markets will be sufficient".'[2]

Professor Johnson concluded his methodological criticisms as follows:

'Given the present and prospective state of knowledge about economic relationships, the labour required for economic calculation, and the fact that the most important decision problems are unique experiments, it is inevitable that economic policy-makers and commentators must rely to a large extent on guessing at the magnitudes of economic effects. What is objectionable is guesswork which produces a final conclusion without either reducing the area within which guesswork is necessary as far as possible, or defining as clearly as possible the nature of the guess and the factors considered in making it. Such guesswork has the undesirable effect of implying that one man's guess is as good as another's, and that there is no great need to try to reduce the area of ignorance.'[3]

[1] *Op. cit.*, p. 140.

[2] *Op. cit.*, p. 141. See also *op. cit.*, p. 43, p. 51, and p. 63, for the method of argument (of Balogh, Harrod and Kahn respectively) criticized by Professor Johnson, and also above pp. 173-4.

[3] *Op. cit.*, p. 142.

It may well be obscurantist to suggest that on this issue, as on most of the other main issues of post-war economic policy, 'one man's guess is as good as another's'. But if, also, reliance '*to a large extent on guessing*' is *inevitable*, it may also be obscurantist not to be prepared to state pretty precisely what the qualifications are which entitle an economist to claim that his guess is better than another's (for example with regard to the prospective economies of scale in a larger European market) and not to explain just why or how these qualifications may make for better guesses.

An exchange of Third Programme talks against, and for, British entry, by Dr E. J. Mishan and Mr A. L. Day respectively, also brought out, rather clearly, the methodological characteristics of the debate. The discussion was confined to the economic issues, and the two participants were agreed on summarizing these in four main points turning on the gains or losses (1) from increased specialization, (2) from larger scale production, (3) from an increased competitive stimulus to efficiency and (4) from a stimulus to growth.

Dr Mishan, throughout, seemed to rely primarily on the claim that those who supported entry into Europe could not 'justify' their support. As regards increased specialization:

'The calculation of gains and losses is difficult. Not only because the relevant figures are hard to find; in any event there must be plenty of guesswork about the new pattern of trade. Even if, by some sort of miracle, we were to have all the relevant statistics given to us from a divine source we should not know quite what to do with them. Economists have no generally acceptable apparatus through which they can feed the relevant data and extract all the right answers. Several economists have attempted calculations, but these are unsatisfactory for a number of reasons.'[1]

Dr Mishan then cited some of these presumably unsatisfactory estimates, and deduced the conclusion that:

'the belief in prospective gains for this country, as a result of increasing specialization within the Common Market, is without foundation'.

[1] *The Listener*, September 14, 1961, p. 372.

Turning to the economies of large-scale production, Dr Mishan found that:

'Again we know surprisingly little.'

Regarding stimuli to efficiency and growth, the argument (like the argument on the central domestic problem as to the effects of very high *versus* not-so-high demand on efficiency and growth) amounted to an exercise, very largely, in guesswork and counter-guesswork. Dr Mishan concluded that the net balance of all the effects either way, favourable and unfavourable, was likely to be small, perhaps on the principle that in conditions of pretty complete ignorance the 'rational' conclusion is that the various effects, altogether, will roughly cancel one another out:

'If one cannot anticipate any gain, neither should the losses be very heavy. And then, more important by far than the economic ones, there are the political consequences. If these were favourable, Mr Macmillan's momentous decision might yet be vindicated as an act of statesmanship.'[1]

Mr Alan Day, replying to Dr Mishan, promptly took over the tactic of demanding *proof*, observing that:

'In no sense did Dr Mishan begin to prove an economic case *against* entry.'[2]

Dr Mishan had confused

'the statement that existing economic theory does not prove a case for a given policy with the statement that there is no economic case for the policy'.

At least Dr Mishan and Mr Day were agreed on the very slight and uncertain significance of rough calculations and quantitative estimates:

[1] *Op. cit.*, p. 373. However, Dr Mishan had elsewhere described the political consequences for Britain as 'giving up our birthright for a mirage of European pottage'. *The Times*, June 2, 1961.
[2] *The Listener*, October 19, 1961, p. 587.

'The rough calculations that can be based on existing economic theory . . . are almost incapable of taking proper account of the effects of economies of large-scale production, and quite incapable of measuring the effects of the stimulus of competition and other dynamic forces.'

Mr Day rejected 'vague intuitive statements' like those of Professor H. G. Johnson who had found it difficult to believe that 'British industry offers substantial potential savings in cost' which cannot be exploited in our domestic market.[1] Mr Day was more inclined

'to accept the opinion of industrialists and technocrats on this particular question, rather than that of economists who have no technical knowledge and no particular practical experience'.

Mr Day concluded that the four economic arguments together 'add up to a very powerful case' and that

'if these arguments are added to the broader political arguments I have deliberately ignored, it seems to me that the case for our entry is overwhelming'.[2]

Meanwhile, Britain's application to join had gone in on August 10, 1961, and negotiations opened on November 8. As the negotiations continued, so did the debate. Of course, discussion was immensely complicated by the uncertainties as to the precise conditions, on a wide range of intricate issues, which would be obtainable in the negotiations. But this did not bring about any diminution of confidence and dogmatism.

A contribution which took serious, if perhaps slightly over-optimistic, account of the conditions which might be obtainable by Britain, and of the alternative policies open to her, was Professor J. E. Meade's pamphlet *UK, Commonwealth and Common Market* (1962), which gave an expert but lucid review of the issues in qualitative rather than quantitative terms. Though coming to a highly conditional conclusion in favour of Britain's entry, Professor Meade gave careful recognition to the unfavourable arguments and possibilities.

[1] See above III (4), p. 172.
[2] *Op. cit.*, p. 589.

Professor Meade, from Cambridge, began, very refreshingly, as follows:

'We have a common heritage with the continental European countries. We also must forget our romantic dreams of grandeur. Moreover, we must fight against our tiresome fault of self-satisfied priggishness; for there are many very liberal men and women actively engaged in the construction of the new European institutions on the continent of Europe and many illiberal and narrow-minded persons exercising influence in the UK.'[1]

Professor Meade proceeded to review roughly the same set of economic points as Messrs Mishan and Day had taken: that is, the effects regarding specialization, large scale, efficiency and growth. On specialization Professor Meade found 'real enough' advantages deducible from the classical case for free trade. Regarding 'economies of scale and the competitive jolt', he concluded:

'We may have something substantial to gain here. But I would not like to guess how large it is or how far the competitive stimulus would in fact raise our rate of economic growth.'[2]

Professor Meade was specially insistent on conditions that would preclude damage to the export prospects of poorer countries:

'I would oppose a change that meant giving up free entry for Indian manufactures in order to allow continental European manufactures freely into the UK with the obligation to impose the common European tariff on Indian manufactures, unless it were combined with other arrangements that offset the restrictive effect upon the market for Indian manufactures.'[3]

As 1962 wore on, and it seemed more probable that Professor Meade's conditions, regarding especially the poorer countries, would not be fully met, he reviewed the alternatives of a

[1] *UK, Commonwealth and Common Market*, 1st Edition April 1962, p. 10.
[2] *Op. cit.*, p. 15.
[3] *Op. cit.*, p. 28.

unilateral reduction of tariffs by Britain, and of working towards the removal of trade barriers through wider multilateral agreements. But he was still prepared to concede to those proposing that Britain join Europe:

'A very strong case can still be made out for the view that we should nevertheless join.'[1]

On the whole those who favoured 'planning' were opposed to entering Europe. On the other hand Mr W. Beckerman maintained:

'Effective national planning in isolation is becoming rapidly out of date, so that one of the advantages of entering the Common Market is the chance it offers of more international planning.'[2]

With the climax of the negotiations approaching, the debate was intensified in the daily and Sunday press. The *Observer* (October 19, 1962) gave the results of a poll of university economists in which 47 came out in favour of Britain joining, 18 were evenly balanced, and 12 (6 from Cambridge) were against.[3] It was suggested, editorially, that the Government could conclude that:

'If the Market is regarded as a beginning, and as an opportunity for new initiatives, it can go ahead confident that it has the great bulk of professional opinion behind it.'

In the correspondence columns of *The Times* there was a wide variety of claims and counter-claims. Arguing from authority, Mr Mishan (October 2, 1962) maintained (in italics):

'No *economist of any standing in this country has alleged, much*

[1] UK, *Commonwealth and Common Market*, 2nd Edition October 1962, p. 13.
[2] *New Statesman and Nation*, May 18, 1962, p. 710. Five years later however, Mr Beckerman seemed to be opposed to entering Europe on the terms which were emerging. See his letter to *The Times*, February 20, 1967.
[3] In some cases, no doubt, Mr Andrew Shonfield's comment was relevant: 'It is particularly hard for British economists, after a century and a half of intellectual leadership, to contemplate the possibility that some new light on this problem may after all be coming from east of the English Channel.' *Encounter*, January 1965.

less demonstrated, that significant economic gains would accrue to this country on entering the Common Market.'

Dr Mishan's claim was promptly challenged by Professor C. F. Carter (October 8, 1962), while the same day Professor J. Jewkes expressed himself as

'Content to go on record as believing that the entry of Britain into the Common Market will, over the next decade, be likely to put us in a better economic position than we will occupy if we stay out with all that that is likely to involve.'

However, Professor Jewkes added:

'Certainly there is nothing in their science nor in their past achievements which gives economists any special claim to be able to foretell the future in such matters.'

A week later (October 15th) a joint letter from Professor H. D. Dickinson, Sir Roy Harrod, Professor R. F. Kahn and Dr N. Kaldor appeared in which the authors claimed, 'while not wishing to express any opinion on the political arguments', that:

'The final choice should not be made on the assumption that there will be any favourable balance of economic advantage for the United Kingdom.'

On October 19th came letters from both Dr Balogh and Dr Kaldor stressing 'dynamic' arguments. As with the arguments over the dollar shortage a decade before, the same 'heads-I-win-tails-you-lose' forebodings were conjured up. Dr Balogh was concerned, if there was a recession among the Six, that the effects of entry would not increase British efficiency and progress, that is,

'if our entry coincided with a setback in the Six or if the policy of a major power among the Six is restrictive . . . (and there are signs that the policy of the most important, Germany, is increasingly dominated by restrictionist financial circles)'.[1]

[1] Regarding investment in innovation, Dr Balogh stated: 'There is nothing in the arguments that we need a larger internal market for such an improvement.' (The *Observer*, October 21, 1962.) Later Dr Balogh maintained: 'There are

According to Dr Kaldor, on the other hand,

'Economic integration invariably favours the most go-ahead industrial regions.' . . .

'It must not be forgotten that for reasons of manpower reserve (if no other) the industries of the Six are likely to continue to grow at a faster rate than Britain; and as innumerable studies have proved, the industries which grow fastest in terms of total output show the highest rates of growth of productivity.'

These various 'dynamic' considerations were supported by Mrs Joan Robinson (October 30, 1962), who held that the argument from the advantage of belonging to a larger market was based on 'a concept taken from old-fashioned equilibrium theory':

'The old-fashioned argument appeals to the "long-run", but real life consists of one short run after another. It is precisely an acquaintance with economic history and dynamic theory which gives rise to the doubts that the economists have expressed.'

By some curious intellectual coincidence, however, this 'new-fashioned', switched-on enlightenment, derived by 'the economists' from 'an acquaintance with history and dynamic theory', had apparently only been vouchsafed to those whose ideological presuppositions inclined them, *a priori*, to be strongly against British entry on political grounds. (Anyhow, in a subject in which, according to Mrs Robinson, the vital consideration is apparently a matter of the right 'fashion', the scope for argument is limited: one man's fashion, if not one man's guess, is as good as another's).

Another lively symposium appeared in the magazine *Encounter*. Most of the numerous contributions were not by economists, but two of them came from Mrs Robinson and Dr Kaldor.

Apart from the argument that the flight of capital resulting

hardly any fields in which Britain cannot support largest-scale industry.' (*Planning for Progress*, 1963, p. 4n.) In 1947 in suggesting a development plan for Europe and its dependencies Dr Balogh had stated 'mass production and standardization was necessary, which depends on the creation of large *regional* rather than *national* markets'. *New Statesman and Nation*, July 26, 1947, p. 75.

from our entry into the Common Market would rule out progress in welfare services at home, Mrs Robinson's arguments, on this occasion, were political and even personal:

'The most important problem for the world (which recent events have underlined) is to work a system of peaceful co-existence between nations. It seems to me that for Britain to join the Common Market would be the reverse of helpful in this respect. Our joining would sharpen the division of Europe, and reduce the little freedom which we still have to attempt to mollify it. . . .

Personally, I have more friends in Asia than in Europe: I do not relish the prospect of having to apologize to them for the shabby way in which they are likely to be treated. For these reasons I regard the prospect of joining the EEC with fear and distaste.'[1]

It was certainly a convenient coincidence for Mrs Robinson that her economic '*expertise*', when brought to bear on the issue in her earlier letter to *The Times*, confirmed and reinforced so precisely the political arguments and personal preferences as expressed in *Encounter*.

For Mr Kaldor, also, political and economic arguments happily reinforced one another. Politically, Mr Kaldor wanted to 'stick to the Commonwealth':

'By staying out of Europe and sticking to the Commonwealth we would be far more influential in guiding the political and social temper of the underdeveloped world than if we were aligned to a group of powers which—rightly or wrongly—is tainted with "neo-colonialism" and whose attitude towards the newly emergent countries rouses deep suspicion.'[2]

On the economic issue Dr Kaldor was quite unqualified and

[1] *Encounter*, December 1962, p. 61. This series of contributions in *Encounter* was opened by a note from Mr Leonard Woolf which began as follows: 'A rational answer to the question whether we should enter the Common Market would depend on (a) an extremely complicated assessment of extremely complicated economic facts, and (b) guesswork on future political and economic events. I have no real knowledge of these economic facts, and economics and professional economists seem to me completely phoney.' (*Op. cit.*, p. 56).

[2] *Encounter*, March 1963, p. 73.

emphatic. The Commonwealth, in Dr Kaldor's opinion, as an economic association was 'gaining added strength':

'From the economic point of view the case against joining the Common Market seems to me overwhelming, and contrary to what some people think, its long-run consequences are likely to be even worse than the immediate effects. . . . In the long run economic integration with the Continent might well mean that we shall become a depressed area from which mass emigration offers the only escape. . . .

If we do not give up our independence in economic, monetary, and financial matters we could raise our economic strength considerably by a vigorous policy of comprehensive economic planning. Contrary to prevailing opinion, I believe that the Commonwealth, as an association, is gaining added strength through the accession of the many newly emergent countries of Asia, Africa, and the Caribbean.'[1]

In January 1963, President de Gaulle pronounced his veto, and, for a time, discussion of the question declined. In July, however, Dr Kaldor added a postscript in interpretation of Mr Macmillan's attempt at joining Europe. Under the title: 'Escape from Socialism', Dr Kaldor claimed that there could be

'little doubt as to the true nature of the motives and interests which caused the sudden wave of enthusiasm for the Common Market a couple of years ago. It was the fear of "British Socialism" '.

With his clairvoyant sense of political reality, Dr Kaldor added:

'There will be plenty of time to "join Europe" if we wish to do so at some later stage, on terms that do not carry the dangers of the present arrangements.'

Dr Kaldor was happy to conclude:

'The whole issue is rapidly being forgotten.'[2]

Three years later, of course, Mr Harold Wilson and his Labour Government, announcing that they 'meant business', sent in another application to join the European Common Market.

[1] *Encounter*, March 1963, p. 73.
[2] *New Statesman and Nation*, July 26, 1963, p. 116.

(3) GOING FOR GROWTH

> 'The pickle in which we find ourselves is the product of confused thought rather than infirmity of will. It is the intellectuals who have fostered the belief that we can have growth without discipline, stable prices with unrestrained demand, over-full employment without inflation and balance-of-payments difficulties; it is these who are ultimately blameworthy if anyone is.'
>
> *Lord Robbins*, House of Lords, July 27, 1966.

We noticed among the early propagations of the growth objective the Memoranda to the Radcliffe Committee of Dr Balogh and Dr Kaldor. It certainly seems to have been a reasonable conclusion from the figures, that for some years the rate of growth of GNP in Britain had been behind that of most other leading countries. But it was far from clear just what the reasons for this phenomenon were, and how deep-seated or remediable it might prove.

Moreover, the actual new objective of 'growth' policy seldom seemed to receive any very searching critical examination, or even precise definition, before being thrust to the top as *apparently* the supreme, overriding objective of policy. Presumably the new objective was to be taken as 'measured' by the rate of growth of GNP, absolutely or per-head, that is, with no regard for quality considerations or the effects of 'externalities'. Above all, little or no reference was made to the possible costs of growth, except as regards the rate of exchange, the rôle of sterling, and free trade principles, and, internally, in terms of some modifications of the processes of free wage bargaining. No costs were contemplated either with regard to the level of unemployment (though 'putting growth first' might in Britain have meant much larger numbers of people changing jobs) or with regard to the distribution of income and current consumption. A more rapid rate of growth seemed often to be presented as something largely painlessly and costlessly super-imposable, without affecting the attainment of other really preciously-held objectives. As Mr Brittan has observed:

'The leaders of the growth movement hoped to gain the benefits of growth without having to pay the price.'[1]

[1] *Inquest on Planning in Britain*, 1967, p. 25.

Sir Roy Harrod was perhaps the most extreme advocate of the growth objective. We have already noted his demand in 1961:

'The planners must plan for a growth rate far in excess of what we have been achieving lately. . . . The idea of overtaking the Americans in their level of productivity is by no means chimerical.'[1]

Two years later Sir Roy was expounding the objective of 'full growth':

'Many economists who would claim to have drawn their inspiration from Keynes have in the post-war period come to substitute the target of full growth for that of full employment, since the latter has been largely, although not entirely, fulfilled. . . .

For full employment we must now substitute growth in accordance with the maximum potential.'[2]

Perhaps this statement of the objective of 'growth in accordance with the maximum potential', assuming throughout full, or very high, employment, could have done with more precise elucidation, particularly with regard to the time elements involved, considering how much else in the management of the economy it was apparently proposed to sacrifice to it (though the readiness to sacrifice was certainly more apparent than real). Later again Sir Roy warned:

'Above all we must avoid making the maximum growth of GNP a "sacred cow".'[3]

However, a few pages later Sir Roy concluded:

'Growth, always subject to any desirable increase in leisure, has priority over all other objectives, some of which are often mentioned as co-equal with it.'[4]

But the 'other objectives' over which growth was to have priority, did *not*, for Sir Roy, include full employment:

[1] *District Bank Review*, December 1961, p. 21.
[2] *Encounter*, January 1964, pp. 47-9.
[3] *Towards a New Economic Policy*, 1967, p. 7.
[4] *Op. cit.*, p. 70.

'Any policy measures deliberately designed to increase the level of unemployment are morally wrong. . . .

. . . I prefer the Swedish target, which they cannot of course achieve fully, of having the unemployed at 0 per cent.'[1]

This is of course an admirable standpoint. But if one is concerned with elucidating the choice of possibilities rather than with expressing moral postures, however justifiable, one will want to know just where this leaves the overriding priority of the growth objective for an economy like the British, where there may be profound historical misallocations of resources and the mobility of labour seems to be slow.

On the left there were further ambiguities. On the one hand, a higher rate of growth, more 'dynamism', or 'getting Britain moving', or 'going', was a main plank in the Labour Party's platform. Usually the definition of 'growth' assumed or implied seemed to be the conventional one in terms of GNP or GNP per head. But it seemed that this highly materialistic objective was to be strenuously sought after and awarded, apparently, very high priority for almost purely spiritual reasons: 'Seek ye first a higher rate of growth of GNP, and the spiritual harmonies of socialism will be added unto you.' But what were the priorities, if a really strenuous seeking of a higher rate of growth, which would obviously take time to achieve, conflicted meanwhile with, for example, a generous anti-poverty programme? Dr Balogh showed a vague awareness of this possible dilemma without resolving it at all precisely in terms of the priority of the 'growth' objective:

'The arguments for planning based on the need for faster expansion are compelling, but they need not lead to *Socialist* planning. Faster expansion could be accommodated without Socialism, without public enterprise or public ownership. It is—as it always was—on the moral and spiritual (or psychological) plane that the realization of the insufficiency, and growing emptiness of a mere continuance of the present trends in the West leads one ever more insistently to Socialism. . . .

Planning in this sense of liberating the energies of the people towards leisure and its more enjoyable utilization, the provision

[1] *Op. cit.*, pp. 16-7.

of a pleasant atmosphere and environment, and deliberate reduction of competitive tensions, all these are difficult to conceive without a very important extension of some type of social ownership in the highly industrialized, rich areas.'[1]

It is certainly difficult to extract any very clear definition of the growth objective, and its precise degree of priority, from such passages, or any clear-cut system of priorities (nor is it easy to discover any *ex post* elucidation in the subsequent decisions of the Labour Government). Subsequently Professor Joan Robinson was caustically critical of the 'growth' objective and its treatment in the National Plan:

'To concentrate upon growth as the criterion of success distracts attention from the allocation of resources between public and private uses and from the distribution of income between families. . . . Even with the low rate, by modern standards, of 2 per cent per annum, national income doubles within a generation. The ideology of growth is designed to prevent us from asking what we want to do with it. . . .

The concept of growth as an end in itself is well exemplified in the so-called National Plan produced in 1965. . . . The so-called planners did not feel called upon to suggest how the projection should be realized, still less whether it would be a good thing if it were.'[2]

Perhaps this *ex post* criticism is a little over-severe. One cannot expect politicians to state their priorities very precisely. But one might have expected from academic economists, if it was elucidation of choice, rather than political influence that they were interested in, that they would have attempted to give a sharper, less blurred and fudged definition of an objective to which they were *apparently* proposing that such high priority should be given.

With regard to economic growth as an objective of high importance, there was quite wide agreement, if little explicit precision on the crucial issues of marginal priorities. With regard to recipes, or measures to promote it, there was little agreement and much fundamental disagreement.

[1] *Planning for Progress*, 1963, pp. 37-8.
[2] *Economics: An Awkward Corner*, 1966, pp. 51-2.

Let us take, first, what was perhaps the most widely publicized recipe for growth, that is, the pushing up of the investment rate or ratio. In fact, tax concessions or subsidies in favour of investment were adopted by both parties and both governments. This was, of course, as we have seen, the 'essentially simple' formula of Dr Balogh:

'The problem is essentially simple. It is only the implementation of an obvious solution which appears to be difficult—and that because the Government has abolished the controls which are necessary for it.

We must increase our investment, especially in our heavy basic industries. If we could devote some 6 to 8 per cent more of our national income to investment we should be safe.'[1]

Dr Balogh had been urging this formula for some years. In 1956, for example, he had argued for a

'rate of increase of productivity of 6 per cent per annum as a target for Britain'[2]

which was to be achieved by an 'easily' induced doubling of productive investment.

Few economists probably would have agreed that the recipe was as simple as that, and some were emphatic as to the dangerous and damaging effects of Government attempts to push up the rate of investment.

Mr Colin Clark was the leading authority who pointed towards labour shortages rather than deficient investment as the source of the British economy's difficulties:

'So far from suffering from under-investment, it looks as if

[1] *New Statesman and Nation*, April 2, 1960, p. 475. Dr Balogh had given the same advice, in almost the same words, to the Radcliffe Committee.

[2] *New Statesman and Nation*, May 5, 1956, p. 484. See also *New Statesman and Nation*, April 14, 1956, p. 361: 'More prudent managers than Mr Butler could easily have induced . . . a doubling of our productive investment. That in turn would have induced (as the example of Germany shows), a parallel increase in productivity to at least 6 per cent per annum.' See the comment of Professor J. R. Hicks, in his evidence to the Radcliffe Committee (III (3), p. 157, above), and the article by T. Barna, 'Industrial Investment in Britain and Germany', *The Banker*, January 1958.

Britain on the whole has suffered from having too much capital equipment and not enough labour to look after it. . . .

Incantations about investment will not solve our problems.'[1]

Further emphatic opposition came from Mr J. R. Sargent in another Fabian Pamphlet published in 1963:

'We should be putting the wrong foot forward, with the risk of falling flat on our faces, if we were to adopt a growth policy which began with a programme of accelerated investment. The moment for this is not yet. The immediate, and increasingly urgent problem is why the increased capital stock that we have managed to install has not given us a bigger increase of output than it has.'[2]

Some three years later (September 1966), with the Government duly flat on its economic face, Professor Sargent, analysing 'why the Grand Design has Gone Wrong', claimed that it was excessive stimulus to investment which had

'thrown the whole growth process off balance, and made it impossible for the incomes policy engine to run satisfactorily at all'.[3]

Professor Sargent went on:

'Under the Labour Government, the intention to raise still higher the proportion of the gross national product invested has been stated in the National Plan, and is to be realized by a new system of investment grants in cash.'

The consequence of this stimulus would be, according to Professor Sargent:

'Certain investments will be undertaken which have a lower productivity than investments undertaken without the subsidy. Average productivity of capital invested will therefore fall.'

[1] *Growthmanship*, second edition, 1962, p. 51.
[2] *Out of Stagnation, a Policy for Growth*, 1963, p. 5.
[3] *The Times*, September 26-27, 1966.

This leads to 'manpower shortage' and the aggravation of wage-push inflation. Professor Sargent concluded:

'The subsidy to investment is a way of kidding ourselves that investment opportunities exist when they do not. . . .

In the prevailing atmosphere we may easily fail to see our trouble is largely a failure of economic analysis—a failure to understand the effects of artificially stimulating investment.'[1]

How far Professor Sargent was right, *ex post* and *ex ante*, is uncertain, and would be keenly disputed. But at least his analysis casts some doubt on the 'essential simplicity' of the growth recipe of raising investment, and suggests the question as to how far the advocates of the growth objective had any reasonably reliable knowledge of how to promote what they were urging should apparently be given such high, and even overriding, priority.

The second main recipe for growth promotion, based on a thorough misinterpretation of French planning, might be called that of collective auto-suggestion, or if we may so call it without offence (following Professor T. Wilson[2]) the 'Christian Science' approach. It involved the same 'psychological' method as was evident in calling crises 'bogus' or 'pseudo' crises, and trusting thereby that they would disappear or cease to be 'crises', with no unpleasant lessons which needed digesting. Similarly, as regards economic growth, 'it was all in the mind'. The remedial process was described as follows by Professor J. R. N. Stone:

'In my opinion the breaking down of these two fears, over-production leading to low profits and unemployment leading to low wages, would transform the economic life of Britain. The practical purpose of our model is to help in effecting this break-down by demonstrating that a well-remunerated and profitable situation *can* exist in conditions quite different from those to which we are accustomed, conditions in fact which would put us nearer the top than the bottom in the scale of economic growth.

I would go further than this and say that a clear indication that our problems of growth *can* be solved and an assurance that

[1] *The Times*, September 26-27, 1966.

[2] *The Times*, March 9, 1967.

the leading forces in the community are setting about its solution are necessary conditions for achieving stability in wages, profits and prices. No thinking Briton can believe that the standard of living in this country can only rise by 2 per cent a year.'[1]

In a later article entitled 'Exploring Britain 1970', Professor Stone explained:

'Our approach is very similar to that shown in the publications to date of the National Economic Development Council: our basic assumptions imply an average growth rate in the economy throughout the 1960s of about 4 per cent per year. From this we have tried to draw as complete a picture of 1970 as we could.'[2]

The method was the 'exploration' of '1970', by means of a highly intricate econometric 'picture' which would generate the assurance in the 'leading forces in the community' that this state of affairs 'could' (in some sense) exist; and this conviction in its turn would or might, so 'transform the economic life of Britain' as to bring about the realization, in 1970, of the econometric 'picture', or something like it. The question of cost seemed to have little or no place in this 'picture'. In fact, it was among the exponents of the more auto-suggestive forms of 'indicative planning' that one found an initially highly-hypothetical exercise merging into, in some sense, a 'possible' target, which merged in turn into feasible policies: so feasible, in fact, that the more attractive and immediately adoptable implications, in the form of large increases in planned or competitively promised public expenditure, along with more ambitious wage and salary claims, were forthwith implemented by those 'leading forces in the community', the Government and the trade unions and professional associations, who proceeded to 'explore 1970' with enthusiastic alacrity.

As regards the NEDC's growth target of 4 per cent, to which Professor Stone's 'explorations' were related, Professor Jewkes (1965) complained:

'When in 1962 the Conservative Government set forth its first

[1] *Manchester School*, January 1962, p. 13. I have ventured to italicize two uses of the word 'can', in which a crucial ambiguity seems to lurk (not to mention the two in the last sentence).
[2] *Sunday Times*, July 11, 1965, p. 24.

five-year economic plan, it declared that this was centred on an annual average rate of growth in the economy of 4 per cent. Those most closely associated with the design and the carrying out of the plan declared that this procedure amounted to a revolution in thought, based on what was described as the "dynamic concept of change". But, despite these sweeping claims, the nature, purpose and function of this 4 per cent has always remained shrouded in mystery. What was meant by the figure? Was it an increase which it was thought would occur; or was hoped would occur; or was feared would not be achieved unless the Government itself engaged in these special measures.'[1]

One might perhaps have hoped that the answers vainly sought by Professor Jewkes might have been discernible in the related 'academic' exercise, much more 'modern' and 'sophisticated' in method. In the article in the *Sunday Times* from which we have quoted, it is simply explained:

'Our estimates are therefore not simple forecasts based on the extrapolation of past trends,'[2]

which seems to leave it open that they might be regarded as in some sense *conditional* forecasts—without the conditions being precisely stated—or persuasive prophecies. Elsewhere however, it was explained (in an elucidation not vouchsafed to readers of the *Sunday Times*):

'We are taking two major risks. First, there is the risk that our projections may be misinterpreted either as forecasts of what is most likely or as statements of what is most desirable. We have tried to make it clear that neither of these interpretations would be correct.'[3]

But if the exercise consisted of a *purely* hypothetical 'exploration' of 4 per cent growth rates, it is perhaps permissible to inquire as to the significance and implications of mentioning a particular calendar year, '1970', in the title of the operation,

[1] *Three Banks Review*, June 1965, p. 8.
[2] Exploring 1970', *Sunday Times*, July 11, 1965, p. 24.
[3] *Exploring 1970, Some Numerical Results*, Dept. of Applied Economics, University of Cambridge, July 1965.

which, as we have seen above, Professor Stone intended should have a strongly persuasive effect in 'breaking down' psychological inhibitions and 'fears'.

If 'indicative planning' was the second general growth recipe, the third can with difficulty be described more precisely than by the heading 'non-indicative planning', or what was simply referred to by Dr Balogh and Dr Kaldor as 'purposive action' or 'purposive direction'. Certainly great hopes were held and propagated for 'planning' in one form or another. As we have seen, in the spring of 1961 in the course of a discussion of a Four Year Plan drafted by Mr Harold Wilson, Dr Balogh affirmed:

'It is of course quite possible to expand production by well over 10 per cent in the first two years of a well-prepared plan. And GATT provides perfectly adequate means of dealing with any resultant balance of payments problem.'[1]

As regards 'the workers' claim for decent wages', it was maintained that

'purposive action could afford to give them rewards beyond their ambitions'.[2]

Absence of planning was apparently partly responsible for 'the Kennedy administration's tribulations and failure to restart growth'[3] (just, of course, when in fact American growth was to 'restart' with remarkable force, persistence and smoothness). As regards the target:

'It should be our endeavour to obtain eventually a growth rate nearer to that in the Common Market—5-5½ per cent per annum—than to the NEDC target of 4 per cent per annum. The latter has been conceived by a Council under the chairmanship of a Conservative Chancellor and must not be permitted to limit our horizon.'[4]

[1] *New Statesman and Nation*, April 28, 1961, p. 662.
[2] *Planning for Progress*, 1963, p. 1. Of course these 'ambitions' must not be too ambitious. In 1958 Dr Balogh had insisted that 'wage-demands must be mitigated first to permit an increase in investment and subsequently (and to a much lesser degree) to keep them within the bounds of the increase in productivity achieved'. (*Oxford Economic Papers*, June 1958, p. 240. See above, p. 163.)
[3] *Op. cit.*, p. 7n.
[4] *Op. cit.*, p. 18.

Centralized investment controls on the Russian pattern were, of course, to be an important weapon:

'This was the way the Soviet obtained its results, and I doubt whether we can do better.'[1]

It was vital to replace decentralized by centralized decision-making (just, of course, at the very moment when the difficulties of over-centralization were forcing fundamental changes towards decentralization on the Russians):

'We have already pointed to the relative inferiority of countries whose economy is based on decentralized decision-making. . . . The conclusion is irresistible that the present trends in the opulent part of the non-Communist world lead towards technical inferiority and spiritual weakness in the face of the Soviet challenge.'[2]

Elsewhere however, a more 'indicative' emphasis could be traced in Dr Balogh's ideas about planning:

'We obviously need a national plan for deploying our resources. By showing that a 5 to 6 per cent a year, or even higher, rate of growth is consistent with stability and balance in external payments, such a plan could alter the present scepticism of entrepreneurs.'[3]

Dr Kaldor, without explaining whether the 'comprehensive' planning he envisaged was more of the 'indicative' or of the 'Eastern European and Soviet Union' type, maintained:

'We could raise our economic strength considerably by a vigorous policy of comprehensive economic planning.'[4]

[1] *Op. cit.*, p. 23.

[2] Op. cit., pp. 45 and 47. In another Fabian pamphlet of the same year discussing 'something which would be recognized by planners in Eastern Europe and the Soviet Union, namely an integrated system of production decisions defining the allocation of labour, capital and materials between producing units and embodying directives and incentives to get them where they should be', it was concluded: 'There is no point in discussing the adaptation of such a system to the UK, not merely because the opportunity is unlikely to arise for applying it, but rather because in most of the countries which do apply it, it is beginning to have a very old-fashioned look.' (J. R. Sargent, *Out of Stagnation, a Policy for Growth*, 1963, p. 43. It is interesting that the rejection of Soviet methods is here based simply on 'fashion'.)

[3] *Unequal Partners*, Vol. II, 1963, p. 269.

[4] *Encounter*, March 1963, p. 73.

Certainly agreement was considerable throughout 1962 and 1963 that there must be no return to the policies of Mr Selwyn Lloyd and that the stop-go cycle must be broken. As Mr J. R. Sargent put it:

'The first thing to do is to carry out a post mortem on Selwyn Lloyd and see that his policies are well and truly nailed down into their coffin. Heartily sick of them as the country was when he was dismissed, the danger that he may walk again, with the added authority of a wronged man justified is serious.'[1]

Above all, as re-expansion moved forward there must be a determination to 'ride out' or 'drive through' any balance of payments difficulties which might threaten, or to adopt special protective measures rather than to bring the upswing to an end by restricting demand. There must, for example, be no restrictions on domestic demand for the sake of making more goods available for export. Sir Roy Harrod vigorously asserted this view in maintaining that buoyant domestic demand conveniently *aided* the expansion of exports, rather than competed with or diminished them:

'One of the ways of helping the expansion of exports might be to keep home demand in continuing buoyancy.'[2]

In the absence of convincing empirical evidence, the precise relationships between the level of domestic demand and exports were inevitably a question of *a priori* speculation and guesswork, and, of course, there was a strong temptation to make whatever assumption fitted best with one's general ideas and inclinations about policy. However, in September 1966, Messrs R. J. Ball, J. R. Eaton and M. D. Steuer presented the results of a thorough econometric study of this question which suggested, in opposition to the optimistic, expansionist view, that exports tended to sag in periods of very high demand. Mr Alan Day in fact maintained that this study had 'demonstrated reasonably convinc-

[1] *Out of Stagnation, a Policy for Growth*, 1963, p. 13.
[2] *The Director*, August 1961, p. 275, cf. also R. Pryke (*Spectator*, July 29, 1966, p. 140): 'There is no reason to believe that deflation has a favourable effect on exports.' Compare Mr Kaldor's view quoted above p. 153n 2.

ingly' that a lower level of demand 'helps our export orders and sales', as well as holding back the demand for imports.[1]

'Hard riding' in the boom had of course been given a bold try by Mr Butler in 1955, but he had eschewed any such devices as import restrictions or devaluation. The question for the 'hard riders' in the early sixties was which particular device to rely on. Some, of course, as we have already discussed, favoured entering the Common Market, a longer term solution at least temporarily in abeyance after January 1963. There would have been wide, though not complete agreement that *some* slight help might be expected from an incomes policy, though many would have held that this was likely to be too little and too late for much reliance to be put upon it in the next upswing.[2] There remained import restrictions (and possibly some form of export subsidies) and devaluation.

The issue of devaluation had been broached at intervals in the early sixties, as for example by Mr R. Neild, (May 1961) then of the National Institute of Economic and Social Research (later to assume an important Government post after October 1964). Mr Neild held that devaluation was a remedy that we must be ready to 'contemplate'. Regarding the effect on exports he was optimistic:

'that a 10 per cent price cut really would increase our sales substantially'.

Mr Neild did 'not particularly welcome devaluation', but he concluded:

'It would be preferable to the alternative measures that we might take if we find that we really are in bad balance-of-payments difficulties, as we may well be, and want a breathing space in which to try to ginger up our economy.'[3]

[1] See R. J. Ball, J. R. Eaton and M. D. Steuer, *Economic Journal*, September 1966, p. 501; also *Economica*, November 1966, p. 388; and A. C. L. Day, the *Observer*, January 1, 1967.

[2] For example, Mr W. B. Reddaway maintained that it would be 'the height of folly to expect more than a very modest contribution from this machinery and it should be regarded as one element in a wider complex of policies'. *Lloyds Bank Review*, January 1966, p. 13. See also on incomes policy, M. J. Farrell, *Fuller Employment*, I.E.A., 1965.

[3] The *Listener*, May 4, 1961, p. 763.

In *The London and Cambridge Economic Bulletin* (June 1962), Professor R. C. Tress and Mr J. M. Fleming saw the main alternative to restricting growth for the sake of the balance of payments as lying in exchange rate variations. The Government must bring themselves to consider that:

'More frequent variations in exchange rate parities as allowed under the rules of IMF are the most obvious candidates for use.'[1]

Professor Meade had for some time been an advocate of the general principles of greater flexibility of exchange rates, as a method of preserving equilibrium in the balance of payments.[2] The idea of 'sliding parities' had been developed by Mr J. Black, and the somewhat similar device of 'crawling pegs' by Dr J. Williamson.[3]

However, in February 1963, an interesting correspondence developed in *The Times* over the merits and demerits of devaluation on the one hand, and import restrictions on the other. The exchange was opened by Dr Kaldor (also to become, like Mr Neild, a Government adviser after October 1964) who argued (February 19th):

'The British economy is incapable of maintaining high rates of economic growth or continued full employment without *either* severe import restrictions *or* devaluation. The introduction of severe import restrictions would run counter to the spirit of the age, to our long-run interest as a trading nation, and to our proclaimed international aim to make trade freer and less discriminatory all over the world. Sooner or later, therefore, the choice has to be faced between the maintenance, for prestige reasons, of a fixed value of the £ and the avoidance of economic stagnation and mass unemployment. . . .

There is a strong case for adopting a floating exchange rate,

[1] *London and Cambridge* Economic Bulletin, June 1962, p 111 (in *The Times Review of Industry*).

[2] See his articles, for example, in *The Three Banks Review*, June 1961; September 1964 and 1966; and earlier in September 1955, his article 'The Case for Variable Exchange Rates'.

[3] See Mr Black's article in *The Economic Journal*, June 1966, p. 288; and J. Williamson, *How to Stop Stop-Go*, 1966.

following the precedent of 1931, and for taking this step *now*, when, thanks to Mr Lloyd, we have plenty of spare capacity and unutilized labour to take advantage of increased export opportunities. . . .

By all means let us adopt growth targets of 4 per cent a year or more. But the stimulation of exports must come first—otherwise the new philosophy will prove just as futile as the policies of expansion which preceded the elections of 1955 and 1959.'

Sir Roy Harrod (February 21st) agreed:

'We are not likely to be able to carry through a growth policy without a shield for our external balance of payments.'

But Sir Roy opposed devaluation on every count: the expense of compensating non-resident holders of sterling; that it would 'reactivate price-wage spiralling' and destroy any prospect of achieving an incomes policy, and that it was not even certain that it would improve our balance of payments. In proposing import restrictions Sir Roy observed:

'Of course we should not impose import restrictions *now*. We should pursue a growth policy steadfastly and impose import restrictions only if and when our current and long-term capital balance gets seriously into the red.'

Moreover, the import restrictions must be 'selective' and 'temporary', and avoid injury to poor countries (refinements which seem to pose rather acute problems of timing, administration and international diplomacy).

Meanwhile, Professor Alan Day (February 26th) gave his cordial support to devaluation, holding that Dr Kaldor had given

'a textbook description of the effects of exchange depreciation by a country with some margin of spare capacity, as in Britain today'.

Dr Kaldor (February 28th) then argued that Sir Roy's reliance on temporary import restrictions overlooked completely the orders of magnitude of the various factors involved. It was not enough to save, by restrictions, say £300 million of imports in the first year. With full employment growth, according to current trends, we would have 'to pile up further restrictions' in subsequent years. To Sir Roy Harrod's argument that devaluation would not lead to a sufficient expansion of exports Dr Kaldor (March 1th) replied:

'When he asserts that it is "inconceivable" that a devaluation could do this, he is flying in the face of all evidence, and of the teaching of all economic textbooks (including his own).'

Finally, after Sir Ralph Hawtrey (March 14th) had advanced his argument that sterling was already undervalued, and that this undervaluation had been a main cause of inflation, Dr Balogh (March 19th) rebuked the devaluationists for their 'rather academic discussion', and showed a remarkable concern for relations with the United States and the condition of the dollar:

'Devaluation, and even more a floating rate could not in present conditions bring more than a fleeting relief. Either would damage the dollar, and embitter relations with America and the sterling area countries.'[1]

Professor F. W. Paish had meanwhile restated (1962) his thesis—highly unfashionable at this juncture—of unused capacity, if steady growth was to be maintained.[2] As we have seen, his argument started from the distinction between the growth of capacity and the growth of production, and assumed (following the tentative conclusions of Phillips, Lipsey and Dow and Dicks—Mireaux[3]) that, in conditions of near-full employment, the most important factor in determining the rate of rise in money incomes was the proportion of productive capacity currently employed, and that therefore there must be some margin of unused capacity at which money incomes will rise at

[1] Dr Balogh added, on devaluation and floating exchange rates: 'After an exacerbation of labour relations due to increasing prices, they would lead, finally, to a steady increase and costs, cancelling such temporary advantages as would be permitted to accrue to us in wages by the retaliatory moves of foreign countries. . . . Devaluation may be forced upon us as a result of mistaken Government policies.' See also his letter to *The Times*, February 4, 1961.

[2] See his essay 'Output, Inflation, and Growth', in *Studies in an Inflationary Economy*, 1962, p. 309.

[3] See above III (3), pp. 144-5.

a rate equal to the growth of capacity. If the margin of unused capacity can be kept close to this level, stable expansion will be possible, since output and income will be kept rising at the same rate. Professor Paish estimated this critical level to correspond to a level of unemployment of about 2-2¼ per cent.

Professor Paish emphasized the harmful effects on efficiency of very high levels of demand:

'In conditions of excess demand, with every firm over-booked with orders, there can be no effective competition. Only if at least a few firms in every industry are short of orders and urgently seeking new business does competition become a reality. In its absence, there is no compulsion on the least efficient firms either to improve their efficiency or go out of business.'[1]

Nor did Professor Paish believe in the simple recipe of raising the level of investment:

'In Britain today, the removal of the particular bottleneck of capital shortage would only too probably reveal a whole series of others lying behind it.'[2]

But Professor Paish was rather a lone voice and his doctrines were highly unfashionable at this particular time.

The second half of 1963 saw a rapid upswing, and the British economy entered the crucial election year of 1964 in a state of boom or rapidly approaching boom. In January Sir Roy Harrod pronounced:

'The days of excess demand are now long since past.'[3]

[1] *Op. cit.*, p. 332.
[2] *Op. cit.*, p. 332. See also *Policy for Incomes* (by F. W. Paish and J. Henessy), third edition, 1967.
[3] *Encounter*, January 1964, p. 48. Those interested in the 'Leading Indicators' technique of forecasting might note that none of the four main post-war booms in the British economy, with their rapidly succeeding crises and collapses, has failed to be preceded by some nine-eighteen months (perhaps rather longer in the case of 1959-60) by a statement from Oxford that 'we are moving out of the inflationary period' (Mr Harrod, May 1949); or that 'inflation came to an end at least two years ago' (Mr P. D. Henderson, May 1954); or that 'it is doubtful if inflation is still a problem at all' (Mr Harrod, April 1958); or finally, that 'the days of excess demand are now long since past' (Sir Roy Harrod, January 1964). For precise references see above I (4), p. 75; III (2), p. 127; and III (3), p. 135.

By April Dr Balogh was maintaining:

'There is a crisis, but this crisis is certainly not one of general over-expansion.'[1]

In May, Professor E. A. G. Robinson praised Mr Maudling's Budget:

'It has been courageous (some critics would say foolhardy) in allowing the economy the chance of another year's expansion above the 4 per cent rate without anything more than a delicate lightening of the pressure on the accelerator.'[2]

Though by now the National Institute of Economic and Social Research was sounding a dissentient warning, the Chancellor was, in fact, only following out the course urged upon him by the hard-riding exponents of growth of all political colours. In June, in *The Spectator*, under the editorship of Mr I. Macleod, the Chancellor was being advised, even more urgently than by *The New Statesman*, to be 'with it,' meaning that he

'must drive straight through fluctuations in the balance of payments'.

Moreover:

'If Mr Maudling is really hoping to win the election he will have to show the public that he is up to date and "with it".'[3]

However, by July, Dr Kaldor was comparing Mr Maudling's financial policies with those of Mr John Bloom, another 'up to date' and 'with it' financier:

'Short-run borrowing is no remedy, if an early improvement in the balance of the accounts is not in sight. . . . Mr Selwyn

[1] *The Director*, April 1964, p. 85.

[2] *London and Cambridge Economic Bulletin*, p. v (*The Times Review of Industry*), June 1964.

[3] See N. Davenport in *The Spectator* of June 5, 1964, p. 771. By November 27 (p. 758), Mr Davenport was remarking: 'Bank rate at 7 per cent again! Mr Thorneycroft and Mr Selwyn Lloyd must be laughing their heads off. If sterling crises can recur with such monotonous regularity in our island history, it is because the trouble is deep-rooted and the remedies, including Bank rate are superficial.'

Lloyd's measures may come to seem mild compared with the actions that will be necessary to deal with the economic consequences of Mr Maudling.'[1]

It should have been obvious for some time that no party could, since the advent in the mid-fifties of sophisticated electoral-economic management, hope to oust its rivals from office except in circumstances of serious economic difficulty. However, some economists were confident that if and when a Labour Government, led by Mr Wilson, took over, the new methods of planning would bring profound and beneficent changes in economic policy. As regards Mr Wilson's 'superior tactical ability':

'In the first place it obtained support of the trade unions for a well-conceived plan for an incomes policy. . . . Wilson went further than any contemporary leader in explaining in detail how planning of the economy is to be evolved under Labour, what reforms of the government machine would have to be undertaken and what far-reaching changes in taxation, investment, foreign trade, and education (to name only the most pertinent) would have to be ruthlessly carried out if Britain were to succeed in transforming herself into a dynamic and social community, and so restore her influence internationally.'[2]

The exploration of 'new frontiers' or new techniques of economic planning, would, it was maintained, bring about a revolution comparable with the Keynesian revolution. The application, for example, of cost-benefit analysis would bring 'a tremendous prize':

'We have begun to grope our way towards a practical concept of economic planning which may prove, in a few years time, to be as revolutionary in its policy implications as was the Keynesian revolution in economics thirty years ago. . . . A tremendous prize awaits the country that pioneers in this field.'[3]

[1] *The Times*, July 28, 1964.
[2] T. Balogh, in *Towards Socialism*, edited by P. Anderson and R. Blackburn, 1965, p. 72.
[3] See P. Hall, in *Labour's New Frontiers*, 1964, p. 173 (quoted by A. R. Prest and R. Turvey, *Economic Journal*, December 1965, p. 728). Of course, valuable analysis of this kind was being attempted regarding the Victoria underground and the M.1 motorway.

The new Government proceeded at once to bring a number of university economists—mostly from Oxford—into Whitehall, as advisers or experts in the various ministries, including, notably, Dr Thomas Balogh as a special economic adviser to the Prime Minister and the Cabinet.[1]

But with the election campaign in the early autumn, then the new Government taking over, and the shortly-following crisis (or 'pseudo-crisis', as it was called in *The New Statesman*) the flow of public admonition and comment temporarily dried up somewhat.[2] In fact Professor Day referred subsequently to the 'conspiracy of silence' which had delayed the sterling crisis:

'All the ingredients for a crisis were there by August, and the most surprising thing is that it took three more months, until November, for the crisis actually to come. By then, any minor mishap could have set it off.'

Professor Day went on to describe the initial achievements of the new Government as follows:

'What the Government has managed to do in its first seventy-five days is to explode the major left-wing myths. One is that we can achieve faster growth simply by talking ourselves into it and ploughing ahead regardless in circumstances which had forced the Conservative Governments to put on the brakes.

The other myth is that our troubles—including stop-go—have been the result of a right-wing conspiracy of the Treasury and the Bank of England to put the international prestige and strength of sterling above all else.'[3]

With the brief and hectic boom, and its burst of growth, due to expire, even though the death agonies were to be somewhat expensively prolonged, scrutiny at the end of the year returned to the 4 per cent growth target. As Professor Day noted:

[1] An apparently inspired account explains the appointment of Dr Balogh (and Sir Solly Zuckerman) as having 'added a new dimension to the Government's capacity for meeting a crisis or planning ahead' and stresses Dr Balogh's influence on Mr Wilson's ideas and speeches when in opposition. See *The First Hundred Days of Harold Wilson*, by A. Shrimsley, 1965, p. 25.

[2] *New Statesman and Nation*, November 27, 1964, p. 820.

[3] The *Observer*, January 3, 1965.

'Recently, in Britain, an important myth has developed around the 4 per cent per annum target for economic growth which plays such an active rôle in political discussion. It is clear that any political party which stated explicitly that its expenditure plans were based on an expected growth rate of less than 4 per cent would be regarded as hopelessly stick-in-the-mud.'[1]

It was not necessarily the figure of 4 per cent that was wrong, highly arbitary though this had been, but the way it had been treated:

'If 4 per cent were treated as a target which could be achieved only at the price of sacrifice of current consumption and of severe disturbance to vested interests and economic and social rigidities, it would serve a useful social purpose. The country could then enter into an informed debate about whether it wanted to give up something now, for the sake of greater benefits in the future.'[2]

The *London and Cambridge Economic Bulletin* was pessimistic:

'The familiar question, whether the two goals of growth at 4 per cent and equilibrium in the balance of payments can be attained simultaneously, seems in danger of being replaced by the question whether either goal can be attained at all, even independently of the other.'[3]

However, in spite of impending difficulties, or the 'pseudo-crisis', Mr Blackaby, editor of the *National Institute Economic Review* called for no retreat from the 4 per cent target, with its confidence-generating properties, in the forthcoming National Plan:

'It may be better not to bother too much about the precise level of the pressure of demand, but to concentrate on bringing about the necessary state of collective confidence which will lead to a

[1] *Westminister Bank Review*, November 1964, p. 2.
[2] *Op. cit.*, p. 13.
[3] *London and Cambridge Economic Bulletin*, December 1964, p. 1. (In *The Times Review of Industry*.)

faster rising capacity trend. The coming Four- or Five-Year Plan —which should be part of the whole process of giving this confidence—should certainly not take any figure lower than 4 per cent.'[1]

Nineteen sixty-five was a kind of twilight year. Was there a crisis or wasn't there? Not for Sir Roy Harrod (July 20th):

'The country's predicament is not a very grave one. The adverse balance of payments is moderate, compared with that which the US has had for nearly eight years. . . . The trouble is that the predicament has been going on for *too long* . . . .

We need not be sceptical about the remedial measures now in hand, but they are bound to be slow-working.'[2]

Sir Roy proposed import restrictions to the tune of £400 million a year, a two-year incomes freeze, and a re-expansion of demand. A few days later Lord Robbins informed the House of Lords that the country was confronted with a crisis 'which was more menacing than any since the war':

'Our position is indeed very serious. There is no easy way out of this business.'[3]

Lord Robbins, however, supported the decision *not* to devalue.

Possibly the hopes of some were raised by the publication of the National Plan in September. Professor Day, a not unsympathetic critic, found himself put 'into something of a predicament':

'The whole exercise was certainly worth doing. But it was also worth doing a great deal better than it has, in fact, been done.'[4]

With admirable generosity Professor Day went on:

'One desirable feature of the Plan's philosophy is that it tries to approach planning on the assumption that it is wiser to make

[1] *District Bank Review*, December 1964, p. 11.
[2] *The Times*, July 20, 1965.
[3] *The Times*, August 5, 1965.
[4] The *Observer*, September 19, 1965.

decisions on the basis of more information, rather than on less. And if one of the consequences of the Plan is to ensure that more of our decisions are made on the basis of a rational view of the probabilities rather than on hunch, prejudice and exaggerated attention to the way things happen to have been going in the last few months, it will be all to the good.'

Obviously 'prejudice' and exaggerated attention to the recent past will usually prove bad guides, though the process simply of drawing up a plan will not necessarily eliminate these, but may in fact dress them up pretentiously in a system of pseudo-consistencies. As regards the much maligned 'hunch', if this means guesswork and judgment, it is quite inevitable in any case. It would seem intellectually unrealistic to suggest that this can somehow be eliminated by the collection of more and more information, or transformed into 'a rational view of the probabilities' unless this latter is simply a more 'professionally' impressive phrase for guesswork or 'hunch'. More information may be better than less, if its collection has not cost too much, and if it is reasonably relevant and unbiased, without overburdening the decision-makers, which again, are matters of judgment—or 'hunch'.

Professor Day went on to complain of the National Plan:

'It shows little sign of awareness of modern techniques such as input-output analysis, and the use of capital-output ratios, and other econometric devices which (for good or ill) play a major rôle in most national plans these days.'[1]

Of course in the parallel exercise of 'exploring 1970', Professor Stone and his colleagues had been making extensive use of these 'modern techniques' and 'econometric devices'. But unless the appeal is for modernity, or for whatever 'these days' is the fashion, for its own sake, the question remains as to the evidence for believing that these 'modern techniques', of themselves would have produced a less unsuccessful plan, the quality of the judgment (or 'hunch') controlling them being no better than that actually employed on the National Plan. Professor Day's frank reference to their use, elsewhere, 'for better *or worse*', seems rather to give the game away, unless, again, one is simply

[1] *Op. cit.*

recommending modernity and fashion for their own sakes.

As we approach the closing months of our period the story becomes more difficult to summarize, and the temptation to comment less resistable. For Sir Roy Harrod the 'not very grave' predicament of July 20, 1965, became 'our last chance' twelve months later, 'a sort of economic Battle of Britain':

'We want foreigners to feel that at long last Britain has regained something of the 1940 spirit.'[1]

In fact, by July 1966, inquest time had arrived again. The coroners were both as widely varying and individually predictable in their verdicts as before. Professor Joan Robinson held that reducing 'military expenditure' was essential for relieving the British economy, which was at least an interesting innovation as compared with the traditional socialist view that it was armaments expenditure that kept 'capitalism' going.[2] Professor Sir John Hicks also called for drastic cuts in government expenditure, pointing his accusing finger rather at the rapidly rising spending of local authorities, who had been free to 'explore 1970' rather prematurely:

'It is dreadful to think how much of our national deficit is ultimately traceable to local expenditure on "civic amenities".'[3]

But Sir John was firmly against devaluation as an alternative:

'It is widely supposed that the only reason why we do not devalue is the obstinacy of Mr Wilson. *But economists may be grateful for the obstinacy of Mr Wilson and for the good advice on this matter we may be sure he is receiving.*'[4]

On the other hand, Professor Alan Day concluded:

'There has, in fact, been an awful sense of inevitability about the

[1] *The Times*, August 2, 1966.

[2] See *Economics, An Awkward Corner*, 1966, p. 72, and *The Times*, August 11, 1966. Professor Robinson concluded that with the problems of sterling and the balance of payments out of the way: 'We could set about to make a country where all can be comfortable, cheerful and free to follow their fancies.' (*Op. cit.*, p. 72.)

[3] *After the Boom* . . . , 1966, p. 16.

[4] *Op. cit.*, p. 21. (Italics added.)

situation ever since the obscurantist economists persuaded the politicians that in some magical and undefined way we could allow demand to roar away and talk ourselves into much faster growth, and since the obscurantist politicians managed to persuade themselves that devaluation would be the ultimate disaster.'[1]

The 'obscurantist economists' was certainly a highly interesting new theme for criticism, which was also developed by Lord Robbins in the House of Lords (July 28th):

'The pickle in which we find ourselves is the product of confused thought rather than infirmity of will. It is the intellectuals who have fostered the belief that we can have growth without discipline, stable prices with unrestrained demand, overfull employment without inflation and balance-of-payments difficulties; it is these who are ultimately blameworthy if anyone is.'[2]

Another profoundly knowledgeable observer commented still more trenchantly:

'Many economists in recent years, British and other, . . . convinced themselves they were ready to add a Post-Keynesian to the Keynesian miracle: they could, quickly and without much cost, raise the full-employment growth rate by macro-economic measures. It would be nice if we could. One day, perhaps, we will be able to. But we cannot yet. Our premature pretension to this secret of secrets, swallowed hook line and sinker by politicians of both parties and commentators at all levels, has yielded a sad episode in the public history of our science. It has cost the British dear in output and prestige and will cost them more yet: loans to be repaid, a dose of unemployment and unrest to be endured. . . . If the Labour Government has fallen memorably flat on its face, who tripped it?'[3]

There were also signs in other quarters that earlier scapegoat-

[1] The *Observer*, July 17, 1966.
[2] See *Hansard, House of Lords*, July 28, 1966. Volume 276, Column 957.
[3] From an unpublished paper on the English economic situation, September 1966, by D. M. Bensusan-Butt of the Australian National University.

hunting diagnoses putting all the blame on industrialists or civil servants, politicians or trade unionists, were coming to be seen as inadequate. Professor Kaldor, exploring again 'The Causes of the Slow Rate of Economic Growth of the United Kingdom', was now (rather than blaming industrialists, as in his evidence to the Radcliffe Committee) looking, like Mr Colin Clark, more in the direction of labour shortage:

'Britain, having started the process of industrialization earlier than any other country, has reached "maturity" much earlier—in the sense that it has attained a distribution of the labour force between the primary, secondary and tertiary sectors at which industry can no longer attract the labour it needs by drawing on the labour resources of other sectors.'[1]

In fact, *The Times* concluded regarding Professor Kaldor's new views:

'Those who like to argue that no one is to blame for Britain's poor economic performance may feel supported.'[2]

This might seem a charitable, if not entirely adequate, note on which to conclude 'this strange eventful history', with the British economy left, if not '*sans* everything', at any rate *sans* growth, *sans* a National Plan, *sans* reserves, *sans* Europe, and *sans* a balance of payments.

Here, however, is one further report, certainly in somewhat grim terms, which, though actually dating from 1963 (or before) seems to apply with quite extraordinary force and even more relevance to the situation three years later at the end of 1966:

'British economic policy is remarkable in a single respect: it is a crashing bore. . . . It is boring in a straightforward sense like the endless repetition of infantile burbling is boring. It just goes on. It is just a repetition. And it has no meaning or purpose.

The basic weakness of Britain after both World Wars has

[1] *Causes of the Slow Rate of Economic Growth of the United Kingdom*, 1966, p. 31.

[2] *The Times*, November 3, 1966.

sprung from the same cause: policies leading to insufficient investment, weakening our competitive position abroad and our capacity to provide a good material standard (or a strong war effort) at home. . . .

Certainly after every crisis Britain's relative position in the world further deteriorated. The attempt to cure recurrent balance-of-payment crises by restrictions on investment necessarily further impairs our relative competitive power, and thus perpetrates our weakness. It has now led us, tails between our legs, to apply humbly for admission to the Common Market "accepting fully all its implications", when we scorned it with contempt only four years ago.

It is quite true, of course, that if our workmen were content with a wage corresponding to the negligible increase in productivity to which this inanity has condemned us, we should get by without balance-of-payments crises. We would, however, only find ourselves becoming progressively poorer and weaker, relative to an expanding world. *Economic policy which is content to register this relative decline by retarding wage increases is contemptible morally as well as technically.*'[1]

We would venture to add just one final quotation of unimpeachable wisdom from the columns of the *New Statesman*, because it marks such a glaring contrast with so much of the economic admonition and punditry of the previous two decades:

'Anyone, economist or layman, who thinks he can see a clear way out is a fool.'

Modernity had, at last, caught up with Galiani.[2]

[1] T. Balogh, *Unequal Partners*, Volume II, 1963, pp. 267-8.
[2] See R. Marris, *New Statesman and Nation*, July 21, 1967, p. 71, and above p. 7.

CONCLUSION

From Economic Theory to Policy? The Strategy of Demand Management. Inflation: Types, Sources, Causes and Methods of Control. Economic Growth, Models and Policies. The Strategy of Commercial Policy. Devaluation in 'Theory' and Practice. Positive Economics and the Predictability Gap. The Obscurity of Policy Objectives. Institutional Change, Utopian and Practical. Forward (or Backward) from Keynes. 'Economics is a Serious Subject'.

(1) FROM ECONOMIC THEORY TO POLICY

Readers will no doubt be drawing their own conclusions from the foregoing survey What follows here is a brief inquiry as to the methods or processes by which the policy proposals and criticisms reviewed above were actually arrived at, and what their relationship is with, or what support they derive from, economic theories and predictions to some extent tested, disciplined or 'scientific'. On the other hand, how far have policy conclusions been based, and *inevitably* based, on guesswork, speculation and 'hunch', and how far has such guesswork been shaped or biased by ideological or political presuppositions and prejudices, or swayed by considerations of fashion?

Ideally, according to the textbooks and the austere methodological essays, policy conclusions are arrived at by combining clearly and explicitly expressed value-judgments, or statements of policy objectives, postulated or advocated, with positive, 'scientific' predictions based, in their turn, on well-tested theoretical generalizations along with their carefully checked specific, initial conditions.

How far do the conclusions about policy which we have been surveying begin to approximate to this standard? Or how far is this standard quite remote from the methods and processes by which these policy conclusions have been reached?

We repeat that the policy questions which we have covered represent no more than a fraction of the range of issues and policies to which economic theories are held to be relevant, and that we have said little or nothing, for example, about questions of taxation policies, policies regarding monopolies and restrictive practices, or the more technical aspects of banking and monetary policies. Also of course, we have omitted completely the applications of economic theorizing to the policies of firms. But the range of pronouncements we have been concerned with surely constitutes a most important type, of the greatest public concern and interest, of the 'fruit', in terms of policy conclusions, yielded by economic theorizing of one kind or another.

From the foregoing survey we may set out five main questions or groups of questions around which the main policy issues can be ordered. This list could obviously be elaborated or extended; but *most* of the questions, general or specific, discussed in our survey, could be arranged under the following five general headings, three internal and two external:

(i) Questions of the level or pressure of demand or activity at which to seek to operate the economy, and of the effects of slightly higher or slightly lower levels of demand or activity on efficiency and growth.

(i) Questions of the types, sources and causes of inflation, and of the effects of alternative methods of attempting its control.

(iii) Questions of the sources or causes of high or low rates of economic growth and of the effects of different measures aimed at promoting higher rates.

(iv) Questions of the general principles or strategy of commercial policy regarding (a) in the earlier part of the period, 'multilateral' and 'bilateral' trade policies and 'the dollar problem'; and (b) more in the later part of the period, regarding economic relations with Europe.

(v) Questions of exchange rates and of the effects of devaluation.

The nature of the economic theorizing relevant to, or used in, discussing these different groups of policy questions differs somewhat from case to case, as does the extent of the interconnections with political issues, and the complexity of the value-judgments, or of the combinations of objectives, involved. But the differences may not be so significant as to preclude some general conclusions.

(2) THE STRATEGY OF DEMAND MANAGEMENT: FROM 97½ TO 100 PER CENT EMPLOYMENT

Under our first heading, that concerning questions of the level of demand, we are not including here the more technical, short-term questions of methods of forecasting and control. We are not discussing, that is, the relatively more technical and tactical issues of how to achieve some particular level of demand or activity with regard to the techniques of which there has doubtless been considerable steady progress resulting from the availability of more accurate and up-to-date statistics, and from twenty years of experience with various fiscal and monetary measures. We are concerned here with what has surely been, for nearly two decades, one of the two or three major domestic issues, the strategic question of what target level of demand or employment to aim at, or of the effects of rather higher, or rather lower levels on efficiency, growth, and other objectives. As usual, positive and normative questions have been mixed together, which it is important, and at least to a considerable extent possible, to distinguish and keep separate—if one is interested in elucidating the choice of policies rather than in persuasion of one kind or another. Anyhow the issue of a high *versus* a not-so-high pressure of demand has been central. Though not always directly posed and confronted it has been an underlying issue in the arguments regarding both the control of inflation, and growth policies.

Desirable target levels of demand and activity are usually expressed in terms of corresponding percentages of unemployment, and it is from here, of course, that the strongly felt normative issues in the debate arise. There has clearly been a considerable change in tastes and norms regarding tolerable levels of unemployment in the two decades we have surveyed. Of course there is nothing illegitimate in moral proclamations to the effect that it is 'intolerable' for governments to 'create' any unemployment, or to allow it to rise above 1½ per cent, or that a target of 2 per cent is a 'cold-blooded' impossibility.[1] However, actual

[1] See above I (1), p. 36. It is curious to find an absolute moral issue being made of the difference between 1¼ and 2¼ per cent unemployment. It would seem more sensible *either* to make a moral issue out of *any* unemployment and hold to a target of total employment, as in New Zealand where 0·5 per cent unemployment provokes angry public protests, *or* attempt to count the cost and weigh up each marginal 0·5 per cent or 0·25 per cent of employment against costs in terms of other objectives—the balance of payments, the growth rate and so on.

policy decisions have to be taken, for example on pit closures in the nationalized coal industry, as against continuing subsidies or higher fuel prices. It could, therefore, be regarded as professionally more appropriate than simply proclaiming moral standpoints, in terms of blood temperatures or otherwise, to make an attempt at analysing, or estimating the costs and benefits in terms of the positive possibilities of combining different levels of employment with varying levels of other objectives. Any such estimates, however, are inevitably based to a very large extent on speculative guesswork. They seem often to differ widely, to be often, though not always, subject to a high degree of political bias, and to have little or no basis in 'scientific' predictions based on well-tested theoretical generalizations and carefully checked specific, initial conditions. On this question, the following statement from one of the most searching economic inquests of recent years (1967) is surely conclusive:

'The trouble is that no accepted body of knowledge exists which would enable one to compare the probable effects of alternative long-term strategies towards demand (not even of that half knowledge which exists in other fields of economics). The research that has been done on demand management could give a Chancellor some useful information on *how* to reduce the pressure of demand over the next twelve months by a given amount, and even on the delayed repercussions that such measures might have in a further twelve months. But there is very little generally agreed doctrine which would help him to decide whether this would be a sensible thing to do or not.

The real intellectual uncertainty concerns the difference—if any—that alternative policies towards demand would make to the growth of productive capacity in the long run. Some economists might argue that the growth of productive capacity is determined by deep-seated technological factors, or by people's basic attitudes to change, and that the management of demand has very little effect upon them.

Those who would accept that demand management might have an influence on long-term growth would disagree about the optimum pressure at which to run the economy. Some are impressed by the benefits of running the economy at a high pressure, with the spur this provides to innovation and labour-saving investment. Others believe that running the economy with a fair margin of unused resources would not only keep costs and prices down, but that it would also make for a more flexible industrial structure."[1]

We noticed in our survey some of the contrasting and, so far, rather inconclusive attempts at estimating the effects of high and not-so-high levels of demand and employment on prices, wages, and the balance of payments, and we shall be discussing these further in the next section. As regards the longer-run effects of different levels of demand on efficiency and growth, views or attitudes conflict even more profoundly. On the one hand it was argued that a very high level of demand encourages a higher level of investment, especially labour-saving investment, and assists towards the relaxation of restrictive practices by labour—and, of course, *vice versa* for not-so-high levels of demand (corresponding to a 0·5 per cent or 1 per cent higher level of unemployment). On the other hand, it is claimed that very high levels of demand promote inefficiency and the hoarding of labour, nullify competitive forces, facilitate the survival of highly inefficient firms, and, in hampering the movement of resources to the more efficient firms and industries, slow down the growth rate.

Such conflicting predictions are obviously and inevitably based very largely on speculation, judgment and guesswork. They appear to be correlated quite strongly with general attitudes towards planning and the price mechanism, and with the kinds of economy and society people prefer. Those who have generally expressed favourable attitudes to planning and central regulation tend usually to be more favourable to very high levels of demand, and to predict that efficiency and growth will be stimulated by them, and are, of course, in any case quite prepared or positively eager for the extension of central regulation and control which will be necessary to counter inflationary effects on prices, wages and the balance of payments. Those, on the other hand, who politically dislike the extension of central regulation and control and put a higher value on decentralization for its own sake, predict harmful effects on efficiency and growth from very high

[1] S. Brittan, *Inquest on Planning in Britain*, 1967, pp. 38-9. See above, also the quotation from G. D. N. Worswick, above I (1), p. 35 (from *The British Economy 1945-1950*, edited by G. D. N. Worswick and P. H. Ady, 1952, p. 9).

levels of demand, and favour rather lower levels, without (with the notable exception of Professor Paish) usually making clear just how much lower levels of employment they are prepared to envisage. On both sides there seems often to be an element of biased or wishful thinking influencing positive predictions, as is always liable to be present when predictions are largely and inevitably a matter of speculation and guesswork.[1]

It does not seem that on these questions the elements of speculation and guesswork will rapidly be reduced or removed, or the operation of bias and prejudice precluded by the establishment of a general consensus based on convincing or conclusive tests, or even that the wide disagreement, simply regarding the positive issues, will soon be significantly narrowed. General hypotheses regarding longer-run effects are exceedingly difficult, sometimes *practically* impossible, to test at all adequately, whether with regard to the longer-run effects of very high levels of demand on efficiency and growth (or, for example, of high progressive taxation on incentives). It might be doubted whether the differences in the positive predictions would really be conclusively resolved even by some huge Utopian 'crash' programme of research, mobilizing for five or ten years a maximum concentration of *expertise*, with no expenses barred. Certainly much interesting material would be produced, but one could not feel at all confident that a significant measure of agreement on positive predictions would emerge.[2]

[1] The evidence for these generalizations (and others that follow) is to be found in the historical survey above. We have considered summarizing the evidence in some statistical or quantitative form, in tables or correlations. But the numbers are comparatively small and the units highly unhomogeneous, and we do not subscribe to the fashion that any figures are better than none.

[2] A. E. Holmans in his very interesting book, *United States Fiscal Policy 1945-1959*, describes a parallel intellectual situation in the United States (pp. 313-5): 'Although all parties of opinion are agreed on the advantages of economic growth, there is, as of 1960, no consensus of opinion about policy to achieve it, even among economists. There are no generally agreed ready-to-hand guides to policy for growth as there are for maintaining stability in the short run. Instead, there are two distinct streams of thought. . . . The two streams may be labelled "Left" and "Right" or "high pressure" and "low pressure". The "Left" or "high pressure" approach relies heavily on a rising volume of aggregate demand, to be maintained by heavy Federal civil expenditure. . . . Most formulations of the "high pressure" aproach assign a small rôle to monetary policy, on the ground that high interest rates restrict investment. . . . The "Right" or "low pressure" approach is entirely different. In this view, the sources of economic growth are the resourcefulness, enterprise, initiative, and

(3) INFLATION: TYPES, CAUSES, AND METHODS OF CONTROL

In Britain in the last two decades questions as to the means and ends of demand management have obviously merged with questions as to the sources and control of inflation. It could justifiably be claimed that in our period some useful distinctions between sources or types of inflation have been developed, and that some significant explanations, or partial explanations, have been advanced, at least reducing at some points the extent of ignorance. But this reduction of ignorance does not seem to have narrowed or relieved the major disagreements on policy, even with regard to the positive elements therein. In fact the usefulness of the main distinction (between 'demand-pull' and 'cost-push') has been, as we have seen, authoritatively called in question by one of the apparently most influential witnesses before the Radcliffe Committee.[1]

Presumably, over the decades, there have been in Britain alone a number of different sources or causes of inflation, and, at different junctures, different sources or causes or combinations thereof, have been operative. On the other hand, some of the main studies have been in terms of wholesale generalizations, covering a whole century of economic history, rather than in terms of case studies. Again, the entire controversy over policy has often been dominated by the element of ideological confrontation, seldom very lucidly and explicitly stated on either side, between those more inclined to rely on the price mechanism and those generally in favour, *a priori*, of more central regulation. As we have seen, one or two of the pioneer econometric studies

savings of the private sector, and not additional effective demand generated by the Government. The rôle of the Government in the process of growth is to promote economic efficiency by maintaining competition, to adjust the tax system so that it does not penalize enterprise, and to keep down the total weight of taxation. . . . The other major contribution of the Government is to prevent inflation, which is held to be inimical to sustained growth, as well as being a cause of social injustice. . . . While the individual hardships caused by creeping inflation are obvious enough, the adverse effect of "creeping" inflation on economic growth is often asserted but seldom demonstrated. . . . The rôles of public finance in the two sets of policies for economic growth are thus in complete contrast. In the "high pressure" system it is the principal method by which the stimulus is applied to the economy; in the "low pressure" system its rôle is an anti-inflationary one.'

[1] See the statement by Professor R. F. Kahn, quoted above, III (3), p. 154.

seemed to indicate that a slight easing of demand pressure, corresponding to a level of unemployment of about 2-2½ per cent, would lead to the elimination of inflationary pressure, or at least its reduction to insignificance. But these results were insufficiently unquestionable to convince or convert the exponents of the cost-push thesis.[1] On the other hand, a subsequent econometric study[2] concluded that demand factors were relatively unimportant in the rise of wages, and that trade union 'pushfulness' was a significant source of inflationary pressure which counter-policies would have to tackle. Again, it does not appear that the new conclusions have converted the adherents of the demand-pull theory. On neither occasion, for all the most skilful scientific testing 'against the evidence of what actually happens in the economy',[3] did one observe (or could one expect to observe) streams of 'cost-pushers' or later, 'demand-pullers', laying down their arms and moving across no-man's land to the opposing lines.

Perhaps some slight distinction can be drawn between the degree of support and assistance from coherent and well-tested theory which the choice of policies regarding the shorter-run control of inflation may obtain, as compared with the strategic choice between very high and not-quite-so-high levels of demand and employment, discussed in the previous section. Perhaps there might be a significantly larger probability that a massive research effort might appreciably reduce disagreement with regard to predicting the shorter-run effects of different methods of controlling inflation, than with regard to the longer-run effects of differing pressures of demand on efficiency and growth.

However, a major complicating factor here is that the problems of the control of inflation lead sooner or later to proposals for, or attempts at, fundamental institutional changes such as an incomes policy, of which the effects neither in the short-run nor still less in the long-run can be predicted other than by the most speculative 'hunch', judgment or guesswork. As a result, eventually, of successful institutional changes the problems of inflation *might* become less serious both for the policy-maker and the

[1] With the important exception, apparently, of Mr J. C. R. Dow.

[2] See A. G. Hines, 'Trade Unions and Wage Inflation in the United Kingdom, 1893 to 1961', *Review of Economic Studies*, October, 1964.

[3] R. G. Lipsey, *An Introduction to Positive Economics*, second edition, 1966, p. 43.

theorist. In doing so, these problems would certainly become very different, as we shall discuss further below.

At this stage we might consider the account of the growth of macro-economic knowledge, or its contribution to more successful policy-making, given by Professor Lipsey in the closing peroration on 'The Progress of Economics', to his textbook:

'There is no doubt that since economics first began some, albeit irregular, and halting progress has been made in relating theory to evidence in the world of economic events. This progress has been reflected in the superior ability of governments to achieve their policy objectives. The financial aspects of the Second World War were incomparably better handled than those of the First World War. The pathetic efforts of successive British Governments to deal with the economic catastrophe that overwhelmed the country after the return to the gold standard and even more so after the great crash of 1929 show measures adopted in all sincerity which in most cases actually served to make things worse. When President Roosevelt tried to reduce American unemployment in the 1930s (with much more vigour than was applied by any British Government over the same period) his efforts were greatly hampered by the failure of most economists to realize the critical importance of budget deficits in increasing the level of the circular flow of income. The contrast between the unhappy period of the 1930s and the present is great. When President Kennedy wished to do something about the high levels of unemployment in the 1960s, his main problem was to persuade the American Congress to adopt what most economists agreed was an appropriate cure—a tax cut; and in 1964, when President Johnson finally persuaded Congress to accept the tax cut, the ensuing rise in output and employment was very close to what the economists on the President's Council of Economic Advisors had predicted it would be. Several times during the 1950s and 1960s successive British Governments have altered the Budget in pursuit of a "stop" or a "go" policy. Many economists are critical of the motives behind these policy oscillations but the fact that each time the economy moved in the direction predicted by economic theory is impressive evidence that we have learned a great deal about the behaviour of the economy in the last forty years."[1]

[1] *Introduction to Positive Economics*, second edition, 1966, p. 859.

All this is admirable and quite undeniable, and of course highly relevant to the hopes, fears and policy problems of the 1930s and 1940s in Britain. But the range and coverage of the achievement here described hardly begins to extend to the problems of British policy in the 1950s and 1960s with which we have been concerned. Certainly the above record of achievement covers the successful policies of the United States Government in raising, by the tax-cut of 1964, both the level of employment and the rate of growth. But with all due respect, the problem then solved might be described as a lower order policy problem, that is, one of overcoming prejudices regarding unbalanced budgets so as to bring the United States up to or nearer its policy possibility frontier, without very significant costs in other objectives. On the other hand, the problems of British policy have arisen from continually pressing against the possibility frontier and trying, largely but not always *entirely* vainly, to raise it. Furthermore, Professor Lipsey goes on to claim:

'Today, we are much less likely to dismiss theories just because we do not like them and to refuse to abandon theories just because we do like them. Today, we are more likely to try to base our theories as much as possible on empirical observation and to accept empirical relevance as the ultimate arbiter of the value of our theories.'[1]

Regarding the important range of policy problems with which we have been concerned in this book, this claim seems more valid as an admirable expression of hope than as a fully-realized achievement.

(4) ECONOMIC GROWTH: MODELS AND POLICIES

In terms of what is often called 'theory' by economists, or in terms more precisely, of non-empirical or quasi-empirical, analytical model-building, the study of growth has, of course, been a major field of activity in Britain in this period. As regards the production of growth models, Britain must rank very high, quite possibly at the top, in any world league table of output-per-head or per-man-hour. Perhaps the (quite invalid) presumption has gained

[1] *Op. cit.*, p. 859.

ground that so much strenuous intellectual production must somehow have so enlarged the understanding of the causes of economic growth as to increase significantly the power to raise or regulate it by the application of a coherent, reasonably well-tested and agreed theory, yielding reasonably definite conditional predictions regarding the effects on growth of alternative policies. Certainly there has, *apparently*, been an increasing readiness to sacrifice or risk other objectives in order to launch policies which, it was held, would raise Britain's rate of economic growth.

Anyhow, Sir Roy Harrod has ranked the development of 'dynamic theory' on at least the same level of significance as that of Keynesian theory, with Keynes appearing as an 'indispensable precursor' of the 'dynamic' revolution or revelation:

'Within the period in which my own attempts have fallen, there have been two revolutions, each seeming greatly to enrich one's capacity for understanding. The first, of course, was the Keynesian revolution. That was an indispensable precursor. The second, not less important according to my judgment, has been the substitution of a dynamic theoretical system in place of a static one.'[1]

Regarding the fruit-bearing capacity, or relevance for policies, of the 'dynamic theoretical system', or of much of growth analysis, one is tempted to repeat the plea which Sir Roy himself made regarding the contribution, to our group of policy problems, of recent mathematical analysis:

'I cannot escape a feeling of uneasiness about the scope and method of economic theory today. It is needful to pay homage to the intellectual distinction of the work of mathematical economists. At the same time I find myself in the awkward position of not having had my understanding of the working of the economies with which we are concerned, whether, for example, our own economy or one or other of those of the less developed countries, greatly enriched, in consequence of this type of work. I am quite ready to admit that this may be because I am incompetent to comprehend it, or because I have not devoted sufficient time to studying it. Nonetheless there remains the nagging

[1] *Topical Comment, Essays in Dynamic Economics Applied*, 1961, p. 1.

thought that, had economics really been enriched to a substantial extent, the findings would, after a lag of a few years, been translated into language comprehensible to what one might call the working economists, *and that their relevance to economic policy-making would have become apparent*.'[1] (Italics added.)

However, regarding the discovery of the causes of growth very great claims have, as we have seen, been made for certain 'simple' and 'attainable' recipes, requiring only 'a relatively small sacrifice in a relatively short time', while it has been maintained that given 'purposive direction', there was 'no real justification for having a fatalistic attitude concerning the rate of economic growth that could be attained in the British economy'.[2] Others, as we have seen, suggested that the raising of Britain's rate of economic growth could be achieved by a process of collective auto-suggestion, stimulated by the contemplation of econometric models of rapidly-growing economies; or it was complained that the 4 per cent growth target set up by the NEDC was too low.[3]

Without attempting any kind of prophecy regarding the future developments and practical fruits of 'dynamic' and growth theory, we would suggest that there is, as regards our period, hardly a relevant point at which its significance for policy will stand comparison with Keynesian employment theory.

If one takes, first, the level of actual policy achievement in Britain in respect of the Keynesian high-employment objective, and in respect of the growth objective, the contrast is too painfully obvious to need further stress. Of course, it *could* be asked just how much the attainment of high-employment levels over much of the world owes to Keynesian theory, but our guess would be that most economists would claim some significant relationship (in particular, for example, in respect of policy in the United States after 1963-64). On the other hand, a claim that the fast growing countries are indebted, for any significant measure of their success, to what is understood by 'dynamic' or growth theory, would seem impossible to entertain.

Secondly, and more significantly, even if 'dynamic' or growth

[1] *Towards a New Economic Policy*, 1967, p. 1.

[2] See the claims by Dr Balogh and Dr Kaldor quoted above in III (3) and IV (3), pp. 152-4, 211 and 217.

[3] See above IV (3), pp. 214 and 217.

theory had provided, or was to provide, much improved predictions relevant to the control of growth rates (corresponding with the assistance that Keynesian theories and their accompanying framework of national income concepts have rendered towards the prediction and regulation of employment rates), it seems extremely doubtful whether a more rapid rate of economic growth would rank as high, on any democratically conceived scale of social preference, as has the Keynesian high employment objective (costs, in terms of other objectives, being taken into account). Of course, only guesswork is possible. But here again imprecision in the formulation of objectives has added confusion to unavoidable positive ignorance. In public discussion in Britain the advocacy of the growth objective has often been mixed up with questions of efficiency and/or the level of utilization, or employment, from which it is quite distinct.[1] Higher efficiency might be desired and its fruits enjoyed without any rise in the rate of economic growth as conventionally measured. But essentially, a more intensive pursuit of the growth objective entails, at high levels of employment, a reduction in current consumption. It is extremely uncertain how far a democratic electorate, of the current British age structure, would support the more intensive pursuit of the growth objective by government policy, if the essentials of the issue were plainly put to it.[2] At any rate, the guess is justifiable that the growth objective would never attain the almost overriding position on a scale of social preferences which much evidence suggests is accorded to the objective of high, full, or even, as in New Zealand, total employment.

Thirdly, regarding the objective of economic growth, there are, of course, all the crudities of its conventional measurement in terms of GNP, and the philistinism of its advocacy without taking full account of these crudities. An operational definition of a generally desirable growth objective, in reasonably unobjectionable terms, is obviously far more problematic than in the case of the employment objective.[3]

Fourthly, it is misleading to discuss the promotion of the

[1] See J. Tobin, 'Economic Growth as an Objective of Policy', reprinted in *National Economic Policy*, 1966.

[2] See *Markets and the Franchise*, IEA Occasional Paper, 1966, p. 29.

[3] See *'Positive' Economics and Policy Objectives*, 1964, pp. 151 ff., for criticism of the growth objective. A powerful and masterly discussion is given in E. J. Mishan's *The Costs of Economic Growth*, 1967.

growth objective as though this was completely costless in terms of other valuable and valid objectives. Conflicts, or costs in terms of other objectives, must be faced, as they often have not been, especially with regard to desired freedoms, the distribution of income, and even, in Britain, levels of employment. An important distinction between the growth objective and the employment objective is that raising the latter from very low levels (say the inter-war average of 86 per cent) involves comparatively minor costs of any significant type—until, in Britain, you get up to somewhere around 97½ - 98 per cent. On the other hand, raising the rate of growth even from the lowest level—or rather even more from very low levels—involves, at once, significant costs in terms of current consumption, or Government spending, in a highly employed economy. We shall discuss the formulation of policy objectives, taking account of conflicts therein in a subsequent section (8).

(5) THE STRATEGY OF COMMERCIAL POLICY

Problems of policy do not, of course, fit neatly into the departmental pigeon-holes adopted for purposes of university administration, and, as we noted earlier, questions of the general principles of commercial policy inevitably contain a large mixture of political issues, partly normative and partly positive, because this is where economic policies shade into foreign and defence policies. This political component certainly weighed heavily in both the groups of problems under this heading which we discussed above: (a) the earlier, post-war questions of close collaboration with the United States in working towards a general 'multilateral' pattern of international trade, as against the framing of 'bilateralist' and discriminatory policies based on the organization of a 'bloc' of whatever Commonwealth or European countries could have been brought together; and (b) the later issues with regard to Britain's economic and political relations with Europe.

As regards (a) the 'multilateral' case was based, as to its economic arguments, in a general way on orthodox international trade theory, going back to the classicals. Keynes himself, in his last article (June 1946) explicitly appealed to 'classical' mechanisms and medicines, though, of course, to a very heavily supplemented and revised version of them.

However, a major distinction must be drawn between an unqualified, dogmatic, *a priori* application of orthodox international trade theory, using it as a comprehensive and conclusive answer to all questions of trade policy, with no significant regard for particular cases; and, on the other hand, deriving from the principles of international trade theory a general presumption or maxim, subject to numerous and important exceptions, and to as much empirical investigation as can be afforded of significant cases. One must at least agree with Dr Balogh, with regard to the application of international trade theory to policy, in his emphasis on

'the failure of empty generalities, the exposure of the grand abstract designs . . . the acknowledgment of the complexity of inter-relationships, of the impossibility of coming to snap-judgments on the basis of simplified assumptions and general models'.[1]

A further difficulty, making for still more uncertainty in predictions as to the effects of different strategies of commercial policy is, of course, that of estimating the attitudes and reactions of other parties, how far agreement will run and how far rules, when negotiated, will be implemented.

There would probably still remain considerable and fundamental disagreement as to how far the history of the last twenty years confirms or refutes the 'multilateralist' or 'bilateralist' cases as developed just after the war. Such predictions or prophesies as were proclaimed on either side often took the form more of prophetic forebodings and were seldom couched sufficiently precisely, with clear and explicit specific conditions, as to be at all conclusively refutable. It might be considered that the huge growth of multilateral trade in the twenty years after the war constituted some kind of confirmation of the multilateralist case, and a refutation of the bilateralist case, but it seems improbable that this would be accepted by the more enthusiastic bilateralists.[2]

[1] *Unequal Partners*, Volume I, 1963, p. 54.

[2] See the quotation from P. Streeten above IV (i), p. 164 (from *The British Economy in the Nineteen-Fifties*, edited by G. D. N. Worswick and P. H. Ady, 1962, pp. 108-9).

Presumably, however, it would be difficult not to admit the falsification of some of the major predictions in favour of discriminatory policies and against 'multilateralism', in terms on the one hand of the American economy's instability, and on the other, of its overwhelming technical 'dynamism' and productivity-growth.

When one comes to the Common Market question in the second half of the fifties, one finds pretty wide agreement that the political issues involved were bound to weigh heavily, possibly outweighing any likely conclusions regarding the economic effects. In some cases economists explicitly confined their arguments to the economic issues and withheld judgment on the issue as a whole, though sometimes they seemed to imply that the political arguments would have to weigh very heavily if they were to turn the balance against the particular economic arguments being advanced. On other occasions an economist would argue strongly regarding the *political* issues alongside his (or her) conclusions on the economic case, with the political and economic arguments nearly always presented as running in harmony and reinforcing one another. In fact, what is disappointing for those who would like to see economics cultivated as a kind of discipline or 'serious subject' (not to say 'science') is that one can find considerably more examples of economists using economic arguments in support of their known political views than one can of those prepared to admit that the economic arguments ran counter to their political attitudes. Usually, though not quite always, if one knew a university economist's political attitudes, one could predict with quite a high probability what his or her assessment of the economic arguments would be.[1]

Professor H. G. Johnson, in addition to noting the 'predictable' character of economists' views on the issue (1960), even held that they may have been to some extent responsible for the

[1] Regarding the evidence for these generalizations we can only refer the reader to the surveys above in III(4) and IV(2), and claim that it would probably be more misleading than helpful to try to draw up statistical tables, or establish quantitative correlations regarding small numbers of unhomogeneous units. As Mr M. Lipton acutely commented: 'On this essentially political issue, there *are* no good economic arguments, only rationalizations of prepared positions.' The Common Market: The Economic Arguments Examined, *Three Banks Review*, June 1963, p. 17.

breakdown of the negotiations over the Free Trade Area:

'It is even possible that unpreparedness and insufficiently cautious expression of opinion on the part of the general body of economists contributed something to the eventual failure of the Government's negotiations with the Six, in that by-and-large economists accepted, or at least did not actively challenge, both the Government's offensively Anglo-centric definition of the problem as one of obtaining the maximum gains from freer trade with Europe at the minimum sacrifice of other British interests, and its vulnerable belief that Britain stood to lose a great deal economically from the establishment of a Common Market without a surrounding Free Trade Area.'[1]

Highly uncertain though some of the points in this argument seem to be, it is difficult not to agree with Professor Johnson when he concludes with regard to the reactions of economists to the Free Trade Area scheme that they seem

'to reveal certain weaknesses of general approach to policy problems of this nature'.[2]

It was said of King William IV that he 'had little information and strong prejudices'. Economists' views on Britain's entry into the European Common Market showed a somewhat similar balance, or lack of it. Removing the lack of information, in really relevant and significant terms, would have been extremely difficult. Again, the issue was so complex, and the effects were of such a variegated, diffuse and long-run character that even a huge concentration of research talent in a ten-year crash programme *might* not very much have reduced disagreements with regard even to the *positive* issues involved.[3] However, as regards the strong prejudices which were brought to bear, some mitigation ought to have been possible, and at least they should not have been allowed so blatantly to bias the conclusions on the positive economic questions as they did in the case of some economists.

[1] *The Free Trade Proposals*, ed. G. D. N. Worswick, 1960, p. 137.
[2] *Op. cit.*, p. 137.
[3] One must, of course, strongly support as much research being carried out as is consistent with a wise and efficient use of scarce resources, while taking a cautious and realistic view of the likely results.

(6) DEVALUATION IN 'THEORY' AND POLICY

The last of our five questions, that of devaluation, has, as we have seen, been discussed on and off over our twenty years, especially before and after 1949, and again from the early sixties onwards. This particular issue might, for two reasons, be expected to have a rather different significance from that of our previous four questions in respect of the relation of theory to policy.

First, under our previous headings it would hardly be claimed that anything like a relevant, established, tested, systematic and agreed body of 'theory' was in existence, whatever hopes might be entertained for certain emerging embryo 'theories'. Under our last heading, a well-established theory of international trade could be used as a basis for certain very general predictions, but even here its precise degree of relevance was hardly clear and undisputed in respect of particular issues involving the strategy of commercial policy. But, as regards devaluation, a reasonably coherent and agreed body of 'theory', authoritatively referred to as 'exchange rate theory', has been in existence throughout the period.

Secondly, in some contrast with our four previous questions, the normative issues and the rôle of ideological prejudices, along with the pervasive planning-*versus*-the-price-mechanism syndrome, though of course present in some degree, are not so intensively involved or so closely interwoven with the positive issues of the effects of policy measures which can with less difficulty be kept distinct.

Nevertheless, at the various relevant junctures, economists have been divided in not obviously unequal proportions between advocating and opposing the devaluation of the pound, though the division does not coincide with such predictable precision with the familiar ideological battle-lines, as on the other four issues. Broadly in favour of devaluation, as regards the 1949 measure, were Professors Robbins[1] and D. H. Robertson. Subsequently, over a considerable period, Professor H. G. Johnson expressed generally favourable views, in principle at any rate, and also, in the sixties, Professor A. C. L. Day, and, perhaps with more reservations, Professor J. E. Meade. Professor N. Kaldor and other economists much more inclined towards 'planning', also

[1] Lord Robbins expressed himself as opposed to devaluation in 1964-65. See *House of Lords Debates*, 1964-1965, Volume 269, August 4, 1965.

expressed support for devaluation at various junctures from about 1963 onwards.

Opposed to devaluation, almost but not invariably throughout, have been the two Oxford experts, Sir Roy Harrod and Dr Balogh, both in 1949 and subsequently. Perhaps the most powerful statement of the case against devaluation came from Sir Hubert Henderson in 1948. Sir John Hicks, after an early advocacy (1947) and some cautious support at the time of the 1949 measure, from the early fifties expressed firm opposition on grounds similar to those expressed earlier by Sir Hubert Henderson. Professor Kahn (1958) also ruled out exchange-rate adjustments so long as there was so little control over wages.

It might be noted here that while the supporters of devaluation seem, on the whole, to have based their case on broadly similar considerations, the opponents have put their main stress on very different lines of argument, at least on some occasions. Sir Hubert Henderson, for example, hardly deigned to mention the analysis of the effects on imports and exports in terms of elasticities of supply and demand, and based his powerful case on the probable 'dynamic' erosion of any possible initial advantages by cost-push inflation, arguing that if the inflationary pressures could be restrained *after* devaluation they could, and should, just as well be restrained *without* devaluation. Sir Roy Harrod, on the other hand, stressed 'perverse elasticities' in criticizing devaluation, in the early fifties at any rate.[1]

The question therefore arises of the significance for policy decisions of the comparatively agreed and established 'exchange rate theory', and its precise relation to the advocacy of, or opposition to, the devaluation of the pound in recent years. We have seen Professors Day and Kaldor invoking 'textbook' theory (including Sir Roy Harrod's own textbook) in support of their case for devaluation.[2] In this connection, also, the following observations by Professor H. G. Johnson (in a review of a work by Professor Joan Robinson) are of interest:

'It is particularly disappointing to find Professor Robinson, who contributed so much to the development of exchange rate theory, failing to impress on her readers the fact that the fixed exchange

[1] *The Pound Sterling*, 1952, p. 34.
[2] See *The Times*, February 26 and March 11, 1963.

value of the pound creates the conflict between full employment and payments equilibrium that has produced incomes policy as a panacea, and continuing to discuss the possibility of a change in the exchange rate as if we were still in the international jungle of the early thirties.'[1]

Professor Johnson's reference to 'exchange rate theory' (to which Professor Robinson had contributed so much) seems to suggest that this 'theory' somehow establishes, or renders probable, or in some way contributes support for, the 'fact' that the fixed exchange value of the pound 'creates' the conflict between full employment and payments equilibrium.

Without entering into the substantive debate on the policy issue of devaluation, it may well be asked whether any 'exchange rate theory' has been developed, or established, with any such agreed content: that is, a theory which excludes the assertion of the counter 'fact', that it is Britain's comparatively high rate of cost-push inflation, and/or low rate of productivity increase, which 'creates the conflict between full employment and payments equilibrium'?

In her treatment of the devaluation question criticized by Professor Johnson, Professor Robinson stated:

'In a situation where there is some unemployment and unused capacity in many lines, a devaluation increases activity and improves the balance of trade at one stroke. But when there is near-full employment already it is liable merely to increase the pressure of demand for labour, while the rise in price of imports increases the pressure for higher money-wage rates, so that before long the competitive advantage of lower home costs is completely lost.'[2]

Surely no 'exchange rate theory', in textbooks or elsewhere, refutes the relevance of these considerations. In February 1963 Professors Day and Kaldor did, in fact, point to the existing unemployment, then over 2 per cent, as an indication of the relevance of 'textbook theory'. But it is a matter of judgment (or 'hunch') whether a margin of 2-3 per cent unemployment would be sufficient to restrain the further cost-inflationary

[1] *New Statesman and Nation*, January 6, 1967, p. 15.
[2] *Economics, An Awkward Corner*, 1966, p. 30.

pressures which might be initiated by a devaluation, the precise strength and repercussions of which would obviously be difficult to predict at all accurately (unless one is accepting as definitively established something like the thesis of Professor Paish).

We emphasize that we are not concerned here to take sides in the substantive policy issue for or against devaluation, or to deny cogency to the case for devaluation in 1963, or at any other particular date. We are simply concerned with the relation between 'exchange rate theory', in textbooks or elsewhere, and policy conclusions; and with pointing out that no policy conclusion follows obviously or easily in favour of, or against, devaluation of the pound (between say 1961 and 1967) *simply* from the logic or geometry of 'exchange rate theory'. A judgment is required regarding, among other things, rates of cost-push inflation, and the prospects of restraining them following devaluation, that is regarding complex processes not at all easily or accurately predictable on the basis of any agreed systematic theory.

In fact, the further question might be raised as to whether 'exchange rate theory' might not more suitably be described as 'exchange rate analysis' or 'exchange rate taxonomy'. Anyhow, whatever is to be regarded as the precise degree of empirical content (if any) of 'exchange rate theory', this, of itself, clearly falls short of establishing any reasonably agreed and relevant predictions which (granted, of course, the relevant value-judgments and policy objectives) would have demonstrated the case for devaluing the pound, in the period with which we are concerned. Of course what is in dispute in the devaluation issue is not any point of logic in the textbook taxonomies. Nor, as we have argued, are the usual pervasive ideological presuppositions, which are often at the root of most of the other policy differences we have considered, of quite so much importance in the case of devaluation—though there may be some inexplicit differences regarding the 'prestige' of devaluation.[1] The positive differences turn mainly, or almost entirely, on differing judgments or

[1] One can perceive how, say, a defender of the Suez operation might be inclined to feel aggrieved by the real or imagined loss of prestige implied by devaluation. Also a dogmatic opponent of every sort or kind of application of the price mechanism, might *a priori*, be inclined against devaluation, though, as we have seen, some quite thorough-going 'planners' have been in favour.

'hunches', to some extent perhaps about the relevant elasticities, but, much more importantly regarding comparative inflationary pressures and all the international repercussions. Whether the decisions made are successful or unsuccessful, will turn on the quality of the judgment that is brought to bear, much more than on any facility in manipulating the taxonomy.

(7) POSITIVE ECONOMICS AND THE PREDICTABILITY GAP

On most, or all, of the positive economic questions involved in the five groups of policy issues just discussed, a number of different hypotheses or tentative theories have been advanced, mostly sharply contradictory of one another. But, as we have seen, there has been relatively very little, and on some points absolutely nothing, in the way of reasonably tested and agreed theoretical generalizations with their relevant checkable initial conditions from which disciplined or 'scientific' predictions can be derived to provide the positive basis for policy decisions. There is, in fact, a large predictability gap which at some quite crucial points does not look like being filled in at any rate for some time to come (and by then, of course, the important policy problems may have moved on elsewhere). This is not in any way to depreciate the significance of much arduous and ingenious work. The land reclamation achievements of the Dutch are among the most remarkably skilful, persevering and heroic labours in Western European history, and many thousands of acres have been reclaimed from the sea. But, if one is thinking of ever proceeding on *terra firma* from Holland to England, these feats are of little relevance.[1] One will always have to face getting across the sea, in one way or another.

It might be urged that although economic theory does not by itself yield any kind of reliable predictions of the specific type relevant to the policy issues which we have been discussing, it provides, in some general way, techniques, 'frameworks', an 'organon', or, what Keynes once called in a grandiose phrase, often quoted in a rather bromide thought-quenching way:

[1] This analogy has been used, in another context of course, by, I think, A. J. Toynbee. But I am unable to trace the precise reference.

'an apparatus of the mind, a technique of thinking, which helps its possessor to draw correct conclusions'.[1]

But as regards the 'correct conclusions' on the positive economic questions involved in our five groups of policy issues, insofar as a general 'apparatus' or 'technique' has led its possessors to 'conclusions', it has led them to n sharply diverging positive conclusions or predictions—($n > 2$)—at least ($n-1$) of which presumably must be *in*correct rather than correct.

Unfortunately, the predictability gap is insufficiently acknowledged and often not even perceived as a gap. It is apt to get plugged with various kinds of dubious temporary filling. For active policy-makers this is quite inevitable. But economists, instead of acknowledging that the gap *can* only be filled by guesswork, speculation or 'hunch', often seem to be engaged in convincing themselves and their political clientele that it has in fact been adequately filled in, when the filling is actually formed mainly or entirely out of ideological prejudices or fashion.

Ignorance, for example, may be pretty considerable regarding the effects of very high demand or not-so-high demand on exports or imports. If for other reasons a very high level of demand is favoured, it is assumed that it will tend to lower costs and so favour exports.[2] Again, ignorance is inevitably profound regarding the long-run effects on efficiency and growth of economies of scale to British industry if it were to become part of a larger European market. So one simply fills in with the economic assumption which fits in with one's political presuppositions.[3]

Even the same economic situation may be described quite differently *by the same writer* depending on the political purpose of his argument, as we have seen with the situations in the summer of 1949 and the autumn of 1951, for example.[4]

Another filler of the predictability gap, which sustains con-

[1] See his Introduction to the earlier Cambridge Economic Handbooks, written, of course, some time before his sweeping criticisms in the *General Theory* of the fundamentally *in*correct conclusions which so many economists had so long drawn.

[2] Ignorance on this question was by no means so extensive following the publication of the articles by R. J. Ball, J. R. Eaton and M. D. Steuer, *Economic Journal*, September 1966, p. 501; and *Economica*, November 1966, p. 388. See above IV (3), p. 219.

[3] See above IV (3), p. 203.

[4] See above I (4), pp. 75-6 and 80-1.

fidence and does something to veil what may be felt as the embarrassing if inevitable nakedness of sheer speculation and guesswork, is simply fashion or 'modernity' (sometimes blended in with ideology, sometimes not). A number of examples have been noted above of a policy, a theory or a concept being condemned or approved on no other explicit ground than that it is 'old-fashioned', on the one hand, or 'modern', on the other. No reference is made to any evidence or tests of any kind which call in question the 'old-fashioned', or support the 'modern'.

Among particular examples we have noticed, there is Professor Robinson's condemnation as 'old-fashioned' of arguments predicting beneficial effects from economies of scale in a larger market.[1] There was no serious attempt to produce significant evidence in favour of one prediction rather than another. Certainly this would have been extremely difficult. So one simply decides between conflicting hypotheses by asking which is the more 'old-fashioned' or 'new-fashioned'. Again when arguing against the possibility of introducing Russian-type planning into this country, Professor Sargent did not mention any questions of efficiency or political values but stressed particularly that it 'is beginning to have a very old-fashioned look'.[2] Again, in the summer of 1964, Mr Maudling was urged to be 'with it' and 'drive straight through fluctuations in the balance-of-payments'. Being 'with it' was apparently the prime criterion; careful, critical inquiry into the evidence (and a balanced judgment) regarding alternative policies came a very poor and impracticable second.[3]

We have seen, too, Professor Alan Day complaining of the National Plan (1965) that it showed

'little sign of awareness of modern techniques such as input-output analysis, and the use of capital output ratios, and other econometric devices which (for good *or ill*) play a major rôle in most national plans these days'.[4] (Italics added.)

One would have thought that there was quite enough scope

[1] See above IV (2), p. 204.
[2] *Out of Stagnation, a Policy for Growth*, 1963, p. 43. See above p. 217n.
[3] See above IV (3), p. 224.
[4] *The Observer*, September 19, 1965. See above IV (3), p. 229.

for criticism in that document without introducing the charge of not being 'modern'. As we have argued, it is difficult to see how these more 'modern' technical and tactical devices—such as estimating capital-output ratios—would have rendered the whole operation less unsuccessful, in view of the broad, strategic misjudgments on which it was based. Anyhow, as we saw, the parallel operation of 'exploring 1970' made full use of such 'modern techniques'.

The rôle of constant changes in intellectual fashion is to give an often spurious illusion of rapid progress in the contribution or potential contribution of economic theorizing to more successful policy-making. Moreover as Professor Samuelson has noted:

'It is safer to be wrong with the crowd than take the chance that you may not be right, all by yourself.'[1]

The extent of the inevitable rôle of guesswork and speculation in forming policy judgments, concealed as it often is by ideological dogmatism or fashion, does not seem to have been sufficiently realized. When Professor H. G. Johnson explains that he is

'not objecting to the procedure of guessing at economic magnitudes as such',[2]

one can only answer that he had better not if he wants economics to have much of significance to say on many of the most pressing actual problems of policy. There might, indeed, be considerable agreement with Professor Johnson when he concludes:

'It is inevitable that economic policy-makers and commentators must rely to a large extent on guessing at the magnitude of economic effects.'[3]

It might only be added, here, that a clear-cut contrast between guessing at the *magnitude* of effects, and at their *direction*, does not seem easy to maintain.

[1] *Problems of the American Economy*, Stamp Memorial Lecture, 1961, 1962, p. 28.
[2] *The Free Trade Proposals*, ed. G. D. N. Worswick, 1960, p. 142.
[3] *Op. cit.*, p. 142.

However, Professor Johnson objects to guesswork if, or insofar as, it

'has the undesirable effect of implying that one man's guess is as good as another's'.[1]

But if one wishes to sustain an objection to the proposition that one man's guess is as good as another's, one must surely be prepared to indicate with some precision: (1) the *kind* of issues on which economists' or *some kinds* of economists' guesses *are* better than other people's; and (2) what exactly it is in their equipment or qualifications which, on some reasonably clearly defined issues, will justify one in holding that economists' or some kinds of economists' guesses *are* better than other people's.

As regards (1), economists pronounce and predict, often with similar degrees of confidence, on very different kinds of issues. They predict or guess at the level of next year's G.N.P. and, equally dogmatically, at the effects of Britain's entry into the European Common Market. As regards the former, though he does not offer any evidence, one may be prepared *very* tentatively to incline towards Professor Samuelson's claim that though economists

'cannot forecast well . . . they forecast the economy better than any other group thus far discovered. Empirical statisticians, clairvoyants, down-to-earth businessmen, hunch-players—all these turn out to have a worse "batting average" than government, academic and business economists.'[2]

On the other hand, with regard to a highly complex, open-ended, politico-economic issue such as the effects of Britain entering the European Common Market, on which English university economists made the most dogmatic and contradictory predictions, one might well be disposed to agree with Professor Lipsey's acceptance of the conclusion (as against Professor Johnson's objection to it) that

'your guess is as good as mine'.[3]

[1] *Op. cit.*, p. 142.
[2] *Problems of the American Economy*, Stamp Memorial Lecture, 1961, 1962, p. 23.
[3] The *Observer*, October 14, 1962, p. 5. See also my discussion in *'Positive' Economics and Policy Objectives*, 1964, pp. 89-102.

In fact, on this kind of issue one might go even further, with Professor M. F. Millikan, and conclude that the economist's or social scientist's predictions or judgments may be inferior to those of 'the successful journalist, novelist, diplomat or businessman':

'Our best formal models are still partial; they explicitly exclude consideration of some of the factors at work in any actual situation. The relative weight of the factors explicitly analysed can seldom be measured, and their combined influence seldom computed. Prediction of a sort is, of course, a necessary component of policy-making. . . . But in social situations such a judgment can seldom be effectively made by "scientific" procedures. If the policy-maker simply desires advice as to what he should do, he had better rely on the intuition of a man of wide experience and demonstrated understanding rather than on the intellectual skills and techniques of the social scientist. . . . A net predictive judgment in most human situations can be made more safely by the successful journalist, novelist, diplomat or businessman than by any social science research team.'[1]

At least in the early 1960s in Britain this was, of course, a terribly unfashionable point of view (in spite of its support by an American social scientist). Obviously distinctions must be drawn between the widely different kinds of predictions, judgments and guesses required in economic policy-making. But those who wish to object to the conclusion that one man's guess is as good as another's, ought to examine these distinctions much more closely than they have.

As regards the second issue which needs examination, that is, the possession of just what equipment or qualifications entitles one man's guess to be considered better than another's, this obviously has also important implications for the education of economists. This question would certainly be much easier to pronounce upon if officially compiled 'batting-averages' as Professor Samuelson calls them (for whole careers and/or for the current quinquennium) could be regularly published for all players by the Royal Economic Society.

Unfortunately one has to conjecture as to what equipment

[1] *The Human Meaning of the Social Sciences*, edited by D. Lerner, 1959, pp. 165-6.

makes for successful guessing, without any agreed assessment as to who the best guessers are, or what their 'batting-averages' have been. We shall only venture here a very tentative personal list of various negative, positive and neutral factors.

Among the negative factors, making for a low long-run batting-average (other things being equal), we would suggest obviously:

(1) ideological dogmatism and party-political fervour; and
(2) subservience to fashion—probably a sign that intellectual cheques are being drawn that are liable to bounce

Among the factors, at best neutral and perhaps often negative, we would place:

(3) mathematical and geometrical facility, which, while there seems to be no reason why it should inevitably work negatively against successful guessing and judgment, in fact seems sometimes to do so.

On the positive side we would put the following qualifications:

(4) institutional experience, when relevant, which comparatively few economists until recent years have had much of in England;
(5) knowledge of historical cases and institutional processes in economic policy, and the critical study of theories and doctrines relevant to economic policy; and
(6) a knowledge of administrative and political processes which should help in the appreciation of the gulf which yawns between bright ideas and successful policies or legislation.[1]

(8) THE OBSCURITY OF POLICY OBJECTIVES

Whether objectives or norms are advocated or simply assumed in the discussion of policies, any precise applications of theory to policy or any precise conditional predictions derived from theories

[1] Cf. the classic pronouncement by Sir James Fitzjames Stephen: 'The one talent which is worth all other talents put together in human affairs is the talent of judging right upon imperfect materials, the talent, if you please, of guessing right. . . . All really important matters are decided, not by a process of argument worked out from adequate premises to a necessary conclusion, but by making a wise choice between several possible views.' (*Liberty, Equality, Fraternity*, second edition, 1874, p. 352.)

as a basis for policies, need to be fitted to correspondingly precise formulations of objectives, or some reasonably clear and explicit scale of policy preferences. But, in fact, intense arguments over economic policies often proceed without any adequately clear statement of the objectives advocated or postulated by the parties to the debate.[1] There is often an extreme contrast between the 'rigour' and precision of abstract models and the imprecision and incompleteness with which the effects and objectives of policy measures are formulated, to which the models and theories are supposed to be providing relevant support. The formulation and examination of criteria or objectives for economic policy has been the concern of 'welfare' analysis, much cultivated in the period we have been concerned with in this book. But it is difficult to discover indications of the actual practical use of 'welfare' analysis in the discussions of policies which we have reviewed. Nor does a study of the extremely abstract assumptions on which most 'welfare' analysis is conducted encourage the hope that anything much of relevance can result to elucidate the choice between actual policies of the kind with which we have been concerned.

Nevertheless, some gradual progress has been made towards the more precise formulation of objectives,[2] though this seldom proceeds as far as explicit statements regarding marginal rates of substitution, or of how much of one objective is to be sacrificed to attain a higher level of another.

Of course the pressures on the party political authorities are very great to avoid commitment to precise priorities involving a readiness to sacrifice some measure of one objective in return for more of another. Politicians will naturally be reluctant to concede that *their* policies will involve the sacrifice of *any* significant objectives, or levels thereof, and will reject and evade the need for choice or the statement of their 'priorities', if and when choice becomes inevitable. They will invoke, if necessary, some sudden great upsurge of economic growth which they are going to engineer, which will render choice unnecessary between, for example, increased investment, more generous anti-poverty measures, larger public expenditure in other directions and increases in taxation. Unfortunately, some 'political' economists,

[1] See *'Positive' Economics and Policy Objectives*, Chapters 3 and 4, pp. 123 ff.

[2] As, for example, in the Radcliffe Committee's discussion of the objectives of monetary policy, Cmnd. 827, 1959, pp. 17-23.

including university economists, fearing perhaps a loss of influence with political patrons, seem to have fostered these Utopian evasions, and to have followed the politicians in veiling in obscurity their marginal rates of substitution and estimates of the costs, in terms of other objectives, of a higher level of one particular objective. This kind of political evasiveness is encouraged further by what has been described by Sir Isaiah Berlin as,

'the natural tendency of all but a very few thinkers to believe that all the things they hold good must be intimately connected or at least compatible with one another'.[1]

Significant examples were noted above in the Memoranda and Evidence of economists to the Radcliffe Committee on the Workings of the Monetary System.[2] In fact, a major distinction is to be drawn between those economists who have maintained that the primary objectives of economic policies have been compatible, for Britain in the nineteen-fifties and sixties, and those who have insisted on the need for choice and hence for precise statements of priorities. On the one hand we have seen it maintained:

'There is no dilemma between growth, stability, and redistribution. In the long run a high rate of growth *promotes* price stability; in the short run demand can be contained through taxation, and a certain rate of wage inflation through redistribution.'[3]

Certainly, on the other side, it has been pointed out that the main aims of policy may be incompatible, or may conflict, at certain proposed levels.[4] But often the compatibility of particular pairs of objectives seems to have been too readily assumed, or urged, in a form too vague to be testable:

First, regarding high levels of employment and price stability;[5]

[1] *Two Concepts of Liberty*, 1958, p. 13.
[2] See above III (3).
[3] P. Streeten and T. Balogh, Bulletin of the *Oxford University Institute of Statistics*, November 1957, p. 339. See also above III (3), p. 151.
[4] See the Evidence to the Radcliffe Committee of Messrs I. M. D. Little, R. Neild and C. R. Ross, cited above III (3).
[5] See the quotation above from Professor Robbins's Evidence to the Radcliffe Committee regarding the consistency between the aims of price stability and 'appropriate' levels of employment and stability, III (3), p. 158.

Secondly, regarding very high levels of employment on the one hand and efficiency and growth on the other;
Thirdly, regarding very high levels of demand and the expansion of exports;
Fourthly, regarding a rapid increase in the rate of economic growth and more egalitarian anti-poverty policies.

In the first case, in particular, reconciliation of conflicting objectives was to be achieved by an institutional *deus ex machina* in the shape of an incomes policy.[1] Of course, legitimate expectations can be held regarding the effects which may result from institutional change. But the effects of institutional changes are likely to be very gradual and difficult to predict. In addition to an incomes policy as an institutional *deus ex machina*, a further comprehensive institutional change, making generally higher levels of attainment feasible across the whole spectrum of policy objectives, was called for in the form of a strengthening of the Civil Service, including more posts for economic experts.

(9) CHANGING INSTITUTIONS

After 1960 in Britain a whole 'grand design' for economic policy was canvassed, with the enthusiastic support of a number of economists, which was based on a systematic refusal or rejection of conflicts or incompatibilities among objectives; or on the notion that insofar as such conflicts or incompatibilities had previously existed, they could comparatively speedily be removed by institutional change. As two critics have put it:

'Choice among the various economic goals was not contemplated. Rather, new institutions were sought by which the inconsistencies among the goals could be eliminated so that all might be attained.'[2]

An 'institution', for example the existing methods of wage regulation, is to be transformed or is simply assumed to be transformed so that, in contrast with the existing processes, it fits into and fulfills its allotted function in a 'model' harmoniously com-

[1] 'The greater equality implied by tax-reform will provide the basis for a national incomes policy.' T. Balogh, *New Statesman and Nation*, September 25, 1964, p. 434.
[2] *Great Britain, Quiet Revolution in Planning*, by E. E. Hagen and S. F. T. White, 1966, p. 13.

bining, say, very high levels of demand and employment, rapid rates of growth and no serious problems of price stability and the balance of payments. Of course, institutional changes are an essential and indispensable means of economic policy-making, and could be regarded as one of the main methods of raising the policy possibility frontier for an economy. Most of the less unpromising recipes for greater efficiency, permitting faster growth, involve institutional or 'constitutional' changes, such as making industries more competitive, 'improving' the educational system and so on. But it may be worth repeating that the effects of institutional changes are likely to be gradual and very difficult to predict, and such predictions can only be justified, if at all, after detailed historical and institutional studies.

We mention here two major examples of institutional transformation which have been much invoked in our period. One of them, incomes regulation, has entered frequently into our preceding historical survey. The other, reform of the Civil Service, we shall discuss here at greater length.

As regards an incomes policy, the possibility has frequently been envisaged of some long-run 'deal' with the trade unions, based on 'adopting' a 'policy of balanced social justice'[1] and at various junctures over the last decade or more, premature optimism has been expressed, encouraged perhaps by the slowing down of wage claims during the 'stop' phase of the cycle, or by some short-run 'plateau', 'pause' or 'freeze'.[2] In fact, it seems that appeals for an incomes policy, sometimes combined with a rather facile optimism regarding its impending establishment (and its effectiveness when established) seem to have amounted to a pretext for evading, in the short and medium run, the inescapable hard choices between conflicting objectives.

As regards a major transformation of the Civil Service, or 'administrative machine', this would make possible much more ambitious policies, based on 'expert' economic planning, and

[1] T. Balogh *Oxford Economic Papers,* June 1958, p. 242. See also above III (3), p. 141.

[2] For example: (1) 'There has been a considerable improvement in the state of awareness of the importance of restrainst over wage increases.' (R. F. Kahn, 1958); (2) 'Both major political parties take inflation seriously.' (Sir Donald MacDougall, 1959); (3) 'Something is due also to the campaign of education, to the leadership of a well-trusted Prime Minister, to the sense of responsibility of many trade union officials.' (R. F. Harrod, 1958). For full reference see above III (3), p. 148.

might bring about a wholesale shift upwards in a country's policy possibility curves, permitting a rise in the levels of attainment of all, or a large number of the main objectives simultaneously (except perhaps for the political objective, or value, of freedom of individual initiative). Much more refined and ingenious tax measures would become administratively feasible, and much higher levels of efficiency in the central allocation of resources, in investment planning, and in exchange or import control, would come within the range of possiblities. If it was complained that the scarce and refined resources needed here are at most times severely limited, then a further institutional transformation, in terms of educational reforms, would be invoked.

Regarding the limits which the capacities of the Civil Service have set on the attainment of more ambitious policy objectives, the two Oxford experts, Sir Roy Harrod and Dr T. Balogh, have, as on other subjects, had most to say.

Sir Roy's views have shown certain changes of emphasis. In 1956 he was referring to

'the sage and mellow influence of Treasury traditions'.[1]

But in 1958, addressing an advertising conference he proclaimed, regarding the level of consumption expenditure:

'Pay no attention to the Treasury; it does not know what it is talking about.'[2]

Later (1963) Sir Roy was expressing much impatience:

'Some of us believe that, despite its high intellectual eminence, thinking in the Treasury is somewhat stale. . . . It appears to continue to be guided by patterns of thought long since obsolete.'[3]

Sir Roy maintained:

'A thorough university training on these relations should be required before people are admitted to those great centres of

[1] *Sunday Times*, June 3, 1956.
[2] *The Times*, May 9, 1958.
[3] *The British Economy*, 1963, p. 189.

power where National Income policies are formed otherwise economic policies may be botched.'[1]

In particular, Sir Roy complained that (a) there was no understanding in the Treasury of 'the vital distinction' between demand and cost inflation; and (b) that the Treasury traditions with 'their affinity with Puritanism' overemphasized the importance of raising investment at the expense of consumption.[2]

However, two years later (1965), having contemplated in the meantime considerable numbers of his colleagues moving—mostly rather briefly—into Whitehall,[3] Sir Roy returned to his earlier views. Before concluding that 'our somewhat tottering economic progress' has been the result of 'inadequacies of the administrative system', Sir Roy posed the rather surprising question:

'Are we sure that the real fault does not lie in the inadequacies of economic science itself?'[4]

Dr Balogh, on the other hand, called, in emphatic terms, for more *expertise* in policy making:

'When I say expert I mean expert. Nothing could be more futile than the substitution of Snowesque scientific dilettantes for Bridgesian humanistic amateurs.'[5]

[1] *Op. cit.*, p. 199.
[2] Of course if Treasury officials had received their 'thorough university training' from Professor Kahn, they would presumably have learned—as he informed the Radcliffe Committee—that Sir Roy's vital distinction between demand and cost inflation was 'unhelpful and misleading' (see above III (3), p. 154). On the other hand, a 'thorough university training' at the hands of Dr Balogh would presumably have instilled the desirability—whether or not on Puritanical grounds—for a much higher investment ratio.
[3] Not only was there a movement into Whitehall, but all round the world the new Ministry of Overseas Development was organizing an outflow of British economists (in spite of the intractable character of Britain's own economic problems). The modern missionaries were quite as confident, if not perhaps as ascetic, as their nineteenth-century predecessors:

'From Greenland's icy mountains,
From India's coral strand
Where Africa's sunny fountains
Roll down their golden sand,
From many an ancient river,
From many a palmy plain,
They call us to deliver
Their land from error's chain.'

[4] *Economic Journal*, September 1965, p. 587.
[5] *Planning for Progress*, 1963, p. 31n.

But *expertise* even of this exalted calibre was far from being enough:

'It would be foolish to expect that economic expertise itself will solve the problem of economic policy-making. Professor (now Lord) Robbins's—or Mr George Schwartz's, or their pupils'—advice would not be better and might be worse than that of those dilettantes who try to play by the ear and who might, by mistake, learn better tunes. It should have become obvious—though it is strenuously denied by the "Establishment" (not excluding Lord Attlee)—that economic policy-making is not a scientific exercise which admits objective impartiality. It is an art inseparable from political assumptions.'[1]

On the other hand, on the subject of this 'inseparability', in economic policy discussion, of 'objective' economic knowledge from political assumptions, Dr Balogh had informed the Radcliffe Committee:

'I shall attempt to indicate what I regard as political in content and what I consider technical and not dependent on political assumptions.' . . .

'There has to be a certain amount of economic knowledge which is irrespective of political viewpoint.'[2]

Whatever the precise significance of these invocations of a bigger and better Civil Service and more economic *expertise* to bolster still further what Dr Balogh referred to as 'the majestic power of a modern state, armed with elaborate administrative apparatus',[3] it does not seem that a mere detached, 'outside' academic observer can predict, with high probability, what effects actual practicable measures of reform may have and how long they will take to work themselves out. However, with regard to this particular appeal for institutional change, in order to raise the whole policy-possibility-frontier for Britain, it should be noted that here again not all economists (or even Oxford economists) were hopeful:

[1] See 'The Apotheosis of the Dilettante, The Establishment of Mandarins' in *The Establishment*, ed. by H. Thomas, 1959, p. 123.

[2] *Committee on the Working of the Monetary System, Principal Memoranda of Evidence*, Volume 3, HMSO, 1960, p. 31, and *Minutes of Evidence*, p. 747.

[3] *Unequal Partners*, Volume II, 1963, p. 262.

'Those who have argued the need to control, reform, or re-man the Civil Service before radical policies can be affected, have probably done a disservice by perceiving the problems of control but prescribing an impossible cure. . . . So much current criticism of institutions is not that well informed.'[1]

(10) FORWARD (OR BACKWARD) FROM KEYNES

It is the pressing claims of a wide range of competing policy objectives, or the fact that throughout much of the post-war period the British economy has been on, or pretty near, a kind of policy-possibility-frontier which can only gradually be raised, which constitutes such a complete contrast with the policy situation which confronted Keynes in the inter-war years. Keynes made the point that when one moves from conditions of unemployment to those of full employment a number of theoretical and policy propositions which held in the one case, cease to hold in the other. This point is very relevant to the question as to how far policy objectives can be treated as complementary or conflicting. Policy problems certainly take on a very different and more complex form when one moves from an economy averaging 14 per cent of unemployment, as in the British inter-war economy which Keynes confronted, to one averaging 1½ to 2½ per cent. The move somewhat resembles one to somewhere near a Pareto-optimal position, from one profoundly sub-optimal.

With unemployment at 10, 15 and 22 per cent for years and decades on end, there was one starkly simple, overriding policy objective on which to concentrate, one which was in the common interests of workers and employers alike and which conflicted hardly at all with any, or most, other *substantial* objectives. Raising the level of employment was, for a very long way, not only compatible with both more investment and more consumption but was helpful or essential for promoting other objectives, such as more rapid economic growth (though this was hardly, of course, an explicit aim at the time) as well as with price stability, insofar as this meant some rise from unduly depressed levels and a 'better' or less unequal distribution of wealth. Such a stark situation introduced and permitted an immense simplification of economic policy issues, a degree of simplification

[1] C. D. Foster, in *Economic Growth in Britain*, ed. P. D. Henderson, 1966, pp. 194-5.

perhaps almost unique in the history of modern economic policy, except, of course, for war conditions which in some ways it resembled.[1] Certainly there were conflicts between drastic reductions in unemployment and the balance of payments, assuming the traditional, classical, institutional objectives of free trade and the gold standard. There were conflicts, also, with the ritual balancing of the budget, and perhaps with a minority of interests in the City and among fixed income receivers. The fight against these was hard enough, but, in waging it, Keynes was largely justified (so, one would guess, a *vast* majority would hold today) in disregarding as negligible the interests and objectives conflicting with his overriding employment objective, and in advocating it as 'the one thing necessary'.

No economist, for most of the two decades following the war, was justified in treating the interests and objectives threatened by his particular policy *nostrum* in the same cavalier fashion, though many did so. In this important respect, therefore, it is not only vain to call for 'a new Keynes' or a 'new Keynesian revolution', it is also misleading to compare, in terms of policies, the Keynesian policy revolution with other more recent policy developments or possibilities. It is also misleading, and historically unjustifiable, to take in vain the adjective 'Keynesian', or its opposite 'non-' or 'anti-Keynesian', as terms of approbation or denigration, for one side or the other, in policy disputes which are of a so vastly different nature from those on which Keynes himself pronounced in the inter-war years.

The uniqueness of the policy situation confronted and attacked by Keynes has not been sufficiently recognized in the two decades after his death, and this has obscured the need to define and choose policy objectives much more precisely, and to make explicit estimates of the cost of attaining a higher level in any one particular objective, in terms of the probable losses in terms of others.

(11) 'ECONOMICS IS A SERIOUS SUBJECT'[2]

Throughout its history, the application of economic theory to policy has depended to a large extent (though, of course, not en-

[1] See *'Positive' Economics and Policy Objectives*, 1964, pp. 146-151.

[2] This was the title of a pamphlet published by Mrs Joan Robinson in 1932. Mrs Robinson wrote (p. 13): 'What the economist, in his capacity of amateur doctor, should do, is to explain frankly the limitations of his knowledge. It is the

tirely) on judgment and guesswork. In the nineteenth century, general qualitative maxims about the workings of free markets, and of restrictions thereon, were propounded for guidance, with exceptions admitted or rejected on the basis of often controversial and conflicting judgments or guesses. Policy decisions were based (insofar as they bore any relation at all to any kind of systematic economic theorizing or thinking) on following out or modifying the general qualitative teachings of what was called 'the science of political economy'. There was little or no attempt at quantification or quantitative estimates, since there was, of course, little statistical basis for them.

As regards, for example, the major decisions on commerical policy of 1846, or even 1932, there was no question of the quantitative examination of the effects of policy measures considered 'professionally adequate' today. Even in the great neo-classical handbook of economic policy, Pigou's '*Economics of Welfare*' (from which, incidentally, the 'welfare' conceptual framework can be stripped, with little or no effect on the cogency of the policy analysis), there are few attempts at quantitative assessments of the effects of the wide range of policies considered. As we saw above (I (3)), the general debate on Planning and the Price Mechanism, just after the war, was conducted largely in terms of general qualitative judgments and maxims.

Anyhow, although the long modern revolution in economic policy had got well under way in the first quarter of this century, still before, say, the onset of the great depression in 1929, the range of policy problems to which it was generally considered that economic theorizing should or could be applied, was comparatively very narrow and restricted in scope compared with the decades following the Second World War with which we have been concerned. In this period two developments, in particular, have transformed the application of economic theorizing to policy.

The first, on the side of the problems to which theory is applied, is the extension of the policy 'revolution', or the much wider scope of domestic policies, and the much more complex, precise and ambitious range of policy objectives aimed at, relating to

unjustified self-assurance of the economists which has alienated the governments and has led them to prefer the advice of bankers, industrialists and other practical men.'

full employment, the control of inflation, and growth, as contrasted with the nineteen thirties, or still more, the twenties; and this at a time when, in addition, the whole strategy of Britain's external commercial policy has had to be fundamentally reconsidered. Inevitably these much more extensive 'macro' policies have impinged much more seriously and problematically on political values and objectives and on questions of administrative feasibility than have the much less ambitious policies of earlier periods.

The second main development transforming the application of economic theory to policy has been still more recent, and is on the side of the criteria or 'methods' aspired to, attempted, claimed or considered 'professionally adequate' by economists: that is the development in the direction of quantification instead of a reliance on merely qualitative judgments regarding the effects of policy measures. As aspirations or attempts, this development may be unreservedly recognized as a main way forward. But actual achievements, claims and immediate prospects need some critical examination. It is claimed that quantification represents a higher level of 'professional adequacy'. But 'professionalism' is often apt to incline, first, towards a certain blinkered narrowness, and secondly, towards an unreadiness to admit to ignorance and to the need for sheer guesswork and speculation. Both such tendencies are serious with regard to economic theorizing and policy-making, where the disregard of non-economic and non-quantifiable effects can be disastrous and where ignorance and uncertainty is likely long to remain a fundamental fact of life.

Moreover, these two developments aggravate one another, since much more comprehensive and ambitious economic policies inevitably have much wider and more pervasive effects on political institutions, values and processes, and 'professional' economists have tended to become less inclined and much less qualified seriously to examine these. In the nineteenth century political economists, in spite of the generally much narrower range and effects of economic policies, took, and were often relatively highly qualified to take, much account of the possible political consequences of economic policies. Whether one agreed or disagreed with their conclusions, at their best, political economists then brought some of the most distinguished and discerning political thinking of their day to bear, where relevant and necessary, on the political aspects and effects of economic policies, and with regard to political values and administrative feasibility. Today, instead of the contributions of a J. S. Mill, Bagehot, or Sidgwick, we have from professional economists either a complete, and possibly disastrous disregard of political values and processes, or we are offered—especially from Oxford and Cambridge—eulogies of the methods of Stalin and Mao Tse-Tung, or of the Suez expedition as a great act of 'statesmanship', primitive grumblings about the inadequate understanding of 'foreigners' or 'the foreigner', or the assumption that what is politically and administratively feasible in England will also prove to be so in West Africa or South America.[1]

However, some signs of a healthy reaction against these dangers, or some forms of them, can be noticed. In another way, also, a hopeful longer-run prospect for the more successful and judicious application of economic theorizing to policy may eventually lie in the new type of economist who emerged, for the first time in Britain in business and government, in significant numbers, in the middle of the nineteen sixties. Until the nineteen sixties, apart from a comparatively very small number of economic advisers, the application of systematic economic theorizing to policy depended, to a very large extent, on the writings of university economists (of the kind, that is, which we have surveyed above with regard to a range of central policy problems). It should make a marked difference to the success with which economic theorizing is applied to policy, to have this done by significant numbers of economists equipped with such basic qualifications and relevant new techniques as a university education in economics can give, but with the vital additional qualification of a continuing close experience of the relevant institutions and processes which policy-making must, if disasters are to be avoided, take fully into account.

[1] Perhaps the prize in this field should go to this exquisite vignette from Cambridge about the direction of labour under Stalin: 'A country woman, in service with a family in Moscow before the war was evacuated and given work in a factory. Later her old mistress had priority to return to Moscow and she was left behind. After trying the regular channels in vain, she wrote to Stalin . . . explaining that factory work did not suit her, that all her village had been wiped out and that she had no friend in the world but her old mistress. Could she go back to Moscow to cook for her? She got a permit within three weeks.' Joan Robinson, *Conference Sketch-book Moscow 1952*, Cambridge, 1952, p. 28. The whole pamphlet is a museum specimen.

However, the emergence in much larger numbers of this, for Britain, comparatively new type of economic *expertise*, will not render obsolete the particular *genre* of writings on policy by university economists, with which we have been concerned in this book. There would probably, on balance, be a regrettable loss, if this type of literature was to disappear altogether. At its best this kind of work *can* have an extremely valuable rôle to play in enlightened democratic policy-making, provided that, in such applications, economics is cultivated as a 'Serious Subject', that is, as a *discipline* and not as a kind of branch of ideological, or party political debate. It is not cultivating economics as a serious subject to use it for rationalizing what party leaders or groups want to hear, or for dressing up particular political preconceptions and prejudices as fashionable *'expertise'*, or for covering over inevitable ignorance with ideologically biased dogmatism.[1] As Pigou once put it:

'To a young man the ambition to play a part in great affairs is natural: and the temptation to make slight adjustments in his economic view, so that it shall conform to the policy of one political party or another, may be severe. As a Conservative economist or a Liberal economist or a Labour economist he has much more chance of standing near the centre of action than he has as an economist without adjective. But for the student to yield to that temptation is an intellectual crime. It is to sell his birthright in the household of truth for a mess of political pottage.'[2]

Of course, such a viewpoint today seems quite intolerably

[1] Mr P. D. Henderson (*Oxford Economic Papers*, February 1961, p. 10) writes: ' "The man who knows not and knows that he does not know" is by no means always a representative figure when economic policy is under discussion. It is arguable that one of the chief benefits of an economic training is a clearer awareness of the limitations both of one's own knowledge and of the subject itself.' Certainly this *ought* to be one of the chief benefits, but it seems often not to have been recently. As Mr G. Hallett in an extremely sensible and penetrating article has put it: 'One reason for the diversity of economic opinions is that many economists tend to be more definite in their prognoses than the available facts warrant.' Mr Hallett continues: 'There is now need for a different type of economics, less dogmatic and doctrinaire, but more eclectic in its theorizing and with more respect for factual knowledge and professional experience.' ('The Rôle of Economists as Government Advisers', *Westminster Bank Review*, May 1967, pp. 10 and 20.)
[2] *Economics in Practice*, 1935. p. 10.

square and 'old-fashioned', not only to 'young men'. But the academic virtues—and they are considerable and invaluable whatever limitations they also impose—*can* be of the greatest service in elucidating the choice of policies. If academic people do not cultivate them and bring to bear the particular contribution they can render, no one else will. However unfashionable in some quarters, they remain of the greatest value for the enlightened debate of economic policy and for the successful application of economic knowledge to policy-making in a free society.

APPENDIX[1]

PIGOU AND KEYNES ON EMPLOYMENT POLICY

I

A review of *Economists and the Problem of Unemployment in Great Britain,* 1885-1929 concluded as follows: 'This, then was the state of opinion in the fateful summer of 1929, when for eight years unemployment in Britain had only once fallen slightly below 10 per cent, and when the world was on the brink of the greatest economic cataclysm of modern times. A majority of economists in Britain supported the general case for public works to combat unemployment (e.g. Keynes, Henderson, Pigou, Robertson, Clay, etc.). Public works policies were opposed by Hawtrey and later by the supporters of the Austrian monetary theory of over-investment. At the same time a considerable body, probably a large majority, of economists held that general wage reductions would, in the then existing circumstances diminish unemployment (e.g. Pigou, Clay, Beveridge and perhaps Keynes).'[2]

In the light of the evidence quoted on which this brief summary rested, there does not seem to be anything seriously wrong with it as far as it goes. But the last sentence on the question of wage cuts could certainly do with more detailed explanation and documentation. In particular, with regard to what is to follow, it would be desirable to make doubly and trebly clear that to record an economist as having 'held that general wage reductions would in the then existing circumstances diminish unemployment' is not to imply that that economist actually advocated or supported general or other wage reductions in those circumstances. It might well have been and was held that although some kinds of wage reductions would have reduced unemployment, it was quite impracticable and undesirable to attempt to implement such reductions, and that there were other easier and socially less inequitable methods of reducing unemployment.

As regards the views of Pigou (and others, for example, Clay) it is worth recalling that the suggestion that high and rigid wages had some responsibility for unemployment in Britain, was originally developed not so much as a deduction from some abstract model of competitive flexibility, but as a simple historical argument of the

[1] This appendix reviews more fully economists' attitudes to employment policy in the nineteen thirties, especially those of Pigou and Keynes, touched on above in I(i). I apologize for some repetitions.

[2] *A Review of Economic Doctrines 1870-1929,* 1953, p. 422.

post hoc ergo propter hoc type, which may have been right or wrong but which is not easy completely to refute. It was natural enough in the twenties to start a diagnosis of unemployment in Britain with a comparison with pre-1914 conditions when unemployment had averaged less than half the post-war figures. It was observed, surely accurately, that wages had been much more rigid since the war, and that this was presumably connected with more powerful trade union policies and with the development of comprehensive unemployment insurance. As Pigou put it (1927): 'If it is correct—if, that is to say, post-war wage policy is in fact responsible for adding some 5 per cent to the volume of unemployment which is normally brought about by other factors—the country is confronted with a problem of a type which pre-war economics never found itself called upon to study. An extra 5 per cent of unemployment—I do not, of course, stress the precise figure—is an extremely serious matter.'[1]

Pigou then considered the remedies of import restrictions and subsidies to wages which he considered might conceivably be effective in reducing unemployment without reducing money wages. But he judged that both of these devices would in practice be 'bungled' by the politicians and so in the long run would work out harmfully. Like Keynes three years later, as we shall see, Pigou did not on this occasion mention public works policies. But he insisted that he was not implying that any decline in working class incomes was in any way desirable or in fact necessary: 'The inference is that it is against the interest of the community as a whole for wage-earners to insist upon uneconomically high wage-rates. That interest requires the restoration, at not too distant a date, of an equilibrium between wage-rates and demand and supply conditions. This does not necessarily imply that wage-earners must forego the benefit of whatever transfer of income from better-to-do-persons to them would be made under a policy of wage subsidies. The same amount of money may still be handed to them under, say, a system of State endowment of large families, or in any one of many ways. Nor does it necessarily imply a reduction in the general level of real wages below which it is now.'[2]

In a lecture published in January 1930, Keynes developed a somewhat similar argument by calling attention to the rise in real wages in Britain 'of some 10 per cent' since the return to the gold standard

[1] *Economic Journal*, September 1927, p. 359. H. Clay argued two years later: 'A great change has taken place during the last twenty years in the methods of negotiating wages. . . . Before the war the policy of maintaining wage-rates in spite of unemployment could be practised only by the organized minority of wage-earners. The majority were unable to resist reductions that were needed to maintain employment.' *Economic Journal*, September 1929, pp. 323 and 332.
[2] *Op. cit.*, p. 366.

in 1925. He expressed 'grave doubts whether an indiscriminate public opinion, reinforced by the votes of wage earners, in favour of raising wages, whenever possible, is really the best means open to us, within the existing framework of society, for attaining what is presumably the object, namely, the betterment of the material conditions of the working class. For the High-Wage Party forget that we belong not to a closed system, but to an international system.'[1] Keynes emphasized that what he called the High-Wage Movement 'has consequently provoked an almost chronic tendency in the direction of dear money', and that the result of the rise in real wages since 1925 had been a fall of profits, 'a fall so severe as to make many branches of English business definitely unprofitable'.[2] Keynes continued: 'What has happened, should, I suggest, be a warning to us for the future. If we want to better the condition of the working class, it is inexpedient to attempt to do it by the method which reduces the rewards of capital below what is obtainable in other countries. Or, at any rate, if we do adopt this method, we must supplement it by abandoning or diminishing the existing freedom of foreign investment. For it never pays to render the entrepreneur poor and seedy. It is impossible in the present order of society to secure the optimum level of output and employment by any other way than by paying the capitalist his full rate, and, if anything, a little over. . . . If we decide that the interests of justice and charity require that the income of the working class should be higher than that which they receive from the economic machine, then we must, so to speak, subscribe to that end. Taxation is a measure of compulsory subscription, and the subscription must be spread over the whole community. But if that subscription is made to fall solely on a particular body of employers then we must not be surprised if the level of employment and output is below what it should be.'[3]

These closely similar views on wages and employment relate, of course, to the period before the onset of the Great Depression at the end of 1929, that is, to an unemployment problem which was regarded as primarily structural rather than cyclical. In the year 1930 unemployment was to rise in Britain at a faster rate than in any year before or since, that is from about 10·4 per cent to about 16 per cent.

II

We have now come to 1930, and it is about Pigou's views on policy at this critical date that recent myths have developed. Since in these

[1] The Question of High Wages, *Political Quarterly*, January 1930, p. 115.
[2] *Op. cit.*, p. 118.
[3] *Op. cit.*, p. 119 and p. 121.

myths Pigou's views are presented by way of a black-and-white contrast with Keynes's views, any errors may also involve getting Keynes's views and achievements seriously out of perspective.

Before we proceed to discuss these myths it might be useful for any readers not recently in touch with the literature to indulge in a couple of preliminary exercises. Most of the leading economists, either as members or as witnesses, contributed to the work of the Macmillan Committee, that is either to its Report and Addenda (published July 1931), or to the various Memoranda and Evidence (taken mostly in 1930).

1. Here are two pieces of dialogue:

(a) W: 'If there is a general state of stagnancy, it might really be impossible for the banks to do anything.

X: Does not this depend on the rate of interest?

W: Undoubtedly in part.

X: Is not that fundamental?

W: There is the state of mind of the business man. The business man might be in such a state that he would not borrow money or use money at o per cent.

X: That is an extremely abnormal state of things?'[1]

(b) Y: '. . . I should have thought it was more plausible to suppose that that high rate of interest was much more responsible for the lack of investment than anything else.

Z: I feel that you may want a frightfully low rate of interest, even a negative one, in certain circumstances to overcome the lack of confidence.

Y: It is rather premature to suggest that.'[2]

Who were or was X and Y with the rather optimistic and classically inclined regard for the effectiveness of flexibility in the interest-rate mechanism? And who were or was W and Z with the rather pessimistic and non-classical scepticism? X and Y were, of course, Keynes, and W and Z were Pigou and Robertson respectively.

2. If Pigou and Keynes were responsible for one each of the following two passages, who was responsible for which passage?

(a) 'I would favour large Government expenditure on really useful public goods. . . . The Government should put in hand and should encourage local authorities and public utility companies to put in hand enterprises of a useful character, even though they are likely to yield a return substantially below current rates, and even though guarantees of interest involving a cost to the Treasury are necessary.'[3]

[1] *Committee on Finance and Industry*, Minutes of Evidence, Vol. II, p. 89, paras. 6613-6.

[2] *Op. cit.*, Vol. I, p. 335, paras. 4837-8.

[3] *Op. cit.*, Vol. II, pp. 92-3, para. 6658 and Note by the Witness.

(b) 'If money incomes have been established at a level appropriate to a certain purchasing power of money and if purchasing power then undergoes a large increase, the fortuitous advantage which will then accrue to those whose money incomes are unchanged may be quite inappropriate to the new situation and without substantial justification. Great evils must needs result, and have resulted, from the excessive rigidity of various types of money-income in such circumstances. . . . A readiness to accept the fact that the value of incomes is something which must be accommodated to changing circumstances is, indeed, an essential condition of the sound working of our economic system.'[1]

Passage (a) is from Pigou's evidence and his additional Note on policy. Passage (b), stressing the importance of income flexibility, is from the famous Addendum I to the Report which, as Sir Roy Harrod puts it, 'the more progressive members of the committee' joined with Keynes (i.e. Sir T. Allen, Ernest Bevin, McKenna, Taylor and Tullock).[2]

It would of course be fantastically misleading to quote this passage from Addendum I on income flexibility without explaining that the signatories went on to advocate not, of course, wage cuts, but, on the contrary, import restrictions and a programme of public works.

But this is precisely how recent myths have treated Pigou's evidence to the Macmillan Committee. Just as there are some significant parallels between Pigou's article on wages (1927) and Keynes's article of 1930, so Addendum I, signed by Keynes, proceeds on a pattern that has some similarities in principle and outline with Pigou's evidence, though of course there are many differences of emphasis and terminology. But Pigou in his evidence proceeded first to examine wage flexibility and concluded that in the then circumstances this was impracticable and undesirable—as did Keynes and the other signatories of Addendum I. Then at the end of his evidence, Pigou made positive proposals for increased public expenditure, as well as for international monetary action and other measures. It would be similarly fantastic to conclude that Pigou had no clear lead other than wage reduction to offer the Macmillan Committee, or that he could only suggest that to reduce unemployment it was up to the workers to shift jobs and locations.

III

We now come to widely current myths regarding Pigou's views on employment policy in 1930, in particular as expressed to the Macmillan Committee.

[1] *Committee on Finance and Industry*, Cmd. 3897, 1931, pp. 193-4, paras. 12-13.
[2] *The Life of J. M. Keynes*, 1951, p. 424.

Professor Lekachman writes of Pigou's evidence to this Committee: 'When he was asked to explain why unemployment was so high, Cambridge's distinguished professor of political economy could extend no aid more useful to his fellow citizens than a diagnosis that "the relative demand for labour in different occupations has altered, and the transfers of labour appropriate to those alterations have not taken place". There was little hint in Pigou's remarks of any novel solution. *If unemployment existed the efficacious remedies were in the hands of ordinary workers and their trade unions. All that workers needed to do was shift jobs and locations judiciously and accept lower wages if necessary, and unemployment would disappear.* The point was made explicitly in the following dialogue:

CHAIRMAN: Would you necessarily create vacancies . . . by the reduction of wages?

PIGOU: I think you would to some extent.

CHAIRMAN: If wage rates were reduced, you think there would be an increased demand for labour?

PIGOU: Then, I think there would be an increased demand for labour.'[1]

One of the editors of the *Economic Journal*, Professor E. A. G. Robinson, in a review on many points highly critical of Professor Lekachman's book agrees with him, or perhaps echoes his conclusions, regarding Pigou's contribution: 'Pigou had no clear lead other than wage reduction to offer to our Macmillan Committee. Contrast today.'[2]

It is necessary first to point out that the omission actually indicated by Professor Lekachman in his quotation of the Chairman's first question consists of the words 'in these other industries'. Again, the words 'in those industries' are omitted (after 'rates') from the Chairman's second question without any indication that the question as quoted is incomplete. Moreover, and again without any indication that an omission is being made, the bulk of Pigou's first answer is also omitted, which actually continues at some length as follows: 'Of course, I am not saying that in some industries there are not vacancies as it is, but you have industries in which the wage rates are now so adjusted that there are no vacancies. It is no use sending coal miners into those industries, because they would not find work.'[3]

[1] *The Age of Keynes*, 1967, p. 51 (Italics added). Possibly this myth has its ancestry in the statement of L. R. Klein that when Pigou 'was called upon to give testimony before the Macmillan Committee . . . he supported a policy of wage cuts'. (*The Keynesian Revolution*, 1st ed., 1947 and 2nd ed., 1966, p. 46). This is a highly misleading statement. But unlike subsequent writers Professor Klein does not say that wage reduction was *all* that Pigou had to suggest.

[2] *Economic Journal*, September 1967, p. 650.

[3] *Committee on Finance and Industry*, Volume II, 1931, p. 48, paras. 5953-5.

Having repaired the quotation it is possible to see something of its immediate context. Pigou was not here discussing general wage cuts but the effect of wage reductions 'in those industries' *not* subject to serious structural unemployment, as contrasted with the coal industry which notably was so subject. Having been interrupted in mid-sentence by Keynes, later in his evidence Pigou went to special pains to emphasize this point: 'This does not, of course, imply that, relatively to the existing conditions, the rates of real wages are too high in the sense I have defined it in the depressed industries. I did not intend to suggest, as any form of remedy, lowering the real wages in the depressed industries. There is no way of saying whether the wages there are too high or not. So, when I came to my division of possible methods of remedy, assuming you can get people transferred, one may assert that unemployment would be diminished if the rate of real wages in the undepressed industries were lowered. Secondly it *would also be diminished if the conditions of demand could be so altered that there should be a higher demand. Thus, either by reducing real wages or by raising the demand, you would employ more people.*'[1]

Immediately before Professor Lekachman's quotation Pigou had explained: 'If you have got unemployment, one can say that the cause of the unemployment is either that the real rate of wages is all right, but there is not enough demand; or if one takes the demand as given one can say that the real rate of wages is too high. . . . So I do not want to say that unduly high wages are the cause.'[2]

Again a little later Pigou repudiated the suggestion that his analysis implied that he was recommending wage cuts to eliminate unemployment: 'There may be other means of doing that.'[3]

Yet again Pigou emphasized this point. When asked whether it was his conclusion that in the existing state of demand for labour the rates of wages in the non-depressed industries were too high, Pigou answered: 'Yes in the existing state of demand. I do not want at this stage to beg the question whether you could not improve the state of demand.'[4]

Again Pigou repeated: 'I am not advocating a reduction of real wages.'[5]

When a member of the Committee suggested that economists did not make enough allowance for the practical impossibility of moving men from one type of industry to another, Pigou replied 'I agree.'[6]

[1] *Op. cit.*, Vol. II, p. 78, para. 6432. (Italics added.)
[2] *Op. cit.*, Vol. II, p. 48, para. 5949.
[3] *Op. cit.*, Vol. II, p. 50, para. 5984.
[4] *Op. cit.*, Vol. II, p. 52, para. 6042.
[5] *Op. cit.*, Vol. II, p. 52, para. 6044.
[6] *Op. cit.*, Vol. II, p. 49, para. 5970.

Pigou's evidence, not unbefittingly for a university economist, was primarily concerned with analysis and diagnosis rather than with policy proposals. But he could hardly have repeated more frequently than he did that he did not advocate cuts in wages. The closing passages in his evidence are concerned with his policy proposals. It may be noted that he did not envisage devaluation (May 1930). But neither did Keynes nor any member of the Committee in the Report and Addenda (published in July 1931—two months before the actual devaluation).[1] Pigou agreed that tariff measures could conceivably help against unemployment but was opposed to them on grounds of probable political mismanagement. He advocated international monetary measures to stabilize prices. He recommended serious efforts to check the flow of new recruits into abnormally depressed industries. And he favoured, as we have seen, 'large Government expenditure' and a programme of public works by the government, local authorities, and public utilities (adding that 'the Bank of England and the banking system should not hesitate to allow the volume of bank deposits to expand so that the money needed to finance these undertakings will not need to be withdrawn from other forms of expenditure').[2] Finally, once again, in the very last sentence of his Note on policy Pigou emphasized that his wide range of constructive proposals '*were designed to enable present real-wage rates to be maintained*'. (Italics added.)

In fact, in their contributions to the Macmillan Committee, Pigou and Keynes were involved in virtually no fundamental or far-reaching differences regarding current policy. Though there were a number of disputes on emphasis, terminology, and abstract assumption, the most important clash between the two was over the historical question of the return to the gold standard. Here again the difference turned largely not on theoretical principles, but on Pigou's severe pessimism, as contrasted with Keynes's comparative optimism, regarding the probable management by the politicians and bankers of alternative monetary policies to that which was adopted of returning to gold at the pre-war parity.

Barely one week after Pigou's evidence to the Macmillan Committee, given on May 28 and 29, 1930, a leader in *The Times* criticized public works proposals on the lines of the Treasury view. Pigou wrote in as follows (June 6, 1930): 'When industry is in

[1] See Addendum I (p. 199): 'We have already agreed, however, that for a country in the special circumstances of Great Britain the disadvantages would greatly outweigh the advantages.' In 1931, at any rate, with unemployment over 20 per cent and still rising, Keynes was *not* prepared to put employment before the exchange rate.

[2] *Op. cit.*, Vol. II, p. 93: Note by the Witness.

equilibrium, the conditions of demand and the rates of wages being so adjusted to one another that, apart from people in process of movement from one place or occupation to another, everybody seeking work can find it, there is a presumption that state action designed to stimulate employment in any particular field will be injurious. It will, in general, merely divert labour from more productive to less productive occupations. This presumption is capable of being stated in a great variety of forms, and is frequently to be found in current discussions of the unemployment problem. There is also a presumption that men set to work in "artificially created" occupations will not be worth their wage . . . and that the "artificial creation" of employment is a waste of national resources. . . . Both these presumptions, whether in pure form or wrapped in the customary wrappings, would provide good reasons for deprecating State action designed to reduce unemployment, whether by Governmental programmes of national development or in other ways—provided that there were no unemployment to reduce! When, however, as at the present time, there is an enormous mass of unemployment their virtue and their relevance are lost. If employment is "artificially created" in these conditions, men are available to come into it, not merely from more useful occupations elsewhere, but from soul-destroying idleness. . . . It is important to be sure that our pre-suppositions are adjusted not to imaginary but to actual conditions.'

One could hardly ask for a less emotional, and more basic and reasoned refutation of the 'classical' fallacy that had come down from Smith, Ricardo, and James Mill. It follows the lines of similar refutations which Pigou had been making since about 1908.[1] So much for wage reductions being Pigou's only suggestion in 1930.

Professor Lekachman also maintains that Mr D. H. Robertson 'allied himself' with Pigou in that he also 'committed himself to the conclusion that the route to full employment in 1939 [1930?] ran through a series of wage reductions terminating in a lower average level of wages'.[2]

[1] See for example his inaugural lecture *Economic Science in Relation to Practice*, 1908, pp. 27-8, and *Unemployment*, 1913, Chapter XI (quoted in *Review of Economic Doctrines 1870-1929*, 1953, p. 416). See also Pigou's lecture on 'Economy and Waste' in *Economics in Practice*, 1935, p. 26 ff.

[2] *The Age of Keynes*, 1967, p. 51. Professor Lekachman quotes Robertson as saying that he considered wages to be in excess 'of what the economic value of the work would be if there were full employment'—a view presumably shared by Keynes. (See Minutes of Evidence, Vol. I, p. 339, para. 4937.) For Robertson's actual evidence to the Macmillan Committee, the actual tenor of which was about the opposite of what Professor Lekachman says it was, see above I(i), pp. 23-4. Contrast Mr M. Stewart on Robertson, p. 290.

IV

Only about two months later a sub-committee of the Economic Advisory Council was set up consisting of Keynes (Chairman), Pigou, Henderson, Stamp, and Robbins to consider the unemployment problem and suggest remedies. At its first meeting (August 10, 1930) Keynes asked Pigou 'to prepare a memorandum outlining briefly the heads of evidence for subsequent discussion'. Pigou's memorandum was ready by September 6th and the sub-committee reported on October 24th.

These interesting and important documents have been reported on by Mr R. Skidelsky in his scholarly and instructive study *Politicians and the Slump* (1967).

Mr Skidelsky's primary interest is in political history rather than economic theory. But he describes Pigou's memorandum as an 'extremely lucid and interesting statement of the economic malaise and of the various alternative remedies'.[1] Mr Skidelsky's account makes it clear that Pigou's memorandum followed very closely, as one would expect, the lines of his evidence to the Macmillan Committee which he had given in May. In fact, Mr Skidelsky's only considerable quotation can be found verbatim in the Macmillan evidence. This is Pigou's 'second best' argument. According to Mr Skidelsky, Pigou and Keynes both 'sought the most direct means of producing employment. Their philosophy was very much as Pigou described it in the following analogy: "A man ordered to walk a tight-rope carrying a bag in one hand would be better off if he were allowed to carry a second bag in the other hand, though of course if he started bagless to add a bag would handicap him".'[2]

Mr Skidelsky notes that Pigou was prepared to advocate a curtailment of foreign lending, and that advancing perhaps from his position in his Macmillan evidence he 'gave cautious support to the idea of a tariff',[3] along with Henderson and Stamp, and of course Keynes. The Committee produced a majority report signed, with some reservations, by Keynes, Pigou, Henderson, and Stamp, who all agreed in calling for an increase in home investment on a large scale. Professor Robbins wrote a dissenting minority report. Mr Skidelsky concludes that 'despite some confusion in analysis and remedy, the economists' report was a radical document with a comprehensive programme of action'.[4] He maintains with regard to economists generally that

[1] *Politicians and the Slump*, 1967, p. 207.

[2] *Op. cit.*, p. 213. See *Committee on Finance and Industry*, Vol. II, 1931, p. 80, para. 6481.

[3] *Op. cit.*, p. 209.

[4] *Op. cit.*, p. 215.

'most of them gave the right advice. . . . The "wrong" advice was given much more frequently by the business community, the City and the Bank of England than by the professional economists.'[1]

V

Continuing evidence of a fairly close compatibility of views on current policy between Pigou and Keynes in 1932 and 1933 may be glimpsed from letters and articles in *The Times*. As we have seen, at the bottom of the slump (October 17, 1932), with unemployment over 20 per cent, there was a letter in *The Times* attacking the orthodox classical maxims of saving and economy in the following terms:

'One thing is, in our opinion, clear. The public interest in present conditions does not point towards private economy; to spend less money than we should like to do is not patriotic.

Moreover, what is true of individuals acting singly is equally true of groups of individuals acting through local authorities. If the citizens of a town wish to build a swimming bath, or a library, or a museum, they will not, by refraining from doing this promote a wider national interest. . . . Through their misdirected goodwill the mounting wave of unemployment will be lifted still higher.'

This letter was signed by Keynes together with Professors Pigou and Macgregor, Sir Walter Layton, Sir Arthur Salter, and Sir Josiah Stamp. The above letter was answered, two days later, by four London University economists (Professors Gregory, von Hayek, Plant and Robbins). They argued in thoroughly classical terms:

'We are of the opinion that many of the troubles of the world at the present time are due to improvident borrowing and spending on the part of the public authorities. . . . The depression has abundantly shown that the existence of public debt on a large scale imposes frictions and obstacles to readjustment very much greater than the frictions and obstacles imposed by the existence of private debt. Hence we cannot agree with the signatories of the letter that this is a time for new municipal swimming baths, etc., merely because people "feel they want" such amenities.

If the Government wish to help revival, the right way for them to proceed is, not to revert to their old habits of lavish expenditure,

[1] *Op. cit.*, p. 209. Reviewing Mr Skidelsky's account *The Economist* (1968) concludes regarding the committee of economists, 'all except one gave broadly the right advice' (January 27, 1968, p. 38).

but to abolish those restrictions on trade and the movement of capital (including restrictions on new issues) which are at present impeding even the beginning of recovery.'

As regards Pigou, previously on June 7th he had claimed—perhaps with some slight, but not much, exaggeration—that '*economic opinion is practically unanimous*' in holding that 'where there are no good personal reasons for private economy, there are, in present conditions, no good patriotic ones; and that the same principle is true of institutions'. (Italics added.)

On January 6, 1933, Pigou contributed an article to *The Times* calling for a policy of expansion. He argued: 'For prosperity to be restored either money costs must fall or money prices must rise. The practical difficulties in the way of the former solution have proved so serious and the friction to be overcome so great that *the main body of instructed opinion has turned towards the latter*' (italics added). With the forthcoming World Economic Conference in view he called for a general step-for-step movement towards monetary reflation. . . . It is imperative for the Government to act.' Certainly he was cautious with regard to public investment policies. He was not prepared to suggest 'that the National Government should float a spectacular loan and devote the proceeds to *ad hoc* public works. But it is suggested that the pressure hitherto exerted in favour of policies of contraction should be lifted; the engines have been reversed long enough; it is time to move cautiously forward.' Subsequently Pigou added the message: 'When in doubt, expand.'[1]

Early in March 1933 there appeared a letter signed by no less than thirty-seven economists from a wide range of universities in England, Scotland and Wales. Many names subsequently more famous were among the signatories, including those of Hall, Harrod, Helsby, Gaitskell, Meade, Carr-Saunders, and Robinson (J. and E. A. G.). They called on the Government for a programme of expansion, holding that 'the Government is singularly well placed to assist in raising demand'. It should do this out of borrowing on capital account which should be separated from the current account items in the budget

[1] In a letter of February 21, 1933. According to Professor Dudley Dillard, in a milder version of the wage-cut myth: 'In his *Lapses from Full Employment*, published in 1945, Professor Pigou says he is in favour of attacking the problem of unemployment by manipulating demand rather than by manipulating wages. This involves a major departure from the classical position and a major triumph for Keynes.' In fact Pigou made it quite clear to the Macmillan Committee (1930), and again in the above article and in *The Theory of Unemployment* (p. 250) in 1933, that he was in favour of operating on the side of demand (or 'prices') and *not* on that of costs or wages. (See *The Economics of J. M. Keynes*, 1948, p. 24 and p. 220.) Keynes had many great and well-deserved 'triumphs', but not this one.

to be balanced out of taxation. Thus quite a large percentage of the university economists in the country at that time were advocating publicly a policy of Government spending and expansion and suggesting a means by which it should be organized by 'deficit finance'. They were opposing the Treasury view on the one hand and the principle of economy in Government spending on the other.

Later in the month (March 1933) Keynes published his own expansionist proposals in his articles on *The Means to Prosperity*. As regards the internal measures, these were essentially the mixture as before, that is the kind of proposals he had been advocating for almost a decade. As Sir Roy Harrod puts it: 'On the domestic side he was still pressing those remedies which he had begun to urge in 1924—large-scale public works on loan account.'[1] Sir Roy points out that in *The Means to Prosperity* the multiplier concept was much more precisely developed than previously. He adds that 'the first inkling' of the idea of 'deficit finance' was introduced. But as regards deficit finance, there had been at least quite clear 'first inklings' in, for example, Keynes's criticism of the May Committee's Economy Report in August 1931. He writes there of governments being forced to borrow as 'nature's remedy' against an indefinite downward spiralling of the slump.[2]

VI

Late in 1933 Pigou published *The Theory of Unemployment*. Another version of the prevailing myth is based on quotations from this book. Mr Michael Stewart has maintained that Pigou's attitude was that 'until wages were reduced, unemployment would persist'; and that Pigou 'concluded that provided there are no obstructions to the free working of the market, "there will always be at work a strong tendency for wage rates to be so related to demand that everybody is employed. Hence, in stable conditions everyone will actually be employed".'[3]

Here again some immediate supplementation of the quotation clarifies Pigou's meaning. He had in fact spelt out much more fully and precisely the deliberate abstractions in his assumptions. The sentence immediately preceding those quoted by Mr Stewart reads: 'With perfectly free competition among work people and labour

[1] *The Life of J. M. Keynes*, 1951, p. 441.
[2] See *Essays in Persuasion*, 1931, pp. 161-2.
[3] *Keynes and After*, 1967, p. 68. No page reference is given by Mr Stewart. The passage is quoted more extensively by Keynes in *The General Theory*, p. 278. But Keynes did not accuse Pigou of advocating wage cuts. The reference is to Pigou's *Theory of Unemployment*, 1933, p. 252.

perfectly mobile, the nature of the relation will be very simple.'

Of course Pigou was repeatedly emphasizing the unreality of these assumptions and explicitly discussing the actual immobility of labour and the powers of trade unions. In fact, in his preface Pigou had emphasized in terms which no doubt look very old-fashioned to contemporary experts, the nature of his approach as a university economist: 'While it is natural and right in the present deplorable state of the world's affairs that many economists should seek to play a part in guiding conduct, that is not their primary business. They are physiologists not clinical practitioners; engineers not engine-drivers. The main part of such contribution as they may hope to make must be indirect; in the study, not in the pages of newspapers or even in the council chamber.'[1]

Anyhow, only two pages before the passage somewhat incompletely quoted by Mr Stewart, Pigou had favourably discussed the same range of policy measures which he had put forward in his evidence to the Macmillan Committe, that is, 'not only the undertaking of large-scale public works, but bounties, guarantees of interest and, if successful in their purpose, protective duties'.[2] Pigou goes further in arguing that these measures would have been effective against the structural unemployment in the twenties before the great increase of cyclical unemployment in 1930.

Mr Stewart maintains that the 'view was almost unanimous' among economists, except for Keynes and Robertson, that government expenditure must be cut in the depression.[3] In fact, as we have seen, a number of leading economists joined with Pigou and Keynes in advocating exactly the opposite policy in *The Times* in October 1932, while in March 1933 a large percentage of university economists had advocated loan expenditure by government. Mr Stewart also maintains that 'most economists' except Keynes and Robertson supported the Treasury view regarding the ineffectiveness of public investment.[4] Again this is almost the diametric opposite of the historical facts. As we have seen, Keynes himself had maintained that 'not one of the leading economists' held the Treasury view in 1929. Furthermore, it may be noted that with regard to the policy of cutting money wages Keynes had maintained (June 1931): 'There is scarcely one responsible person in Great Britain prepared to recommend it

[1] *Op. cit.*, p. v.
[2] *Op. cit.*, p. 250.
[3] *Keynes and After*, 1967, p. 66.
[4] *Op. cit.*, p. 66. Contrast R. Skidelsky's well founded conclusion: 'There is no doubt that the Treasury view was rejected by all the leading economists. Pigou subjected it to detailed analysis in 1927 and found it to be fallacious.' *Politicians and the Slump*, 1967, p. 25. (See presumably Pigou's *Industrial Fluctuations*, 1927, II x.)

openly.'[1] (This statement by Keynes was undoubtedly somewhat premature in view of the economy campaign and the cuts in the pay of public servants which we put through only a couple of months later—though these cuts were in the name of public economy, rather than of wage flexibility as a cure for unemployment. But Keynes's generalization was far nearer the truth than its opposite would have been, or such fantasies as that all economists except Keynes were calling for deflation or wage cuts.)

Subsequently Mr Stewart refers to the 'sheer indecency of calling for wage cuts'—as he alleges Pigou and Robbins were doing at this time. But of course Mr Stewart has to agree, that *according to Keynes's own analysis*, in real terms, 'if there is to be an increase in employment there must be a fall in average wages'.[2]

Finally with regard to the suggested black-and-white contrasts between the policy views of Pigou and Keynes at this time, we may cite a letter from Keynes in *The Times* of July 28, 1933. A *Times* leader had rather rashly attempted to suggest a distinction or divergence between the views of Pigou and Keynes with regard to the monetary processes involved in an increase of public investment. Keynes promptly replied: 'Your leading article today suggests a difference of opinion between myself and Professor Pigou which does not, I think, exist. Like him, I contemplate that public works would be paid for out of loans. How far the "creation of new money" would be necessary as a complement of this policy depends on the meaning of these words. . . . The main point, however, is that which has been emphasized by Professor Pigou—namely, whether there are not many enterprises which would pay for themselves if we were to credit to their cost what they would save the Treasury in unemployment relief, and, I should add, what they would earn for the Treasury in the increased yield of taxation.'

VII

The broad measure of agreement on employment policy between Pigou and Keynes thus continued on through the bottom of the slump. From 1934 the economy was slowly moving out of the depths

[1] See *Unemployment as a World Problem*, edited by Q. Wright, 1931, p. 31.

[2] *Keynes and After*, 1967, p. 68 and p. 116. Mr Stewart's comments on Professor Robbins seem to be less wide of the mark. See *The Great Depression*, 1934, p. 186. Possibly Mr Stewart's belief in these myths stems from their propagation by Dr T. Balogh who long previously had proclaimed: 'Keynes fought single-handed against all his learned colleagues, who wanted to cure the great deflationary crisis with more deflation.' (*The Listener*, August 19, 1948, p. 255.) Dr Balogh seemed to suggest a comparison with his own position in 1948.

of depression. Whether for this reason, or because of the ferocious and apparently fundamental disputes that broke out with the publication of *The General Theory* in January 1936, Pigou seems to have contributed little or nothing further to current policy discussion by way of letters and articles in *The Times* or elsewhere.

In *The General Theory* Keynes was concerned to emphasize to the full what he considered to be fundamental disagreements on terminology, assumptions, and historical criticisms. This represented a complete and sudden *volte-face* compared with his policy writings in previous decades, which had repeatedly and strongly emphasized agreement. As we have seen, in 1929 Keynes had emphasized that 'not one of the leading economists' accepted the Treasury view (which had been attacked by Pigou in 1908). In 1930, at a crucial phase, an agreed report signed by Keynes, Pigou and three other leading economists, had put forward a cogent and radical programme to counter unemployment. In 1931 Keynes had maintained that 'scarcely one responsible person' was advocating wage cuts. In 1932 with Pigou and four other leading economists he had signed a letter attacking the economy campaign. In 1933 Keynes had rebuked *The Times* for suggesting that there was any disagreement between himself and Pigou regarding public works policies or the monetary processes involved. Just previously in the same year, thirty-seven university economists—then a large proportion of the total—had advocated in the columns of *The Times* measures for Government loan expenditure. Now, however, in *The General Theory* Keynes saw himself as having to convince 'my fellow economists' of fundamental errors 'in orthodox economics', as represented particularly by Pigou. He maintained that he was attempting 'to bring to an issue the deep divergences of opinion between economists which have for the time being almost destroyed the practical influence of economic theory, and will, until they are resolved, continue to do so'.[1]

But on policy issues only a fairly small minority of university economists, in particular at The London School of Economics, disagreed at all significantly with Keynes's policy proposals. There was probably then far less disagreement and divergence among university economists on the main policy issues than in the 1950's and 1960's. Again, at the beginnning of the century, on the tariff reform issue, the minority of university economists in favour of tariffs was probably much weightier, and had much more to say for itself, than the minority in the early thirties. The massive obstacles to the adoption of expansionist policies in the thirties lay not with academic opinion, but in Whitehall, the City, and Westminster—to whom of course

[1] *The General Theory of Employment, Interest and Money*, 1936, p. vi.

The General Theory was not addressed and on whom it could have had little or no *direct* impact. Shelves-full of often highly abstract literature have been devoted to the differences between Keynes and 'the classics' (with whom Pigou is, we would suggest, quite misleadingly included) with regard to analysis, abstract models, terminology, and critical-historical judgments. Perhaps it signifies something about what economists often mis-call 'theory' that whether all these 'fundamental' differences had any implications for policy or for policy-relevant predictions—and if so precisely what—seems to have been very little investigated. Again, there has been some expert study of the changes in terminology and abstract model-building between *The Treatise on Money* and *The General Theory*. But again, whether these changes had any significant implications for policy, and if so precisely what were the corresponding shifts in Keynes's predictions and policy proposals, does not seem to have received much attention.

Keynes, however, suggested in *The General Theory* that Pigou and others were apparently not *logically* entitled to have joined with him, as they had, in opposing the Treasury view and wage cuts, and in advocating public investment. In fact, Keynes rather backhandedly praised Professor Robbins (certainly one of the few university economists who actually seems to have advocated wage 'flexibility' and to have opposed public works) for 'almost alone' maintaining 'a consistent scheme of thought, his practical recommendations belonging to the same system as his theory'.[1] Pigou in his review of *The General Theory* complained: 'When one of the arraigned persons had palpably not made a particular mistake, the method of lumping enables Mr Keynes to say that he ought to have made it, and that, in not making it, he was false to the "logic" of his own school—has allowed his "good commonsense to overbear his bad theory".'[2]

Keynes did not anywhere state—he would not and could not possibly have done so—that Pigou had been advocating wage cuts. This outright fantasy has been left for a later generation. The furthest Keynes went was in stating that Pigou 'believes that in the long run

[1] *Op. cit.*, p. 20n.

[2] *Economica*, May 1936, p. 116. See also *Employment and Equilibrium*, second ed. 1949, p. 86: According to Keynes, '*logically* the "classical school" are bound to reject Government attempts to alleviate a slump by means of Public Works and to welcome economy campaigns in times of depression. . . . This, of course, is a travesty.' It certainly is a travesty in the case of Pigou. But it is far from being a travesty in the cases of Smith, James Mill, Ricardo, and of many others, including numerous passages in neo-classical writings and some in Marshall.

unemployment can be cured by wage adjustments'.[1] But no one is more celebrated than Keynes for his emphasis on the insignificance or practical irrelevance for mortals of propositions about 'the long run', and this must apply, therefore, to his own attribution or accusation regarding Pigou. The trouble was, apparently, not that Pigou was disagreeing on policy regarding the effects of wage cuts as applied to the British economy *as it actually existed*, but that he *might* disagree, or *would have* disagreed in the case of some economy very different from the actual British economy in the 1920's and 1930's. In the 1920's and 1930's, in any case, general wage cuts and general wage policies were simply assumptions employed in highly abstract analysis, not a realistic policy possibility. There was then no machinery, and hardly any suggestion of machinery, for implementing general wage cuts. It has only been with the emergence of incomes policies in the transformed situation of the late fifties and sixties that general wage policy has become a serious policy possibility.

The question then arises as to the significance for policy of *The General Theory*, and the changes in policy based upon any new predictions it provided, as contrasted with the predictions and policies on which Keynes had been in broad fundamental agreement with Pigou, and which had had their fullest theoretical foundation in *The Treatise*. Mr Michael Stewart at least sees that there is a question here. His answer however seems so far-fetched as only to emphasize the relevance and point of the question. Before *The General Theory*, Mr Stewart maintains, Keynes 'could not really answer' the Treasury view against public investment that 'there was only a certain amount of savings in the economy available for investment'. Mr Stewart goes on: 'Keynes could not really answer this theoretical case, and although he continued to advocate public works in the early 1930's, he was in the position of a man calling on emotional grounds for a course of action that the intellect showed was wrong. The subordination of emotion to reason represented by government policy in the early 1930's is a sufficiently rare phenomenon in politics to call for encouragement and praise; it must have been particularly galling to an arch-intellectual like Keynes that it should happen in a case where he was stubbornly convinced that reason had got it wrong.'[2]

We need not go back to the early critics—such as Bentham and Lauderdale—of Smith, Ricardo, and James Mill, the principal originators of the Treasury view or of the theory of saving under-

[1] *The General Theory of Employment, Interest and Money*, 1936, p. 278.
[2] *Keynes and After*, 1967, pp. 66-7.

lying it. We have seen that Pigou (from 1908) and others had repeatedly refuted it (but presumably we are to believe that Pigou, too, had simply been moved by gusts of emotion). Mr Skidelsky is certainly justified when he writes that it was 'rejected by all the leading economists' during the slump. To claim that Keynes before and all through the slump was 'subordinating reason to emotion' is simply to repudiate a decade of Keynes's writings which repeatedly started from, and ended with, a confident appeal to reason and reasoned commonsense against the crass unreason of mass unemployment amid mass poverty which existed in Britain and the world.[1]

The question remains then as to what precise new and significant development with regard to policy *The General Theory* introduced, and whether the ferocious disagreements with Pigou and others, which *The General Theory* brought about, were reflected in any fundamental new divergences on policy disruptive of the previous very considerable measure of agreement? What new and different predictions, relevant to actual possible policies, did *The General Theory* provide, as contrasted, say, with *The Treatise on Money?*[2] We are certainly not saying that the right answer to this question would be a negative one, though we would suggest that it would be in much more limited terms than current conventional orthodoxy implies. Anyhow, here is a question the examination of which would at least be historically more justifiable than the concotion of myths about Keynes's contemporaries.

VIII

By the time of the publication of *The General Theory* in January 1936, the economy was well advanced on the upswing, though in

[1] It seems pedantic to cite references on such a point, but those who do not know them might look, for example, at pp. 118-167 of *Essays in Persuasion*, 1931.

[2] These questions are, for example, comprehensively begged in the following: He (Keynes) 'thought it a matter of great importance—of real, urgent, political importance—that people should know that he was saying something fresh. If he had been polite and smooth, if he had used proper scholarly caution and academic reserve, his book would have slipped down unnoticed and millions of families rotting in unemployment would be so much the further from relief. He wanted the book to stick in the gizzards of the orthodox, so that they would be forced either to spew it out or chew it properly. Pigou spewed it out.' (J. Robinson, *Economic Philosophy*, 1962, p. 80.) The question is, of course, just what it was 'fresh', *in terms of actual policies* for the unemployed, that *The General Theory did* say, 'fresh', that is, compared with the actual policies that he, and the 'orthodox' Pigou, had been advocating for years. Of course there was much that was fresh in the book, but the question remains as to what significant new predictions, relevant to employment policies, that it brought.

the UK the average unemployment in that year was still around 13 per cent. Nineteen thirty-seven was a peak year and unemployment was back at around the 1928-29 level of about 10·8 per cent. Keynes's next major contribution in the way of current policy proposals was his article 'How to Avoid a Slump' (*The Times*, January 13, 1937). This article is of great interest, first because it is probably Keynes's only, or much his most significant, contribution to current policy for dealing with the upper turning-point of the cycle, as contrasted with the depths of the depression. Secondly, it must be one of his last important pronouncements on current domestic policy problems under fully peace-time assumptions.

Keynes begins by remarking that we have 'climbed out of the slump'. There was not 'a precarious boom'. There was 'nothing wrong', but the time had come to level off activity and above all to take precautions against a descent into another slump. Keynes maintained: 'We are in more need today of a rightly distributed demand than of greater aggregate demand.' He maintained that economists were 'faced with a scientific problem which we have never tried to solve before'. He claimed (again emphasizing broad agreement on policy questions, as contrasted with the pressing of extreme disagreements in *The General Theory*) that, 'we have freed ourselves—this applies to every party and every quarter—from the philosophy of the *laissez-faire* state'. He added somewhat modestly and tentatively: 'Perhaps we know more.'

Keynes went on: 'Three years ago it was important to use public policy to increase investment. It may soon be equally important to retard certain types of investment, so as to keep our most easily available ammunition in hand for when it is more required. . . . Just as it was advisable for the Government to incur debt during the slump, so for the same reasons it is now advisable that they should incline to the opposite policy. . . . Just as it was advisable for local authorities to press on with capital expenditure during the slump, so it is now advisable that they should postpone whatever new enterprises can reasonably be held back.'

It is very interesting with regard to Keynes's conception of 'full employment' that at this time about one year after *The General Theory*, in his next major policy pronouncement, he was concerned with damping down public expenditure and curbing borrowing and deficits when unemployment was still at a level of about 11-12 per cent. Incidentally, it is a curious contrast that eight years previously in 1929 when unemployment had been at about the same level he was urging a drastic programme of public works (although since then his ideas had developed in the direction of the stagnationist view of a drying-up of profitable investment opportunities).

Keynes urged in rather modern fashion the 'riding-out' of balance-of-payments difficulties: 'Above all it is desirable that we should view with equanimity and without anxiety the prospective worsening of our trade balance.' But then of course the state of the reserves was fairly healthy: 'We have today a plethora of gold.'

Keynes's most emphatic warnings were against a rise in interest rates to curb the boom: 'We must avoid it, therefore, as we would hell-fire. It is true that there is a phase in every recovery when we need to go slow with postponable investment of the recurrent type, lest, in conjunction with the non-recurrent investment which necessarily attends a recovery it raises aggregate investment too high. But we must find other means of achieving this than a higher rate of interest. . . . It is a fatal mistake to use a high rate of interest as a means for damping down the boom.'

Looking further ahead to countering the danger of depression, though there are some hints of a stagnation thesis, Keynes's proposals again amounted largely to the medicine as before. He wanted a Board of Public Investment to prepare detailed schemes which could be put immediately into operation as required (a proposal which had appeared in the Liberal Yellow Book of 1928).

A couple of months later (March 11, 1937) Keynes supplemented this article with another examining the possible effects of the Government's proposal of a loan of £80 million for rearmament expenditure. This article is very interesting as a pioneer exercise in national income forecasting. Keynes made use of the multiplier concept, estimating it at between two and three, which he figured would imply a total increase in national income of between 4 and 5½ per cent. Keynes concluded that the rearmament loan 'need not be inflationary. But unless care is taken, it may be rather near the limit'. Unemployment was then at about 12½ per cent, Keynes estimated. But he added: '*We cannot safely regard even half of the unemployed insured persons as being available to satisfy home demand*' (some being unemployable or seasonally unemployed, or unemployed in the export industries). (Italics added.)

At the end of the year (December 28, 1937) Keynes again agreed in a letter that curbs on public expenditure were probably desirable: '*It is very generally held today* that there is a good deal of advantage in retarding expenditure by such bodies when other sources of demand are strong and in accelerating it when other sources are weak. This is probably a reason for not pushing such expenditure at present' (italics added). Unemployment at this time was about 11-12 per cent, and probably rising again.

However, nearly a year later (September 1938) Keynes was complaining: 'We are still allowing a great volume of potential wealth to evaporate unrealized.' He argued that we could not hope to keep pace with a form of government (in Nazi Germany) 'which has devised means of producing and maintaining full employment'.

Keynes's articles in 1939 may also have some interest with regard to his ideas about full employment.[1] But they were concerned with a twilight period of mobilization between peace and impending war and so it is difficult to draw conclusions about his views on peace-time normality.

Keynes's great emphasis on avoiding a rise in interest rates in 1937 may well have had some theoretical connections with the arguments in *The General Theory*. We have no evidence regarding Pigou's agreement or disagreement. But it certainly is not clear that any fundamental differences regarding policy in 1937 would have emerged between Pigou and Keynes, or that the measure of agreement *on policy* between 1930 and 1933 had appreciably or significantly lessened in any way as a result of the new ideas in *The General Theory*.

IX

The General Theory therefore appeared just one year before the launching of the rearmament programme which could be said to have marked the beginning of the end of mass unemployment, though this end was delayed for about another three years. One can only speculate as to what would have happened regarding Keynesian policies and the level of unemployment had the Second World War not broken out when it did. As Keynes was to complain in 1940: 'It is, it seems, politically impossible for a capitalistic democracy to organize expenditure on the scale necessary to prove my case—except under war conditions.'[2] Certainly Keynes's great leap forward in applying his theory or analysis to operational policy-making came with the transition to the war economy, notably his articles 'The Income and Fiscal Potential of Great Britain' (December 1939), 'The Concept of National Income' (March 1940), parts of 'How to Pay for the War' (1940) and finally the Budget of 1941. These were, of course, among Keynes's greatest constructive achievements, and perhaps, historically, the greatest and most effective of all practical operational applications of an appropriately devised framework of economic concepts to govern-

[1] See articles in *The Times*, April 17 and July 24-25, 1939, and in *The Listener* for June 1st, where with unemployment at about 1½ million (c. 11 per cent) Keynes judged that the 'number of unemployed should fall in the course of the year by 500,000 as a minimum. . . . It is not an exaggeration to say that the end of abnormal unemployment is in sight.' See above p. 26.

[2] *New Republic*, July 20, 1940, p. 158; quoted by A. E. Holmans, *United States Fiscal Policy 1945-1949*, 1961, p. 318.

ment policies (though hardly of solid 'laws' or functional relationships).

Of course it may well be claimed that the development of the national income framework stems in part from *The General Theory*. It could also be claimed—and has been—that the discussion of basic national income concepts such as saving and investment, was among the most obviously unsatisfactory parts of the book. The pioneer attempt to quantify Keynesian concepts in terms of a national income framework seems to have been Mr Colin Clark's treatment based on the Fundamental Equations in *The Treatise on Money*.[1] It might be asked whether there is an advance, rather than the opposite, in *The General Theory* on the definitions of *The Treatise* with regard to the setting up of a satisfactory national income framework. However, there is obviously much scope for argument here, probably to a considerable extent inconclusive.[2] But whatever conclusion is come to on this question it is surely impossible to justify the view that Keynes's policy proposals before *The General Theory* were based on 'emotional grounds' which 'the intellect showed was wrong'. (Presumably the 'intellect' referred to was represented at the time by Ramsay MacDonald, Snowden, Jimmy Thomas, Baldwin, Neville Chamberlain, Montague Norman, the City of London, Sir John Anderson, and the authors of the Treasury White Paper.)

There were three main policy doctrines regarding unemployment which may be called 'classical'—or certainly the first two of them may be. These were (i) that public investment could not raise the level of employment and investment but only divert part of an apparently fixed fund of investment resources; and (ii) that governments should practice economy and cut down spending especially in depressions—

[1] See *The National Income 1924-1931*, 1932, Chapter XI.

[2] Professor G. L. S. Shackle in *The Years of High Theory*, 1967 (Chapters XI-XV) argues in detail on behalf of *The Treatise* as against *The General Theory*, for the 'clearer vision' (p. 148) of the former as contrasted with the latter's 'many pages of irrelevant, confused and fallacious argument' (p. 143) about the definitions of saving and investment. Professor Shackle even considers it worth framing the question regarding *The General Theory*: 'Was it necessary or worth while? The *Treatise* had efficient machinery, easier, indeed, to grasp than that of the *General Theory*. This was not altogether an advantage, in the circumstances of the time and for the purpose in hand. The mystique, the ascendancy of the later book arose partly from its seeming difficult' (p. 162). Professor Shackle of course answers his question in the affirmative. But the criteria of 'High Theory' on which he bases his comparison seem, as far as we can judge, to be somewhat different from the operational, predictive, policy-relevant criteria with which we are concerned here. Professor Shackle, however, is undoubtedly right about the yearning for a mystique, which is still so powerful as to fashion its history in terms of fantasies rather than facts.

the classical built-in destabilizer. These doctrines were both well rooted in the Turgot-Smith theory of saving and investing, to the effect that all savings pass smoothly and 'immediately' into investment, a theory which may well be called 'classical' since it was above all propagated by Smith, James Mill, and Ricardo, the latter expressly applying it in Parliament to employment policy in the post-war depression after the Napoleonic wars. These doctrines remained influential right down to the 1930's, and, of course, had been trenchantly restated by the Treasury in opposing proposals for public works in 1929. By this time, however, they had lost much of their grip on academic circles, except in London, but were still dominant in Whitehall, the City, and Westminster. Keynes was, or would have been, thoroughly justified in attacking a still influential 'classical' theory based on these two policy doctrines derived from a completely unrealistic 'classical' theory of saving and investment. But in *The General Theory* he concentrated not so much on these two doctrines (on which of course Pigou was emphatically anti-classical) as on a third 'classical' doctrine to the effect that general wage cuts would relieve unemployment (though he had claimed in 1931 that 'scarcely one responsible person' was actually advocating this policy). The wage cuts doctrine involved assumptions, as Pigou explicitly recognized, of perfectly free competition and perfect mobility in the labour market. Pigou also recognized, of course, that these assumptions were completely unrealistic, though it is true that a few other English economists, notably at the London School of Economics, urged wage 'flexibility' as a cure for unemployment (without apparently taking account of the complete unreality of the assumptions needed). But as Professor Samuelson has said: 'Had Keynes begun his first few chapters with the simple statement that he found it realistic to assume that modern capitalistic societies had money wage rates that were sticky and resistant to downward movements, most of his insights would have remained just as valid.'[1] Of course, Pigou would have completely accepted such an assumption as realistic, as he repeatedly stressed the point himself. All Keynes's main policy conclusions, with which fundamentally Pigou agreed, would have remained just as valid and well founded.

Although he did not allow it to affect his current policy conclusions, just why Pigou devoted such elaborate efforts and emphasis to the perfectly competitive and flexible model may well be a very cogent and justifiable methodological question. One can only point out that the perfectly competitive reference model has been used,

[1] *Keynes's General Theory, Reports of Three Decades*, ed. R. Lekachman, 1964, p. 332.

with would-be ultimate policy relevance, by many economists since the 1930's, as in 'welfare' analysis—where it has been concluded that only poll taxes are compatible with 'optimal' conditions. It would be as justifiable to charge the many distinguished exponents of 'welfare' analysis with being 'classical' for starting from the perfectly competitive reference model, as it is to call Pigou 'classical' for *his* use of it. Furthermore, it would be hardly more fantastic to charge the users of this model in 'welfare' analysis with actually having proposed that all taxes except poll taxes should be swept away forthwith from the British and United States economies, than it is to charge Pigou with actually having advocated wage cuts, during the depression.

Anyhow, whether or not Pigou is to be described as 'classical' in a Keynesian sense (a term which can indeed historically be given a very valid and weighty content) we have seen that in his day Pigou, in 1930, gave what nearly fourty years later can be recognized as thoroughly sound and relevant policy advice, in broad agreement, of course, with Keynes, Professor Robinson has invited us to 'contrast today'. There is indeed a contrast, but unfortunately it seems to work in the opposite direction to that which he implies. One may venture the judgment that if English economists in the sixties had been giving nearly as well-founded and widely-agreed advice as Pigou contributed in 1930 (and if indeed this advice had been acted upon) British economic policy would have been considerably less unsuccessful than it actually has been. In the thirties most university economists were certainly, constructively, and on the major issue, well ahead of other opinion in Whitehall and the City. In important respects, and with some exceptions, this was not the case in the sixties. Another 'contrast', highly unfavourable to the later period, might well obtain regarding some university economists' standards of historical scholarship.

INDEX OF NAMES

INDEX OF SUBJECTS